Studying Digital Media Audiences

Although many digital platforms continue to appropriate and reconfigure familiar forms of media experience, this is an environment which no longer consistently constructs an identifiable 'mass' audience in the terms understood by twentieth century audience researchers. The notion of 'audiencing' takes on different characteristics within a digital environment where platforms encourage users to upload, share and respond to content, while the platforms themselves monetize the digital traces of this activity. This environment demands new ways of thinking about audience and user engagement with media technologies, and raises significant questions on methods of conceiving and researching audience-users. This volume addresses ongoing debates in the field of audience research by exploring relevant conceptual and methodological issues concerning the systematic study of digital audiences. Drawing from work conducted by researchers based in Australia and New Zealand, the book uses theoretical frameworks and case study material which are of direct relevance to audience researchers globally.

Craig Hight is an Associate Professor in Communication at the University of Newcastle, Australia. His research interests have focused on audience research, digital media and documentary theory. He is currently researching the relationships between digital media technologies and documentary practice, especially the variety of factors shaping online documentary cultures.

Ramaswami Harindranath is Professor of Media at the University of New South Wales, Australia. He has published widely on audience research; global media, economy and culture; diasporic media and cultural politics; multicultural arts and cultural citizenship; South Asian politics and culture; and postcoloniality. He is currently completing a manuscript entitled Southern Discomfort, which re-assesses the concept and politics of cultural imperialism.

T0175004

Routledge Studies in New Media and Cyberculture

For a full list of titles in this series, please visit www.routledge.com.

Studying Digital Media Audiences

Perspectives from Australasia

Edited by Craig Hight and Ramaswami Harindranath

Routledge
Taylor & Francis Group

LONDON AND NEW YORK

First published 2017 by Routledge

2 Park Square, Milton Park, Abingdon, Oxfordshire OX14 4RN

52 Vanderbilt Avenue, New York, NY 10017

Routledge is an imprint of the Taylor & Francis Group, an informa business

First issued in paperback 2019

Copyright © 2017 Taylor & Francis

Library of Congress Cataloging-in-Publication Data
CIP data has been applied for.

ISBN: 978-1-138-22456-8 (hbk)
ISBN: 978-0-367-87819-1 (pbk)

Typeset in Sabon
by codeMantra

Contents

List of Figures and Tables

Figures

Tables

Acknowledgments

The editors wish to acknowledge Marsden funding administered by the Royal Society of New Zealand (project UOW1008 'Playing with reality? Online documentary culture and its users'), which supported this publication.

Introduction
Studying Digital Media Audiences

This volume begins with two assumptions. Firstly, that the insights gained from audience research are an essential contribution to debates over the nature and significance of digital media. Such research remains vital to interrogate a range of accelerating changes in social, cultural political and economic practice which are embedded within, driven by or refracted by multiple and proliferating services of digitized media technologies. There is scarcely an area within contemporary modern societies which is untouched by digital media in one form or another, and research into the human dimensions of these structures, frames and dynamics is an indispensable part of providing an accurate and insightful understanding of their nature and implications.

Our second assumption is that audience studies as a field of enquiry, as a broader agenda, set of ethical practices, and array of research paradigms and techniques, remains a work in progress. At a time of accelerating changes within media ecologies, there is a necessary project of reconsideration, revitalization and extension of the work of audience research which remains essential to its continued relevance. To conduct audience research means to continue to address the challenges of what terms such as 'audiences', 'consumption', audience activity' mean within a rapidly and continually evolving digital context. This volume is intended for existing and aspiring researchers in this broader field of possibilities.

We could approach 'digital media' (an inadequate label encompassing a range of technological and audience practices) from at least two distinct but overlapping perspectives. One the one hand, much of digital media is informed by continuities with earlier media structures and content patterns. From this perspective, the 'digital' represents extensions of well-established audience consumption habits, and associated forms of engagement, reception, interpretation and response. We see familiar generic forms, in which content is structured and designed to appeal to specific and familiar target audiences. And this is a perspective which highlights the potency of twentieth century mass media within an expanded and layered media ecology; television, in a number of guises, remains a major cultural force; music continues to be distributed in formats (think vinyl) whose existence confounds predictions of their demise; the market for print publishing continues in a tense balance with e-publishing; cinema is a key part of global cultural consumption patterns, even as distribution fractures across mobile and streaming options. And these are all forms whose reach is extended through digital platforms where acts of audiencing are deeply embedded within both global and local cultural exchange. Here it is not difficult to find evidence that supports the view that social media are still beholden to contemporary mass culture generated through familiar means; Twitter, YouTube and other social media are platforms dominated by responses to conventional commercialized media content. From this perspective, audience research should focus on how to adapt and apply the rich existing set of research paradigms, techniques, and instruments developed in response to developments in twentieth century mass media.

A contrasting perspective emphasizes the emerging configurations of online, mobile and platform-based media encompass distinctive new forms of media experiences, where participation and interaction assumes divergent forms derived from the emerging affordances of, and increasing intersections between, social networking, locative media and gaming technologies that play out within the full complexity of social, political and cultural contexts. For instance, even as we write, virtual reality and augmented reality – think Pokémon GO – are attracting renewed interest and appearing in forms gaining mass global appeal and participation. Regardless of whether or not this is really a 'game-changer', the lines between global and local, individual and collective, fiction and nonfiction, entertainment and surveillance are blurred in provocative ways here. From this perspective, models of audiences derived from twentieth century mass media have only a tenuous relevance to explaining the nature of media or how audiences re-imagined as users, navigators, and players engage with broader contemporary social, cultural, economic and political concerns.

What is certain however, is that the notion of 'audiencing' takes on different characteristics within a digital environment where platforms encourage users to upload, share and respond to content, while the platforms themselves monetize the digital traces of this activity. This environment demands new ways of thinking about audience and user engagement and interaction with, and use of, media technologies, and raises significant questions on methods of conceiving and researching audience-users. As with any form of newer media, there is also a need for caution with regard to the rhetoric suggesting that these new forms are inevitably and inherently more participatory with media-publics, more accurately reflective of viewers / readers / navigators / contributors and their interpretive repertoires, or more enmeshed within social, cultural and political contexts. There are new challenges here, new theoretical and methodological seductions to be wary of, and demands for conceptual models which scaffold upon the more familiar terrain of audience research into radio, newspapers, television and cinema rather than neglecting a rich literature and proven research traditions. The rapid nature of changes and developments in media technologies pose conceptual and methodological challenges for the study of current audience practices. Audience researchers have had to be more reflexive in their pursuit of strategies that might provide insight into macro patterns without losing a sense of the fluidity and fractured nature of engagement with digital platforms at the level of the individual and collective audience.

'Digital media' is also a broad umbrella for a range of technological, economic, social, cultural and political configuration of factors which are undergoing accelerating change. There is no doubt this is a complex ecology, offering multiple possibilities for interventions by researchers. And many of the platforms which are the focus of the research chapters in this book are themselves in the process of being transformed; Facebook has reached saturation point within particular global demographics, YouTube has moved away quite significantly from its non-commercial origins; while Twitter, Snapchat and WhatsApp struggle to develop sustainable business models which would engender their longevity as popular platforms. The patterns of many social media reveal the same trends toward increasing concentration of ownership as earlier media eras, even as these intersect with new issues, such as Big Data privacy concerns and (in a post-Edward Snowden era) their relationships with state enforcement agencies globally.

As has been well-demonstrated by more perceptive digital theorists there are complex dynamics between the 'old' and the 'new'; not just in terms of a recycling of familiar media forms in new guises but the exploitation of new distribution streams for older media content, or explorations in the interplay between previously distinct media in ways which are both familiar and startlingly new. These are exciting times for audience researchers contemplating an expanding and rapidly changing universe of mediated connections in diverse social and cultural contexts. Not only the object of study but available tools for exploring digital media are expanding. Alongside that are developments in data and data collection, made available to researchers by digital media technologies – Big Data for large-scale quantitative analyses, databases with extensive verbal data from platforms such as Twitter, access to online forums and archives. Digital technologies as both tools for data collection and analysis as well as platforms that enable audience activity and interaction – these have significantly altered the ways we research audiences and to the very questions we pose.

This book is intended to serve as something of a bridge, from an earlier era of audience research, focused particularly on mass media, into the future, where we anticipate a period of continued and perhaps accelerating change and experimentation in digital platforms from communities of users. There is an urgent need here for audience researchers to likewise continue to develop and experiment with research approaches toward the nature of engagement with contemporary digital platforms and media, to accumulate insights which can inform research into newer digitized forms of social, political, cultural and economic activity.

How To Read This Volume

The work in this volume covers a variety of issues for contemporary audience research; reconceptualizing and retheorizing 'audience'; the nature, constitution, and characteristics of digital audience data; tools for analyzing data; and digital methodologies for audience research. This volume raises fundamental questions about how to conceive digital audiences, the validity of Big Data, the variety of tools and methodologies at our disposal and their relative merits, the continuing significance of context – social, cultural, political. These are some of the issues tackled in the essays collected in this volume.

This collection has been inspired and driven by new work presented at a research symposium held at the University of New South Wales, in 2014. This event highlighted the value of perspectives from the margins of globalized media flows. The chapters included in this volume are built on original research in Australasia, drawing from work conducted by researchers based in Australia and New Zealand, but using theoretical frameworks and case study material which are of direct relevance to audience researchers globally. This collection comprises internationally known and emerging scholars from Australia and New Zealand who are currently engaged in conceiving and researching digital audiences, centered on localized research concerns through which global concerns are addressed.

Each of the chapters articulates and demonstrates a theoretical and methodological approach toward audience research in the digital era. Part of the agenda of this volume is to showcase research in action; to demonstrate the nature of research acts using digital tools, chiefly new forms of software, which demand technical up-skilling on the part of researchers more trained in humanities and social sciences; or to encourage collaborative work with computer scientists and programmers.

Each researcher makes interventions into a broad array of possibilities for investigating notion of 'audience' entangled in mobile, interactive networked media embedded within uncountable microcontexts of social, political, cultural and economic circumstances.

In Chapter 1, Athique addresses the drift toward Big Data within contemporary audience research and its underlying reliance on a host of assumptions not only about quantitative, data-driven research approaches, but also their acceptance of the paradigm of 'users' generated by the major social media platforms. In an era dominated by the monetizing of data exhausts generated by users engaged in online activity, the danger is to mistake the data profiles of users for the users themselves and to rely on either the residual category of a generic 'user' or a loose deployment of the term 'community'. Audience researchers operating in effective 'collaboration' with the generators of Big Data need to develop amore critical and reflexive understanding of the nature of the data they might harvest, and the relative value of data-driven methodologies for cultivating insights into the nature of contemporary audiences. Despite a host of ontological and epistemological dilemmas in play within this environment it nevertheless remains a rich field for new forms of audience research. Athique argues for engaging with such data as a means of exploring the notion of user-led transnationalism.

In Chapter 2, Ruddock argues for a reconsideration of the relevance of George Gerbner's work for the study of digital audiences. Gerbner's perspective on violent and sexual media content moved beyond a media effects paradigm, to argue instead that such content derives from a narrow commercial agenda targeting mainstream audiences, an agenda which has negative implications for cultivating the popular (and political) imagination. Outlining the set of assumptions behind Gerbner's Cultural Indicators Project (CIP), Ruddock argues that this is a communication model which makes sense in the digital era, which fosters more directly the conditions for audience activism centered on broadening the range of media content provided by a mediascape dominated by commercial interests. This, then, is a conception of audiences that prioritizes their agency, both in terms of recognizing their selections within commercialized content and in their ability to provoke changes in the nature of media production.

In Chapter 3, Goggin engages with the apparently new development of the location-based augmented reality (AR) game Pokémon GO via a broader thinking of what mobile means in relation to digital media audiences. He provides a context for understanding the game itself by discussing the emergence of mobile media audiences, and the increasingly prominent role location has played in these formations. He traces the emergence of Pokémon GO through the recent history of mapping, locative media, and augmented reality technology, and discusses the specific case of Pokémon GO against the histories of mobile gaming. He concludes with some remarks on the discursive, business, technology, and design strategies evident in Niantic's effort to configure and sustain the phenomenal success of its Pokémon GO launch.

In Chapter 4, Harindranath examines a host of assumptions underlying concerns over the use of the internet as a radicalizing tool for Islamic fundamentalist groups. He places such concerns within historical traditions of 'effects' research in particular, demonstrating how they are motivated by a familiar set of assumptions about 'vulnerable' audiences.

Arguing that there has been too much emphasis on media technologies and content, and too little on the broader socio-cultural and political context, this chapter addresses current conjunctures that inform responses to digital overtures from extremist groups. These include the paradoxes underlying the use of images by Islamic extremists, the global struggle over hegemonic control of images, the mediatization of global conflicts and how these, along with ongoing debates on multiculturalism and immigration marginalize communities and affect the self-perception of specific ethnic and religious groups in the West. Harindranath argues that there is a need here to carefully theorize the complex dynamics between lived experience, extremist social media, the perception of digital images, and radicalization.

In Chapter 5, Woodford, Prowd, and Bruns outline a number of possibilities for using data-scraping techniques to investigate audiencing practices operating through social media platforms such as Facebook, Instagram and Twitter. Each platform offers possibilities for engaging with post-demographic audiences, those generated through the specific nature of social media platforms, through user profiles and other forms of activity fostered online. Their research suggests the possibilities for quantitative techniques of gathering data on diverse aspects of 'audiencing', and focuses especially on users' online 'conversations' on Twitter, and how these might be mined for insights into broader patterns of television reception. They demonstrate the potential for Application Program Interfaces (APIs) to generate new audience research strategies, including building databases of audience patterns which can be later mined for other connections between data points across the Australian Twittersphere. These provide the basis for longitudinal research on social media activities and their relationship to other media forms. The authors also provide a useful reflexive commentary on these techniques, highlighting the challenges of using tools (APIs) provided by social media platforms themselves and their implications for exploring 'audiencing' practices associated with social media platforms.

These concerns are taken up in the following chapter (Chapter 6), which also overlaps with Athique's opening discussion to this collection. Drawing from the relatively new paradigms of software studies and critical data studies, Hight examines the implications of considering the datafied 'audiences' which are generated both by software-based platforms, and by research practices which are themselves embedded within software. He discusses YouTube as a distinctive data assemblage generated by the dynamic collaboration between a highly sophisticated and largely automated infrastructure and a globalized population of users. The key argument here is that as researchers look to either study the nature of YouTube as a video distribution infrastructure, or to use the platform as a mechanism for exploring a variety of social, political, economic and cultural issues related to audio-visual content, we need to develop a critical understanding of YouTube as infrastructural software, and as a key site within the broader ecosystem of the Big Data analytical models which constitute the social media economy. This chapter examines YouTube from the margins, both in terms of audience researchers within the academy necessarily operating as a 'third-party' researchers (outside of the platform and its commercialized data management policies), and from the perspective of a New Zealand-focused case study. Both of these positions reveal the challenges intrinsic to the practice of generating useful data from YouTube, and the manner in which researchers need to address the nature of technologies not only in media practices but also in their own research practices.

Pearson and Moskal, in Chapter 7, work through a mixed-method analysis of a failed attempt to introduce a small-scale social network at a New Zealand university. Their research demonstrates the value of engaging conceptually, testing these through mixed methods, and an iterative approach to analysis. Pearson and Moskal are able to deal holistically with an entire network, and use an approach combining both qualitative and quantitative techniques which are not so easily used with Facebook and other platforms of a similar scale. Drawing from social network analysis techniques and qualitative data from interviews with (non)participants, the case study reveals rich material for examining the relationship between a network and the broader social and institutional context in which it has been established, to reveal multiple causes of failure, and to provide a narrative for the life cycle of the network overall. They argue that socio-personal and structural constraints on actors both on and off the mediated network, and the proportions of types of actors at the genesis of a network, are both important influences on the overall success of such networks (especially for closed networks).

Goodwin, Griffin, Lyons, and McCreanor are part of a larger multi-disciplinary team of researchers investigating Facebook and its relationship to the social and cultural dimensions of drinking cultures in New Zealand. In Chapter 8 they utilize qualitative research as a means of framing and reflecting upon the nature of Facebook postings and their significance within the social circles represented through text and images. They explore how young people's agency operates in relation to the kinds of content posted online, and how these are negotiated by specific groups of New Zealand-based users. Moving beyond a focus simply on user's online profiles, their research highlights the need to have a mixed-method approach, to not assume that Facebook data can stand on its own, but needs instead to be couched within a broader understanding of the social discourses which are refracted through such media platforms.

In Chapter 9, Zappavigna demonstrates the potential for detailed qualitative and quantitative analysis of data culled from social media platforms. As with Woodford *et al.*, she engages with the audience of one medium (television) who are employing the affordances of another medium (Twitter) to engage in commentary and conversation during broadcast, a practice termed 'second screening'. She uses the Twitter conversations generated by viewers of an Australian cooking gameshow to suggest the layers of potential linguistic interpretations available to 'searchable' online audiences. Zappavigna employs Halliday's concept of linguistic metafunctions, to explore how hashtags enact three simultaneous communicative functions: marking experiential topics, enacting interpersonal relationships, and organizing text. In the process, she demonstrates both the complexity of the nature of contemporary audiencing, and the value of a theoretically-driven mixed-method approach to the gathering and analysis of Twitter data.

Turnbull and Moore, in Chapter 10, also discuss a research project centered on Twitter, but in their case they work to establish a very different form of relationship with research participants. They discuss working with students to reflect upon the nature of what networking means, how their participatory activities create new kinds of relationships with other members of a user base, and the value of providing a reflective space for users to consider the nature and implications of their own activity. They explore the nature of 'audiencing' as a diverse series of media practices, and examine the performance and practice of using Twitter as a platform for the public expression of a professional persona in the specific context of an Australian Media and Communication Studies undergraduate curriculum. This essay includes a discussion of the use of learning assessment strategies enacted with Twitter and the role of 'small data' and limited data sets in contributing to students' understanding of the shared construction of knowledge and their ability to develop critical self-evaluation skills.

Finally, in Chapter 11, de Bruin reports on a small-scale qualitative research project that is designed to be a part of a much broader contextual frame, one focused on the nature of historical changes in media use through the examination of micro-contexts of audience practices. This project considers how individuals are embedded within a variety of broader cultural frameworks which inform the choices they make in choosing multiple opportunities to access and make use of media content. De Bruin explores the implications of changes in 'mediatization' across decades, through its implications for a group with a liminal identity; migrants travelling from one small country (Holland) to another (New Zealand). His research generates a broader narrative highlighting the changes in people's immersion within media flows and use of media forms within 'national' frameworks which transcend geography. In broader terms, this case study not only demonstrates the continued value of qualitative approaches to digital media audiences, but suggests that there are nuances to the motivations, meanings and implications of users' encounters with media that are not easily quantified, or able to be explored through the data-scraping techniques featured in other chapters in this volume.

1 User-led Transnationalism, Big Data and the World Wide Web

Adrian Athique

The global nature of the World Wide Web is undeniably one of its most fundamental characteristics (whether as a medium of information, entertainment or interaction). Paradoxically, our understanding of the new audience formations emerging from digital media systems has tended to centre around either the residual category of a generic 'user' or a loose deployment of the term 'community'. Equally, and with some cause, the majority of digital audience studies have been primarily attentive to the unique interactivity of the engagements formed with digital media systems. It is fair to say, however, that the radically global nature of the medium has been too rapidly naturalized and should receive greater analysis and emphasis in discussions of digital audiences. It now seems that the most likely trigger for a reappraisal of user-led transnationalism is the rapid emergence of a new quantitative digital research paradigm based upon 'data mining'. In this context, the new methodological possibilities offered by the various 'scraping' techniques demonstrate new potentials for mapping audiences at a global scale. In discussing the significance of these developments for audience research, this chapter interrogates the interface between the user-led transnationalism of the World Wide Web and the re-appearance of audiences as 'Big Data' formations.

YouMedia and Transnational Fan Cultures

For audience researchers, probably the most discussed 'point of convergence' in the Internet era is that which has occurred between fan subcultures and mainstream audiences. It appears that the contemporary 'mainstream' is not, after all, a dispassionate and generalized alternative to cult behaviors, but actually a vast overlapping field of fan cultures of many differing kinds. Consequently, the devotional and over-invested behaviors of fans can no longer be easily stigmatized. At the same time, this also means that the enabling anthropological concept of subcultures as singular communities for close study is also dead in the water. After all, belonging to only one fan culture would scarcely round out anyone's social media profile. As a consequence, our intensive interest in interactivity needs to move beyond user-engagement with media content and trendy systems to focus more squarely on the qualities of interaction across a media-rich environment. The comfortable assumptions around agency and activity that currently prevail simply won't be sufficient for much of the work that actually needs to be done in an era of interactive audience research. With digitality, as much as popularity, inflecting our experience of everyday communication, the conceptual precision between 'active' and 'interactive' audiences itself, needs far greater clarity of purpose. Some extensive categorical work will be required in the coming years, allowing us to distinguish effectively between witting and unwitting interactions, between public speech and trails of data exhaust and between inputs prompted by users, by interpersonal protocols or by the system itself.

In a consumer society, all social actions are inevitably social transactions, and this necessarily results in the conflation of roles. Thus, viewers, voters, shoppers, and subjects have become simultaneous framings that have increasingly dissipated the previous notions of audiences, publics and citizens enshrined in the social contracts of the post-war era. At the tipping point between the two world orders, the great transnational shift of the 1990s rested upon a purposeful union of digital technologies and market expansion. Consequently, the phase of globalization that followed can be characterized not by its internationalism per se, but by its peculiar logics of mass mediation, faux individuation and the commercialization of all speech. All of this tends to sound somewhat sinister, and it has certainly drawn the ire of the socially minded in various guises. Nonetheless, the premise of this programme is unequivocally liberal: the empowerment of individuals through assisted consumption, with their collective aspirations guaranteed by market mechanisms which bring equilibrium to the personal, domestic and political domains. In this present configuration of digitality, the 'meaning' of the media culture is taken to exist not so much within the content of various platforms, but within the 'interactivity' (or even 'hyperactivity') of media users. By this logic, audiences realize agency not by choosing to read or think in different ways, but by doing a lot of clicking and commenting. Opportunities to do so have proliferated exponentially, as a procession of multimedia gadgets and software applications have targeted the enthusiasm for online entertainment and interpersonal communication.

In the gold-rush of the 'Web 2.0' economy of the 2000s, Internet startups mushroomed like rock bands in the late 1960s, all seeking to build their own social media fanbases before 'selling out' to entertainment corporates and other major league investors. As part of that process, the public love affair with digital technologies has produced its own series of fashions and crazes, with fan cultures building around the styling of personal media devices and the various semantic rituals embedded in platforms such as Twitter, Facebook, Flickr, Viber, WhatsApp etc. By taking part in this vast workshop of communication, Internet users engage with a vast 'participatory culture', an entirely novel media system centred upon the contributions of its audience.[1] This particular socio-technical interface has arisen from the commercial dynamics of consumer electronics, and this seductive convergence of technological novelty, popular culture and public speech has fashioned a union between 'Trekkies' and 'Techies' at a number of levels. The predominant 'user paradigm' then, is intended to embody the consumer utopias envisaged in Alvin Toffler's ideal type of the 'prosumer'. Thus, the success of Web 2.0 portals over the past decade has been founded upon their capacity to extract value from the established transnationalism of youth culture, and the rich folklores that have been constructed cumulatively over the last half century. The social and economic motivations of a user-led system of this kind have been most usefully exemplified by the amateur video-sharing site YouTube and the rich participatory culture that it facilitates.[2]

YouTube functions as the primary site of contemporary fan culture, with a universal premise and a global footprint. It is able to do so because the other key aspect of Web 2.0 has been the reorganization of what was previously a fragmented and disparate body of online material into a series of 'gateways' that simultaneously aggregate and personalize the content of the World Wide Web. This 'channelling' of the Internet medium has produced 'pinch points' where public activity on the web can be commercialized. In order to manage content at this scale, the visibility of videos on YouTube is organized via a recommendations system that combines Google's search algorithms with the system of customer votes (or 'likes') also seen on social media platforms like Facebook and with the customer prompting system pioneered by Amazon in the 1990s. As with most 'Web 2.0' platforms seeking to derive value from their users, the personal profiles of YouTube members are primarily structured around consumption habits. Self-presentation in this domain takes place via our endorsement of particular films, shows and music. Those sharing an interest in a particular artist can use YouTube to quickly gain access to their entire back catalogue, clips of TV appearances, unreleased bootlegs, homemade 'talk to camera' album reviews, cover versions or mash ups by other fans, documentary features and tutorials for undertaking various 'tribute' productions. Attached to all of this material is a string of commentary provided by YouTube users.

This treasure trove of fan discourse and debate offers a rich mix of personal recollections linked to particular songs, appreciative and amorous statements, queries around particular material, arguments over the relative value of artists and the vigorous correction of erroneous statements by more expert fans (the ubiquitous 'uber nerds'). Each forum produces its own cascade of armchair experts, narcissists, activists, humanists, bigots, trolls and bunnies. Thus, participatory culture has proved to be something of a bear pit. Given its universal accessibility, this unruly field of discussion is also a global phenomenon. Taking aside the procession of 'world's funniest' clips and stunts delivered to your phone handset, YouTube has not become an alternative universe of citizen media, but rather a vast conglomeration of fan culture. The parallel replication of fan cultures across the world, and their aggregation via the World Wide Web, is instructive in terms of how we might understand the innumerable 'public spheres' being constructed around the consumption of popular culture at a global scale. What fans say and do around different examples of popular culture offers a prime example of their imaginative engagement with a wider society. Indeed, there are remarkable consistencies between the emotional registers of message boards on popular music and video content and those attached to the pages served up by NGOs or providers of international news. Even where these 'virtual communities' maintain a relatively limited referential geography, the vast chamber of the World Wide Web reinforces the grandiose tendencies of youthful expression.

User-led Transnationalism

The fact that such engagements now commonly take place within a unified global media system necessarily inculcates an innate consciousness of the globalization of possibility. Thus, at a mundane level, our everyday encounters with the hurly burly of fan debates in online forums underline the reality of global constituencies. To receive personalized evidence that your own objects of self-realization are equally meaningful to someone on the other side of the world is simultaneously both banal and profound. Far more accessible than the complex operations of global value chains, such moments are proof positive of globalization. Across the board, the expansion of conversational scale that such forums represent is quite possibly the most salient feature of the World Wide Web. Within each self-referential strand of the pop culture fabric, the primacy of national frames is often less determining than other points of commonality or difference between users. Nonetheless, the strategic use of national flags in online debates is itself a perpetual reminder of the global scope of our everyday text debates. People are almost universally compelled to state where they are from in the course of any substantial interchange with other users, and this locative aspect of self-presentation remains tremendously important to the meanings being drawn by others. From the amicable and cosmopolitan to the jingoistic and barbaric, the online interactions of a vast global public reveal, for the very first time, the operation of grassroots 'international relations' in real time.

The profusion of transnational interactions via bulletin boards, file shares, creative collaborations and various forms of virtual sociability provides us with a rich and easily accessible field of transnational communication. The individuation of the programming, and its vast cumulative range, offers insights into almost every conceivable topic. Invariably those insights are earthy, emotive, fragmented and inconsistent, thereby getting to the heart of the modern experience. Firmly in the popular domain, the interactions between these new audience formations take us beyond the dry justifications and language of policy and treaty that typically characterize studies in international relations. We should remain aware, of course, that much of this material, tending towards the irrational and the extreme, is unlikely to be representative of the 'considered opinions' favored by critical theory. Equally, these distinctive disembodied textual exchanges are medium-specific and should not be taken as evidence of 'natural' behaviors. Nonetheless, with their characteristic suturing of the personal, cultural and political, the vast body of transnational interactions taking place via the internet are tremendously valuable as a field of public speech into which the social imagination of globalization is being collectively projected. This is immensely valuable to the privileged few who have access to the birds eye data, even as most of us tend to miss the significance of this in the intense personalization of our media experience. At the very least, the network geography of user-led transnationalism further requires that any such future epistemology of audience behaviors must account for interactivity on a global scale.

Of course, the great paradox of a media system increasingly driven by the personal profiles of individual users is that most Web 2.0 portals are presented as entirely generic formats. Barring changes of language and script, YouTube or Facebook present themselves as universal standards for users across the world. Far from being culturally neutral, these platforms are infused with the 'Californian ideology' of Silicon Valley, in that they prescribe a certain form of individualism where freedom is made synonymous with an expansion of choice. On the screen in your hand, the individual capacity to shuffle our favorites, playlists and address books and to conduct arguments with our own personal public certainly feels very much like the empowerment of a unique personal space. Just as Raymond Williams saw the television set and the private car as technologies that provided for the privatization of public space, the era of mobile media takes individualism to a global scale.[3] We are now offered a 'roaming' media environment where our media applications and personal profiles operate seamlessly as we move around the world. Regardless of where you travel, your own personal media channels will maintain your personalised cultural domain and the privilege of micro-managing it. You can paint your own cloud. This is where our intense interest in the popular and personal provides the primary terrain for managing the inherent contradiction between the hyper-liberal ideology of networked individualism and the functional imperatives for the standardization of data.[4]

Big Data

For the technorati, whose desired crop is readily comparable data, social information must be collected somewhat generically. Equally, since the underlying economics of Web 2.0 rely upon the real-time application of targeted marketing via automated algorithms, the input variables must also operate in a recognisable series. That is why the prevailing form of 'identity' in digital culture is standardised through this clumsy mash-up of the fan survey, dating ad and CV formats. By firmly anchoring all user activities to a set of profiling systems, this vast audience is systematically captured as an informational commodity.[5] The business models of Facebook and Google are only viable because we have already accepted the global domination of the relatively small number of information technology giants who set and maintain protocols and operating standards for the World Wide Web. As such, we should not forget that this systematic capture of the Internet's audience is a direct consequence of an integrated transnational media system. The 'necessary convenience' of these services consequently allows them to operate as gateways to a vast realm of human experience, thereby aggregating a majority of Internet users into the critical mass which allows for their secondary commercialization. In that respect, the global scale at which contemporary social media platforms operate is inconceivably vast (two billion is an abstract only tangible, perhaps, to a seasoned quant). Nobody has ever had so much data, nor had it in an individuated and relational structure so purposefully designed for correlation. Despite the obvious shortcomings of commercially-defined user profiling, it remains the case that sufficient scale confers value to even the most clumsy survey instrument.

Unlike an earlier era where market researchers would examine consumers in direct relation to a given product, the vast datasets being constructed from the social media era are purposefully intended to automatically correlate past and potential behaviors in relation to all or any products, activities or actions. This constitutes something of a tipping point in the informational economy. It becomes possible only because processing power has increased exponentially (as anticipated by Moore's law). It becomes possible only because data storage has become inconceivably vast and cheap. It becomes possible only because a user-led medium of record removes the need to employ millions of data entry clerks to capture the data. With this architecture in place, the engineers of Web 2.0 have consciously initialized a chain reaction in the generation of data. The ultimate output of this vast experiment is a mode of informatics where various logics of correlation can be deployed to create new knowledge from the raw material.[6] Whereas Web 1.0 was a radical experiment in free speech and global connectivity, the users of Web 2.0 are all participants, witting or otherwise, in a series of universal lab tests exploring the possibilities of Big Data. Notably, the evident focus upon the benefits of Big Data techniques for businesses, managers and consumers consistently implies the creation of new value from existing and/or self-replenishing stores of data. Without the continuing flow of user-generated content, the alchemical processes of Web 2.0 would break down entirely.

Fundamentally, Web 2.0 has nothing to do with self-realization, cultural bonding or the uncovering of meaning, but everything to do with the quantification of social behaviors on a global scale. This has little, if anything, to do with the traditional concerns of academic audience research but everything to do with the quantification of social behaviors for the purposes of extraction. As you might expect, such a program has no more time for national sovereignty than it has for personal privacy. A handful of Internet companies now know more about the functional behaviors of media audiences than all the academic researchers in the world combined. Most critically, Big Data analysts at the major multinationals are not interested in the indexical truth of the data (its connection to reality) but almost wholly in the calculative potentials of the data itself. Their interest in the activity of digital audiences may be entirely different from ours, but it is no less intense. This is necessarily the case, since the value of their numerological techniques is largely being realised through behavioral predictions. For our part, the pervasive nature of these practices indicates that there is no escaping the implications of Big Data for audience research as an academic practice.

Low Standards

Whereas the expanding domain of Big Data has something of an omnipotent air about it, it remains the case that most of the datafication projects currently in train necessarily suffer from the vast outsourcing operations that make them possible in the first place. The reliance of content aggregators on a combination of volunteered inputs and the wholesale scraping of inputs from disparate sources across the World Wide Web necessarily impacts upon the integrity of the data being collected. Big it may be, but essentially, this is all stolen data and, as you might reasonably expect, this means it is dirty data. A shopping history is not a very accurate rendition of an individual's taste, since the majority of purchases may well be for others. A list of favorite bands or movies is not a very deep reading of cultural orientation, given that people will often tend to 'like' the most popular acts as a result of peer pressure or indifference. The degree of investment, so central to the notion of fan cultures, is absent in the majority of inputs. The standardized format of most 'membership' profiles limits the nature of information collected, and the gaps in this data tend to be very important. In recent years, the more widespread looting of webmail and cloud storage through text searching means that the more standardized formats of profiling have to be correlated with volumes of personal and professional communication, which is by its very nature very complex and context-sensitive data. Such correlations tend to proceed via text-searching mechanisms, which further disembed the data object from its origins.

In the social sciences, we have to account for the knowing qualities of human subjects, that is, the transitive dimension of the 'data mining' experiment.[7] Users have become aware of the pervasiveness of data trails, and there is now an obvious 'chilling' effect, where even the most average college student understands that making too many jihad jokes online could make it difficult to take holidays that require air travel. At a more general level, it is already evident that as our awareness of secondary data processing and the permanency of our user history have started to sink in, people have taken evasive action online.[8] For some users, the constant prompting for elaborate inputs of personal information initiates a tendency towards wilful misinformation. The number of people who faithfully and consistently enter personal information are probably as rare as the numbers who actually read the terms and conditions agreements when they 'join up'. For those who remain willing, it is still quite difficult to be consistent when responding to innumerable surveys whose questions are preset and ultimate purpose unknown, even to the people designing them. Some users are stepping outside, by turning to private browsing technologies like Duck Duck Go, Tor and ProtonMail for reasons that are not so much nefarious as indignant. If we suspect that our book purchases are scrutinized for both commercial and paramilitary purposes, then we become naturally more suspicious of the questions put to us by academic researchers, and more careful about how we deploy participant information in publications.

Obviously, there are innumerable ethical dimensions to these developments, but even were we to sort these out it remains the case that the ubiquitous pressures of a global information society are affecting the spirit in which data is solicited and offered. Consequently, this places limits upon the integrity of the data itself. At the same time, by falling back upon the scraping of 'free' information provided in less fraught exchanges, as in social media platforms, we become restricted by the cellular architecture of those systems. For example, there is an enormous difference between the viewpoint of a single user moving through the interlinked pages of a social media system and the tiny number of people with access to the bird's eye view of that system. Collecting data from within the system is very difficult to do in any systematic sense, and the nature of the information is limited by the format parameters and the consistency of inputs. This is particularly frustrating since the scale of data being collected suggests that the answer is probably in there somewhere. At a more fundamental level, audience researchers can become lost in Big Data because the questions we ask tend to be premised upon the idea that the information 'out there' is descriptive of a social reality that we perceive as human beings. For the serious Big Data enthusiasts, however, the obvious disconnections between social reality and human complexity are largely irrelevant. Data analysts are not interested in the indexical truth of the data (its connection to reality) but almost wholly in the calculative potentials of the data itself.

We see this numerological tendency in the distinction that Mayer-Schonberger and Cukier make between causality and correlation - a distinction which marks a rupture between the positivism of natural science and the numerology of computer science.[9] Causality is the establishment of a likely reason for an event, via a controlled experiment where all variables are accounted for. Such controlled experiments are inherently difficult when it comes to social science because of the complexity of social variables and the knowing nature of the subjects themselves. Nonetheless, this work is intrinsic to the legacy of natural science and the various 'positivist' traditions in sociology. The essence of positivism is the desire to know why something happens, or why it is, and to establish the answer upon an empirical basis through experiments that can be repeated with the consistent results. Essentially, this is how 'social facts' are manufactured (be that about audiences or anything else). Correlation, by clear contrast, is about identifying trends in various forms of information and comparing them to establish patterns. These patterns can then be used to make predictions about what might happen next, even though this does nothing to establish the origin of such trends or the actual reason why any event will occur. In that sense, correlation plots current trends to predict the future, without worrying a jot about causality. Thus, for numerologists, the dirty nature of our data becomes relatively unimportant. They simply assume that once the scale of collection becomes sufficiently large, the data is all equally dirty and thereby that the trends they are following remain valid.

Numbers and Networks

With its interests in rearranging numbers to see the future, the convergence of 'data mining' and 'predictive analysis' clearly marks a revival of numerology for the purposes of divination.[10] Since the application of this numerological premise is typically a universal abstraction, there is little or no mention of cultural diversity in the various explications of Big Data. There is an implicit assumption that what rings true to a data analyst, programmer or executive in Silicon Valley constitutes the truth everywhere. The various 'universal' platforms of the social media age thus make scant, if any, concessions to the complexities of human cultures. Rather, there is a sense that the automated capacity to switch language script within a universal interface addresses the functional aspects of cultural geography, and that this is sufficient for the purposes of standardising user data. Thus, in marked contrast to the earlier audience research traditions in anthropology and cultural studies, the proponents of Big Data display a marked indifference to the deeper meanings of the actual content being carried on various platforms and the differing social systems that shape media reception across the world. Of itself, the use of datafication to 'solve' and therefore 'leapfrog' the linguistic barriers that have shaped human history infers that cultural difference can be rationalized by information technologies as a functional rather than subjective obstacle. Nonetheless, every time Big Data applications 'functionalize' and 'solve' such problems by applying one filter or another, they remove a large portion of the information that we have previously regarded as central to understanding the phenomena of audiences.

Pressed on this, the new audience quants could perhaps provide us with a set of parameters claiming to account for culturally specific viewing patterns if they wished to, but one suspects that colleagues in the humanities might remain unconvinced. The 'one size fits all' logic of Big Data notwithstanding, there are also some important questions to be raised when it comes to the geography of Big Data. Two billion Facebook pages is a big achievement, but this is still only one third of the global population (even assuming that each profile represents a unique and living user). The contours of the digital divide may have changed a good deal over the past decade but the world is not undivided when it comes to Internet access. Even more than that, if we are to rely so heavily on the inputs of shopping carts and pop fandom to establish social identities, then it remains difficult to establish how 'big audience research' of such a kind will capture the perspective of subsistence farmers in Ethiopia, for example, even where they have access to television or internet. Uneven geographies and demographies are an inevitable consequence of the narrow interests who operate scraping technologies. The common modes of 'collection' for Big Data are not sufficiently attuned to populations who remain comparatively less enmeshed in the digital mall that has been packaged as Web 2.0. When it comes to the everyday business of scraping, the Americans and Europeans are the most surveilled people on Earth, but for those who shop less there is less to scrape and, as a consequence, Big Data is an incredibly skewed sample for any behavioural universe.

Notwithstanding this uneven capture of human populations, the specific geographies of digital interaction have great potential for audience research and certainly merit some further Attention. When we look at network platforms in geographic terms, there is clearly additional value being generated in the spatial information embedded in network communications. Critically, as a medium of both communication and of record, the Internet shapes our communications in a network form, but it also captures their form continuously in real time. For audience researchers, this means that online audiences are automatically recorded as a rolling map of terminal locations and information flows. Were we able to access this data, and manage its volume and complexity, we would be able to see the unique spatial record of every audience configuration occurring online. Obviously, to the human eye these maps are a massive jumble of dots and lines that bear little correspondence to a concept of audience that we can grasp with any meaning. From a Big Data perspective, however, these graphical accounts can be correlated through powerful computers that can compare the almost innumerable records of sociability that now exist. Where patterns begin to emerge, a typology of networks begins and from this comes a characterization of what audience formations on the Internet actually look like. To take this exercise to the Big Data level, it becomes necessary to correlate social network records for every individual subscriber within this system, By doing so, we would hope to identify the underlying geographies of exchange and association within a worldwide field of popular culture.

Social network matching of this kind is a complicated exercise conceptually. It requires careful parameters, sophisticated algorithms and powerful processing.[11] More than that, it requires access to high level data. Nonetheless, while you couldn't do this kind of work for a ten thousand dollar research grant over the Easter recess, this kind of work is nothing like the 'Manhattan Project' of a global ethnography. Approached in this way, geospatial studies of transnational media audiences have become not only conceivable but eminently doable. We can expect, then, that this kind of work will be undertaken increasingly over the next few years. As a result, we will be able to learn much about the geographic bias of different cultural forms, from linguistic idioms down to punk bands. In the more finely grained studies, we may be able to capture the kind of inter-group dynamics that inspired social network analysis in the first place. If we then proceed to combine the possibilities of mapping new audience formations with the capacity to scrape and sort digital content, then our spatial knowledge of various networks of association can be augmented with the capture of everyday speech within those networks. Further, the integration of interpersonal communication with entertainment implies that we may also be able to map the varied forms of distribution by which cultural works circulate within social networks (whether by purchase, broadcast, gifting or stealing).

Materialism and Discourse

Notwithstanding the inherent limitations of data collection from the World Wide Web, it is obvious that these practices represent new potentials for enumerating, tracking and mapping transnational audience formations. With adequate resources and access, any online audience can be captured in data transfer records and mapped out visually, revealing in the process the complexity and density of communication in that cluster, along with the physical location of each member. In this form, then, we can now not only conceptualize transnational audiences, but actually see them. At another level, however, the embedding of these vast conjoined systems implies that the presence of the transnational is already acute within these networks, and thus a mutual awareness of the global scale becomes part of the relative positioning of all the individuals that we encounter. We get the sense that everyone is conceptually mapping global formations from different vantage points within the system. Arguably, it is meaningful evidence of how and why they do this that constitutes the great feedback loop in digital anthropology. Does such usage of Big Data, then, effectively close the loop between the underlying anthropological premise of audience studies and the emergence of an interactive global media system? Perhaps not quite. If this was to be our aim, we would have to ensure some capacity to move from the bird's eye view of Big Data back to the subjective, environmental and embodied domain of culture as a human experience.

In that respect, it is important to read the growing number of works that interrogate digitality within highly particular cultural and material locations. Daniel Miller's studies of social media in Trinidad and John Postill's work on the suburb of Subang Jaya in Kuala Lumpur are useful exemplars.[12] At this local scale, the fundamental shift from virtual and anonymous internet profiles to personalized and intimate media experiences clearly signifies the re-embedding of digital networks into the practices of everyday life (not as an 'other life').[13] In the process, our understanding of the central 'Big Data' platforms in social media becomes subject to material conditions, cultural norms and social rituals where local specificity is intrinsic to their operation. It still matters that Facebook is meaningful in highly specific ways in specific districts of Malaysia. This kind of ground-level understanding of user-led transnationalism requires us to capture not just the local network map, but also the rich interiority of mediated human networks and the environments in which they operate. Thus, at some level, we shift back down to the digitally-enhanced village and its workings. The nature of this material favors comparison over blunt correlation, but at the same time the increased volume of material that becomes available as a consequence of the World Wide Web makes even intensely localized studies subject to 'infoglut', and the new methodological challenges that go with it.[14]

Whereas the emerging practices in digital anthropology rely upon the architecture of Big Data as a means of both collection and stimulus for its participants, the conjoined thick description of interpersonal relationships and material environments serves to re-embed the data account within the physical (and thereby the intransitive within the transitive dimension). In the process, this ground-up approach allows us to reinterpret the macrological phenomenon of the World Wide Web at the micrological scale of material intimacies. Such a shift is not entirely unlike the affective domain that Facebook delivers to its users at the front-end. The nature of this work involves the de-centering of a universal 'user experience' within actually-existing cultures and societies, and this 'localization' process is increasingly having to account for the transnational scope of the communications process in developing societies, a development that Madianou and Miller seek to capture under the heading of 'polymedia' in their work on transnational Filipino families.[15] Where these situated accounts become more challenging for researchers is when it comes to the strictly mediated communities that only exist virtually. That is, those networks of interactants who share nothing in terms of intimacy, geography, culture, or polity. There are now numerous examples of transnational formations oriented primarily by enthusiasm for a particular set of mediated practices (variously receptive, collaborative, distributive, and/or dialogic). Such online engagements between participants here, there and everywhere cannot be accessed through any form of locality, as mediation itself is their only instance of communality.

Furthermore, participation in a transnational virtual community is most likely only a fragment of a wider multi-channel experience for these users. For an anthropologist, this would scarcely be a major trope of social identity. Nonetheless, some of the larger portals on the World Wide Web have memberships that rival and even surpass nation states, and we have not yet established the extent to which this mobilizes new supra-national sensibilities or whether it merely constitutes a banal transnationalism. This is a vitally important question, which requires access to the discursive realm of user-led transnationalism. This domain has been open to the 'rat's eye' view since the advent of the public Internet. For those prepared to track through, read and log the flow of transnational interactions, there is much that can be learned of the unique protocols of simultaneously international and interpersonal dialogues between users spread across the globe. This kind of labor intensive work remains light years from the capacity that we now have to track these interactions in terms of numbers and nodes. That is not to say that it is easy itself. With so many of the environmental and contextual clues stripped away, there has been considerable debate on the methodological limitations of virtual ethnography in this form. Nonetheless, these are appropriate techniques for indicative studies of user-led transnationalism, notwithstanding the increasing distortion of popular forums by government 'cyper-troopers' and, more recently, algorithms that spam these networks with the official line.[16]

To move beyond small samples and essentially manual methods of collection and analysis, it becomes necessary to consider a set of automated processes that might enable us to work with this material at a larger and/or more longitudinal scale. Making the transition to a 'Big Data' mode of qualitative research is no easy task, since the complexities of human communication have proved to be a consistently difficult problem for computer scientists to 'solve'. Whilst it has now become perfectly possible to harvest large volumes of online commentary from appropriate forums and on defined topics, the subsequent business of analysing the data in a fashion that illustrates the dynamics of transnational interaction is by far the hard task. Brian Yecies' recent work on user-generated commentaries on Korean popular culture within Chinese language web forums provides a useful illustration of both the technical and conceptual challenges that this work engages.[17] The parameters of collection are one thing, the linguistic issues another, and the transition from enumerating sentiments (in roughly positive / negative terms) to a deeper contextual analysis of intercultural discussion and subjective positioning is perhaps the greatest challenge of all. To some extent, the toolkit established for the purposes of testing market sentiment is sophisticated enough that it will rapidly supersede traditional processes of audience research by industries such as Hollywood. For scholars of cultural studies, however, an effective means of translating so many thousands of qualitative responses into a deeper understanding of cultural politics has yet to be established.

Bulk Billing in Audience Research

Taking account of these various examples and approaches, it is clear that audience research has entered a paradigm shift. We now conduct our business in a context where an automated account of audience activity is being collected on a universal scale, and not predominantly by national actors (nor, for that matter, by universities). As a consequence, common media formats, universal communication protocols and the incredible aggregation of users by contemporary web portals are bringing the top end of the transnational spectrum into focus. For those able to access and, more critically, to effectively manage this bulk of information, there are new possibilities for recording transnational interaction as a percentage of media consumption, of monitoring indicators of its activity levels as a live feed, of mapping the communicative structures of transnational interactions, and of tracking processes of cultural translation in real time. Thus, our field of enquiry seems poised for a shift from musing in detail on small samples to brainstorming new ways to sift and present data on a vast scale. The practical challenge is how to granulate the harvest. The conceptual challenge is how to situate the individuals and the social formations encapsulated in Big Data. These issues must be resolved because, taken by itself, it is hard to see how scraping away at the big picture can tell us much about social meanings. Certainly, correlation can give much in the way of context, but that is not the same thing.

At the most fundamental level, the simultaneous evolution of digital research methods and new audience formations via the internet signifies the extent to which we may find ourselves increasingly studying data about audiences, instead of the audiences themselves. What can be more tempting than the capacity to sit at your laptop and drop into rich conversations about media culture taking place on the other side of the world? What can be more tempting than the capacity to access a database and get real time representations of transnational audiences for specific forms of content? The clear and obvious danger of such pleasures is that the essentially human concerns of audience studies could be forgotten in the convenient euphoria of Big Data. Thus, our longstanding concern with meaning might be ill served by entering this goldmine of functional data without a map of our own. In many respects, it is starting to look like we are coming full circle to a world of 'mass effects' research driven by *a priori* assumptions and tested on sophisticated correlations of dirty data garnered from a reasonably unethical trawling operation. The prevailing emphasis on correlation over causality, and on data manipulation over data integrity may be suited to behavioural studies of shopping with limited aims, but these are shaky foundations for any understanding of global cultures. Indeed, such tendencies are precisely what the proponents of active audience theory have sought to counter for the past fifty years.

In the digital aftermath of cultural studies, then, what we may be left with is a radically decontextualized numerology that begins with the online consumption of popular culture. If we proceed uncritically, then the various data formats now emerging will become self-referential enquiries that increasingly forget the independent existence of the phenomena that they were originally conceived to study. It is in this fashion, very precisely, that data overtakes reality. A more productive approach would be to direct our attention towards the potentials of digital research tools as we see them. In many respects, the real utility of 'Big Data' on audiences lies not its sheer bulk but in the fact that it is granular. This means that well-designed studies can operate at several scales, and might therefore be able to furnish understandings in areas that remained practically out of reach just a few years back. For those questions we haven't yet thought to ask, there are also new potentials here for exploratory work, leading perhaps to more sophisticated understandings of key concepts like interactivity, community, crowd and public. For those of us interested in the phenomenon of user-led transnationalism, we certainly cannot ignore the emerging capacity to grasp the depth and scope of transnational social interactions in a digital age. This may well prove critical for understanding the cultural geography of the World Wide Web, not to mention the subtle variations in the politics of culture that inevitably point to the future.

Notes

1 See H. Jenkins "The Cultural Logic of Media Convergence", *International Journal of Cultural Studies*, 7 no. 1 (2004): 33–43.
2 See J. Burgess and J. Green, *You Tube: Online Video and Participatory Culture*, (Cambridge: Polity, 2015).

3 See R. Williams, *Television: Technology and Cultural Form* (London: Collins. 1974) and also A. Athique, Digital Media and Society (Cambridge: Polity, 2013), 111–123.

4 See, for example, B. Wellman, Barry (2003) 'The Social Affordances of the Internet for Networked Individualism', *Journal of Computer-Mediated Communication*, 8 no. 3, at: http://onlinelibrary.wiley.com/doi/10.1111/jcmc.2003.8.issue-3/issuetoc; viewed 12 February 2012.

5 As per the logics outlined in R. Zafarani,. M. A. Abbasi, and H. Liu, Huan *Social Media Mining: An Introduction* (New York: Cambridge University Press, 2014).

6 See D. Neef, *Digital Exhaust: What Everyone Should Know About Big Data, Digitization and Digitally Driven Innovation* (New Jersey: Pearson 2014) and also T. H. Davenport, *Big Data @ Work* (Boston: Harvard Business Review Press, 2014).

7 See T. Benton and I. Craib, *The Philosophy of Social Science: The Philosophical Foundations of Social Thought* (Houndmills: Palgrave Macmillan, 2010) 134–5.

8 See M. Andrejevic, "Surveillance and Alienation in the Online Economy", *Surveillance and Society*, 8 no. 3 (2011): 278–87.

9 V. Mayer-Schonberger and K. Cukier, *Big Data: A Revolution That Will Transform How We Live, Work and Think* (New York: John Murra, 2013).

10 For example, E. Siegel, *Predictive Analytics: The Power to Predict Who Will Click, Buy, Lie, or Die* (New Jersey: John Wiley and Sons, 2013).

11 On the technical side, see S. D. Roy and W. Zeng, *Social Multimedia Signals: A Signal Processing Approach to Social Network Phenomena* (Heidelberg: Springer, 2014).

12 D. Miller, Daniel, *Tales From Facebook* (Cambridge: Polity, 2011) and J. Postill, John *Localizing the Internet: An Anthropological Account* (New York: Berghahn Books, 2011).

13 See H. Horst and D. Miller (eds) *Digital Anthropology* (London and New York: Berg., 2012).

14 M. Andrejevic, *Infoglut: How Too Much Information is Changing the Way We Think and Know* (London and New York: Routledge, 2013).

15 M. Madianou and D. Miller, *Migration and New Media: Transnational Families and Poly-Media* (Routledge: London, 2012).

16 See A. Rutkin, Aviva, "'Botivist' Calls You to Arms", *New Scientist*, 227, no. 3041 (2015): 24 and V.S. Subrahmanian, V.S. et al. "The DARPA Twitterbot Challenge", *IEEE Computer Magazine*, arXiv:1601.05140v2, 2016) and R.Tapsell "Negotiating Media Balance in Malaysia's 2013 General Election", *Journal of Current Southeast Asian Affairs*, 32 no. 2 (2013): 39–60.

17 Z. Yang, Zie and B. Yecies, Brian "Mining Chinese Social Media UGC: A Big-Data Framework for Analyzing Douban Movies Reviews", *Journal of Big Data*, 3 no. 1 (2016): 1–23 and B. Yecies, Brian, Z. Yang, M. Berryman and K. Soh, Kai "Marketing Bait (2012): Using SMART Data to Identify *e-guanxi* Among China's Internet Aborigines", in N. C. Tirtaine, Cecilia and J. Augros (eds) *Film Marketing into the 21st Century* (London: British Film Institute, 2015).

2 Audiences and Australian Media Policy

The Relevance of George Gerbner

Andy Ruddock

Introduction

This chapter outlines the relevance of George Gerbner's work on television violence to audience informed, policy-directed Australian media research. Gerbner founded the Cultural Indicators Project (CIP) in the 1960s. He is best known for his work on violence in broadcast television. However, from a contemporary perspective, there are reasons to think that his ideas about the social significance of popular culture, and the avenues it opened for audience activism, were better suited to the digital age. At the very least, it's easy to show how Gerbner illuminates key issues in Australian media policy, as it is made over to serve digital audiences. Gerbner innovated American policy debates by connecting screen violence to the political import of popular entertainment; often with a special focus on gender relations. Today, a similar project is afoot in Australia: Academics have made incursions into public policy by shepherding debates about sex and violence toward issues of social inclusion. This strategy shares with Gerbner the conviction that familiar concerns about violence, pornography and copycat behavior fail to address the deeper cultural impact of screen cultures. In Australia, we are asked to think not only about if pornography and action-based content provoke misogyny and aggression, but if they might also play positive social roles. Gerbner, on the other hand, was keener to rethink the kind of damage that such content might exert on people who, at face value, don't do anything after exposure. Despite these differences, it's worth noting that Gerbner's main contribution to media policy was his characterization of 'mass' media as key nodes in processes of social communication. Gerbner also aspired to include media users in the formulation of media policy. In combination, these aspects of his work offer that Gerbner's views on how violence expressed the political logic of commercial media continue to illuminate the role that audiences play in digital cultures.

Bringing a CIP perspective to Antipodean conversations adds historical weight to the notion that policy should use nuanced understandings of what violence and pornography represent, as core elements of media culture. It reminds us that questions of social inclusion lie behind the issue of media effects, and that in this sense the contemporary policy landscape may have changed less than the technologies it addresses. But it also queries Australian enthusiasm for non-adversarial, consumerist relationships between audiences and industries. A CIP view offers an adversarial alternative. Moreover, the option it offers complements the strategies contemporary digital audiences use to challenge dominant sex/violence screen representations. Therefore, this chapter will make the case that including Gerbner's ideas in discussions over the health of Australia's digital media ecology offers alternative visions for what audiences can do in public cultures still dominated by corporate storytelling, other than those currently proffered in consumer-based approaches to media and education policy.

Sex, Violence, and Media Policy

Australian academics have outlined innovative options for managing screen sex and violence; 'risky' content that has always provoked scholarly debate and public concern. The affects of convergence on content classification,[1] and the value of pornography in healthy relationships,[2] are two notable examples. Audience research has played a key role in each project. The absence of compelling evidence that screen violence and pornography harms its audience has been noted;[3] so, too, the possibility that such content might do its viewers some good.[4] These positions emphasize the positive role that commercial media industries play in democratic societies. But they are also convenient to a changed environment that has vastly expanded rates of exposure.[5]

Whatever their motivations, initiatives to reconcile new media industries and public interest are controversial. Graeme Turner criticized a tendency toward unwarranted optimism about media and well-being, fuelled by 'anecdotal evidence and self-serving industry spin from the entrepreneurs of cool capitalism'.[6] From an audience's perspective, the question becomes how to articulate these reservations, while acknowledging the value of avoiding the impulse to prejudge 'risky' content as inherently bad. One option here is to use the language of the CIP. Some Australian work encourages policy decisions informed by the pleasure that audiences derive from violent and sexually explicit materials. The CIP explains why it is just as valid to listen as other audiences voice the discomfort they experience through unwanted exposure caused by limited choice. Both, positions, I suggest, are equally valid. Moreover, recent examples of digital activism show how audiences are starting to use Gerbner's ideas to affect changing production practices.

The argument evolves as follows. First, I explore recent Australian media research on the management of violent and sexually explicit materials. Second, I explain why Gerbner's work is significant to these developments, since it reimagined the geography of audience studies, particularly around the concept of message systems. The last section of the paper explains why Gerbner's reconceptualization of media risk suggests that we need to spend as much time listening to what the public doesn't like about screen sex and violence, as to the enjoyment they get from such material. It also explains how digital media set the foundation for the kind of audience-driven media activism that Gerbner wanted to provoke.

Australia Media Policy and the Question of Media Effects

In Australia, questions about what media violence and pornography are, and what they do to their audiences, have been used to contemplate cultural rights. Croucher and Flew's *Classification-Content Regulation and Convergent Media*, a report prepared for the Australian Law Reform Commission (ALRC), sought to improve the quality of audience experience and the vitality of Australia's media industries by updating the nation's content censorship and classification scheme. The lessons of international audience research on the effects of violence and pornography played a key role here in serving two principles: that 'Australians should be able to read, hear, see and participate in media of their choice'[7] and that 'Communications and media services available to Australians should broadly reflect community standards, while recognizing a diversity of views, cultures and ideas in the community'.[8] Sex and violence were key indicators of the latter; the report noted that Australia's existing regulatory framework acknowledged public fears about scenes of sexual violence. This brought pornography into the debate. Whether or not we agree, some argue that demeaning, misogynistic sexual violence is a signature of mainstream pornography.[9] Even performers see danger and exploitation, sometimes bordering on coercion, as a professional hazard.[10]

At any rate, violence and pornography have emblematized the balance between commercial and public interest in Australian policy reform. This is an audience affair, because research on what aggressive performances, sexual or otherwise, *do* to their viewers informed Croucher and Flew's recommendations. Drawing on Gunter,[11] the authors noted that exposure to violence is connected to three kinds of harm: aggression, desensitization, and fear. However, the report concentrated on the former, noting 'that there are inherent difficulties in making recommendations about content classification policy and regulation based on claims of media effects on human behavior'.[12] The absence of solid findings of harm was juxtaposed with the likelihood that exposure also lead to pleasure, empathy, and learning. Effectively, the report presented a binary view of what screen violence is, as a message; an injunction to aggression, versus a commonly enjoyed source of imaginary pleasure that does no harm, and indeed might do some good. Inattention to fear and displeasure limited the report's value as a source of public information about the variety of reasons why we should care about media violence.

This was a significant absence, because the report was part of an equally significant academic trend. The ALRC review maintained that the absence of compelling evidence on the dangers of media sex and violence, and absence of research into the good that this content might do, underpinned the legitimacy of pursuing a rapprochement between public and industry, rather than protecting the former against the latter. Research on pornography, examining how consumers use it to support relationships, has taken this position from media to education policy.

Alan McKee is a crucial figure here. There is research suggesting connections between pornography use and positive social outcomes - such as a more tolerant view of same-sex relationships.[13] According to McKee, such effects aren't surprising, because porn is entertainment, similar in form to other sources of media pleasure. Some might feature violent actions directed by men toward women, but most people prefer porn that is consensual, light hearted, irreverent and non judgmental.[14] Moreover, its users, or at least the ones that he researched, are a moral bunch who abhor exploitation.[15] Ergo, a vibrant pornography industry that responds to its consumers is perfectly in keeping with policy values that reconcile economic vigor with social well being.[16] Naturally, this leads to radically new policy options. In terms of what it is, the case that pornography is an open space of entertainment and pleasure, and one of the few arenas where diverse sexual identities are expressed without judgment, lends a different view on content classification; many of the things that we might see as 'violent' in porn are nothing of the sort, and reflect a narrow view of what consensual sex can be. The effect here operates against the interests of inclusive culture: common sense views on the unacceptable end up being exclusionary, by underwriting heteronormative views of what healthy sex is.[17] Once we allow that a lot of what looks like harmful porn to heteronormative viewers is benign and helpful to others, then new policy options become clear; for example, instead of worrying about steps to keep pornography away from younger audiences, perhaps we should consider how sex education can embrace it.[18]

Evidence of the effects is again key to this position. McKee argues the case that porn provokes aggression against women relies on flawed experimental evidence.[19] Effects are found when audiences are exposed to extreme images that they would not choose to access, under conditions that are nothing like the natural habitat of the porn user. As with Croucher and Flew, the gist is that the absence of sound evidence as to porn's dangers, balanced against the lack of attention to porn's healthy pleasures, makes a valid case for moving the policy question beyond the fields of risk and restriction.

Australia has seen a valuable rethink of what screen sex and violence is, and what it does among audiences. This has made the case that nimble, consumer-centered commercial media industries are good for national culture. So may they be; but it's worth pointing out that there are other ways to redefine the ontology of violent entertainment, and its impact, that lead to alternative conclusions. Crouch, Flew, and McKee critique effects research that treats scenes of sex and violence as simple messages about how to behave. But more complex views of what such content represents provides a way to rethink harm, as well as pleasure, and this is a vital consideration in the current policy moment. Enter George Gerbner.

The Cultural Indicators Project

Gerbner altered the policy application of North American mass communication research by connecting media violence to political socialization. Like Croucher, Flew, and McKee, he believed the behaviorist effects studies missed the point about why and how media matter to most people, most of the time. Unlike Australian scholars, he used this as the basis for reconceiving harm. Between the late 1960s and late 1970s, Gerbner and his colleagues at the University of Pennsylvania used content analysis and surveys to urge scholars, politicians, media and the public to stop worrying about the behaviors of individual audience members and start fretting about the effect of violence on the public imagination.[20]

Gerbner's work on violence was motivated by the question of how creativity and public inclusion could flourish in the face of media industries that were commercially hostile to both.[21] Gerbner maintained that commercial message systems limited the diversity of public storytelling, to undemocratic ends: violence was but a symptom of this effect.[22] Quantitative content analysis showed that violence indeed dominated American broadcast television, and surveys comparing the world views of people who watched a great deal, versus those who did not, suggested that this had tangible effects on perceptions of social reality. In particular, the plethora of television violence 'cultivated' the perception that the world was a far more dangerous place than was actually the case, for most viewers.[23] Croucher and Flew mentioned this 'mean world' syndrome, but did not elaborate on the provenance or political inferences of the concept. This is significant because the implications of the 'mean world' syndrome, as elaborated by Gerbner *et al.* are considerable when considering the nature of audience experience.[24]

Gerbner's content analyses – a series of annual 'violence profiles' drawn from samples of prime-time US television – defined violence as a story, rather than an action.[25] Looking at patterns of who tended to do it, and who suffered, Gerbner and his colleagues defined television violence as a power parable; women, the young, the old, and people of color were most likely to be the victims of onscreen assault and murder, and white middle-class, middle-aged men tended to be the only group that benefitted from violence.[26]

The main 'effect' of these stories was to make viewers afraid and suspicious. Surveys found that the more television people watched, the more that they came to accept its version of social reality as the truth; thinking the world was a far more violent place than was actually the case, and adopting pessimistic beliefs, such as the view that most people were self-seeking, and not to be trusted. In this sense, violence was but a symptom of the political problem posed by commercial media; a preference for predictable, uncomplicated content produced a public culture that offered few debates or options for social action, promoting nothing other than consumerism and an acceptance of social inequality as 'just the way things are'.[27] Putting it another way, where effects studies asked how violence made people do things, Gerbner argued that the main outcome was to discourage audiences from doing much of anything.[28]

Gerbner wanted his evidence to energize media professionals and audiences into demanding a more vibrant public culture. Gerbner was a fastidious note-taker who left an extensive archive of memos, letters, emails and unpublished materials. A tiny fraction of these resources has been uploaded to a digital archive, compiled at the University of Pennsylvania. Using this content, and an authoritative guide written by Morgan,[29] several important dimensions of Gerbner's work are clearer now than they have been in the past. In particular, it reveals four points of compatibility between cultivation and critical understandings of digital audiences.

First, Gerbner saw media communication as a link in a complex chain of social communication. Gerbner's early model of communication shared much in common with Stuart Hall's encoding/decoding model; both scholars thought that reality was constructed through a series of encoding/decoding moments that carried the material world through the cultural industries and their publics.[30] Gerbner's account of the risks of media violence was not based on a simplistic understanding of media content that ignored the complexities and ambiguities of meaning. In his research on confession magazines of the 1950s, for example, Gerbner used interviews with editors and corner store retailers to solve the riddle of how a media form that aimed to frighten women into compliant domesticity became so popular with the very audience it set out to pacify. The staple feature of these magazines were stories about 'good' girls who were subjected to horrific ordeals when they rejected patriarchy. One story, for example, details the torment of a young woman who travels to Europe alone, where she meets a nice young Austrian man who turns out to be a vicious Nazi. Gerbner noted a contradiction, however; these horrible tales were carried by magazines that always showed happy women. Through speaking with shopkeepers, he found that the architecture of the supermarket demanded that the lurid content of these magazines be disguised with happy covers maintaining the prevailing consumer mood. Hence, the 'preferred meaning' of confession magazines – 'women,

it's a scary world, stay at home and consume' – emerged through the negotiation of media content, space, and the aspirations of different groups
positioned at different distribution points.[31]

The magazine study established the most important aspect of Gerbner's
thinking; that operation of media power depended on its mode of distribution. From this perspective, Gerbner fits into a tradition of critical
message system analysis, beginning in the work of Harold Innis, em-
bracing key cultural studies figure James Carey, and continued in Evgeny
Morozov's work on the conservatism of digital media.[32] Gerbner believed his role was to question the role of television in democracy, at a
time when many people accepted its benefits as a given. The connections
between the personal and academic convictions of Gerbner and Innis are
striking; both were combat veterans who had seen 'improved' systems
of communication destroy lives, landscapes, and cultures.[33] Both were
keen to resist the idea that more efficient communication systems were
intrinsically better. And both were interested in how dystopian views
of media history facilitated the understanding of empire. In Gerbner's
case, these ideas found early expression in comparative analysis of the
depiction of the teaching profession on US and Soviet Union screens.
Gerbner – who had been fired from his first academic post for alleged
leftist tendencies – used content analysis to make the point that in the
USSR, drama tended to show teachers as respected, happy individuals
who knew that their work had social value. In American screen fiction,
they were more likely to be sad and lonely malcontents who only found
happiness when they quit teaching.[34] The lessons were that the cultivation of responsible social values could not be left to commercial media, and that the only way to manage content in pro-social directions
was to influence its modes of production and distribution.

Nevertheless, Gerbner believed that people could change media industries. He may have been a pessimist, but the poor Hungarian refugee
who became a hero, by personally arresting the prime minister of the
Hungarian fascist wartime regime, was no fatalist. He hoped the violence profiles, which showed the limited roles offered to women actors,
and the narrow license afforded to creatives, could be used as evidence
by bodies such as the Screen Actors Guild to agitate for change. In his
later years, Gerbner turned his attention to the creation of a 'Cultural
Environment Movement'; a network of grassroots community organizations that sought to agitate for more imaginative public storytelling
from the television and film industries.[35] Despite his conviction that the
total commercial media system was endemically disingenuous, vis-à-vis
the rhetoric versus the practice of social responsibility, he never thought
that the people who worked in the cultural industries were the problem,
or that audiences were helpless. Toward the end of his life, Gerbner came
to believe that citizen action promised more than policy as a means of
changing media industries. When it came to forging democratic media

systems 'independent citizen action, rather than corporate or government regulation can build appropriate mechanisms'.[36] Gerbner's concern was that legislative efforts to classify and control access to images
of sex and violence were ultimately ineffective because they failed to
address how the proliferation of such content reflected the requirement
in monopolized, globalized, commercialized media industries to produce stories that sell. Stories about women in peril, for example 'not
only teach lessons of vulnerability, mistrust and dependence but also
help sell burglar alarms, more jails and executions promised to enhance
security'.[37]

The headline finding of the 'mean world syndrome' – that the more
television Americans watched, the more afraid and manipulated they
became – meant that for many years, qualitative researchers put Gerbner
in the very effects box that Croucher and Flew critiqued.[38] Perhaps this
is why the ALRC review did not pursue fear as a concept worth much
consideration. This is a missed opportunity, since a broader understanding of Gerbner's work tells a story of shared interests between the CIP
and critical audience studies. Moreover, this is important at a time when
key figures like Liz Bird and Graeme Turner urge us to return to questions of how media culture confines social imagination and opportunity.[39] The notion that screen violence needs to be recognized as a story
that speaks to the nature of popular entertainment, and its social role,
can be used to frame a different kind of relationship between audiences
and industries, other than a consumer/industry partnership grounded
in pleasure. Incorporating Gerbner's work with recent Australian developments, reframing sex and violence as entertaining stories that reflect key tendencies in the nature of commercial popular culture, offers
two different views on the role of audiences in cultural industries. The
language of pleasure involves them as knowledgeable consumers who
choose content. The language of complaint involves them as activists
who seek to act on its creation and regulation. Consider, for example,
Gerbner's vision for the Cultural Environment Movement, which was
the endgame of several decades of work using violence to argue that
popular entertainment stifled artistic creativity, political imagination
and public participation:

> Placing cultural policy issues on the social-political agenda. Sup-
> porting and if necessary organizing local and national media coun-
> cils, study groups, citizen groups, minority and professional groups
> and other forums of public discussion, policy development, repre-
> sentation and action. Not waiting for a blueprint but creating and
> experimenting with ways of community and citizen participation
> in local, national and international media policymaking. Sharing
> experiences, lessons and recommendations and gradually moving
> toward a realistic democratic agenda.[40]

The point is that Gerbner's violence work eventually showed how focusing on displeasure, fear, and lack of choice fashions active roles for audiences in cultural policy, based on the notion that audiences, writers, and performers all wanted to see a more creative public culture, less shackled by the obligation to make and consume 'stories that sell'. If such hopes seemed pie in the sky in the nineties, they seem eminently possible in today's world, where creative and audiences have allied to affect such changes, based on lack of choice, in stories about sex and violence. To validate this interpretation of Gerbner's work, consider two projects that demonstrate how the language of cultivation helps explain the dilemma of pornography and violence, taking audience experience of these phenomena as entertainment forms into account.

Anger and Activism

On the topic of gaming, the absence of choice in a sea of formulaic, frequently offensive violence is a matter of concern *to gamers*.[41] A rancorous conflict has emerged between effects scholars who feel a link between game play and aggression has been established beyond reasonable doubt,[42] versus colleagues who feel this is a politically motivated, deceptive argument.[43] These quarrels have spilled out of academe into the public sphere, due in good measure to the escalation of rampage shootings as bitterly familiar media events.[44] Intriguingly, though, some gamers do fear their pleasure is implicated in these catastrophes; at least insofar as gaming is a suggestive reference point in cogitations on the causes of violence. In some online gaming communities, the Sandy Hook tragedy prompted a desire to take greater ownership of this discourse. Writing for *Rock, Paper, Shotgun*, games journalist Nathan Grayson issued a distinctly Gerbneresque plea for reflection:

> We take tremendous joy in virtual violence. We squeal with glee when life-giving liquid squirts out of men's necks. Does that cause violence? Probably not.... But it gives violence an active, constant role in our day-to-day lives ... it would be impossible for frequent immersion in violent scenarios – fictional or not – to not have some kind of effect on us.[45]

Where the potential of gaming as a vehicle for consciousness raising is clear, the squandering of this potential by commercial gaming industries is a problem, seen from the gamer's experience. Grayson's web comments sparked a discussion where a couple of noteworthy arguments emerged. First, the dominance of unimaginative violence (that is, shooting, stabbing, punching, and kicking that makes no effort to encourage gamers to think about morality) means the industry keeps gamers in the firing line on gun crime. Second, the reality of life for most gaming enthusiasts is marked by frustration, born from a lack of choice, as they sift through hours of monotonous barbarity in search of the odd jewel. Overall, the idea that violence expresses a lack of creativity in media industries, and that this lack of creativity constitutes a failure of responsibility toward public culture, is one that some gamers, in this instance at least, recognized.[46]

Similar initiatives have been noted in studies of pornography. Ethnographies of sex industry retailing tell fascinating stories of production, distribution, and consumption loops. These specify the circumstances that afford creative relationships between producers and audiences. However, such mutually enriching connections are based on the consensus that the mainstream commercial porn market hinders the telling of different stories about non-heteronormative sexuality. Strikingly, elements of this work echo Gerbner's finding that small corner stores were key players where feedback altered the content of 1950s confession magazines. In a similar vein, Comella's study of Seattle-based feminist retailer 'Babeland' described how the store became a physical space that altered content by bringing producers and consumers together.[47] The 'Babeland' study demonstrated that women audiences – or at least the ones who frequented that store – were not able to choose the content that they wanted to see, until the store itself was able to create a visible market for that content. The formation of small markets was vital to the opportunities that McKee has championed. Only when producers and audiences meet to discuss what they like to see, *and what they don't*, can the criteria for good, even educational pornography be developed. Consequently, this work has made a crucial specification to the idea that commercially healthy media industries operate in the public interest; in the case of pornography, the American experience suggests that this happens when community-centered industries create niche markets by cultivating their own audiences, giving them a voice that speaks to the *lack* of pleasure that they get from mainstream pornographic fare.[48]

Conclusion: Cultural Indicators and Australian Audience Studies

In Australia, listening to audiences' experiences with screen sex and violence has played a key role in staging normative questions about entertainment and public interest. To develop this worthy trend, it's important to understand that starting policy discussions by asking the audience does not mean privileging choice and pleasure. Displeasure, distress, boredom and lack of choice are equally significant, and Gerbner's CIP is a useful tool for addressing these themes. It is a research model that used violence to outline how media industries set the rules of social discourse. Gerbner's thinking prefigured many contemporary issues relating to digital audiences, and are highly relevant to debates about the potential risks of exposure to violent media content, which continue to drive academic engagements with media policy. If nothing else, his views on how screen violence works as a cultural message system explains why scholars like Turner are wary of using the lessons of audience research to explore synergies between industries and audiences.

Croucher and Flew and McKee used weaknesses in behavioral audience studies to argue that Australian culture can flourish through the partnership of vibrant media industries serving knowledgeable audiences who should enjoy access to a range of properly labeled stories about sex and violence. This may well be true, but as it stands, the argument does not take on board other accounts of how violence and pornography damages its audiences in non-behavioral ways.

Gerbner's ideas on how media entertainment affects audiences who don't 'do' anything need to be part of the conversation. This is all the more important since key elements of the classification/pornography argument rest on principles that Gerbner would agree with; Australians should be able to access the media content that they enjoy; the assessment of risky content needs to listen to the audience; pornography isn't radically 'other' from other forms of media entertainment. The thing is, Gerbner used these ideas to advocate for an adversarial relationship between audiences and media creators versus media businesses. Audiences can't access the content they want because commercial industries won't make it, and the prevalence of violence is a symptom of standardized public storytelling. Recent examples of audience and artist activism in gaming and pornography indicates popular agreement with these ideas. Gerbner's vision for a Cultural Environment Movement was ahead of its time. At any rate, a robust engagement with media industries and policy in Australia would do well to hear what Gerbner had to say about media violence as a catalyst for political engagement, and spend time with audiences who don't like what they see on their screens.

Ultimately, Gerbner's saw audiences as vital links in blended chains of media and social communication, which is the crux of the question of why digital audiences matter. Gerbner's insight on this 'mattering' can be seen through a couple of examples. First, his notion that repeated exposure to the same content cultivated political relationships – often damaging ones that centered on gender – remains highly relevant when considering the impact of digital culture. Interestingly, in the field of online pornography, researchers who have very different views on the impact of such content, be it good or bad, agree that increased exposure to it plays a role in normalizing pornography as an integral part of popular culture.[49] Again, commercially oriented pornography contributes to discourses of sexuality. Hence, the observation that one of the main media effects is to naturalize the language of the market as the language of culture remains relevant to discussions on digital content, like online porn, regardless of how one views its effects.

Second, his notion that media violence tells a political story, and that being able to 'read' that story should provide an impetus to citizen action, can be seen at work in fields such as gaming activism. His efforts to involve the public in challenging dominant modes of production and distribution foundered, because they were ahead of their time. Feminist gaming activists such as Anita Sarkeesian ground their work in the observation that the repeated use of sexualized violence in gaming is an expression of a creative failure that spawns little other than misogyny. Her brand of crowd sourced industrial interventions, using digital media resources, is precisely the kind of action that Gerbner wanted audiences to take. Thus, appreciating Gerbner is a valuable way to connect contemporary considerations about digital audiences to more enduring themes on the relationship between media narratives and public well-being.

Notes

1 Croucher, Rosalind, and Terry Flew. "Classification-Content Regulation and Convergent Media." Sydney: Australian Law Reform Commission, 2012.
2 McKee, Alan. "Censorship of Sexually Explicit Materials in Australia: What Do Consumers of Pornography Have to Say About It?". *Media International Australia* 120 (2006): 35–50; McKee, A. "The Positive and Negative Effects of Pornography as Attributed by Consumers." *Australian Journal of Communication* 34, no. 1 (2007): 87–104; McKee, Alan. "Pornography as Entertainment." *Continuum: Journal of Media & Cultural Studies* 26, no. 4 (2012): 541–52; McKee, Alan, Sara Bragg, and Tristan Taormino. "Editorial Introduction: Entertainment Media's Evolving Role in Sex Education." *Sex Education* 15, no. 5 (2015): 451–57.
3 Croucher and Flew, "Classification-Content".
4 McKee, "Censorship", Mckee, "The positive and negative", McKee et al., "Editorial intro".
5 Wright, Paul. "Pornography and the Sexual Socialization of Children: Current Knowledge and a Theoretical Future." *Journal of Children and Media* 8, no. 3 (2015): 305–12.
6 Turner, Graeme. *Reinventing the Media*. London: Sage, 2015. Location 3019.
7 Croucher and Flew, "Classification-Content", 80.
8 Croucher and Flew, "Classification-Content", 82.
9 Bridges, Ana J., Robert Wosnitzer, Erica Scharrer, Chyng Sun, and Rachael Liberman. 2010. "Aggression and Sexual Behavior in Best-Selling Pornography Videos: A Content Analysis Update." *Violence Against Women* 16:1065–1085. Dines, Gail. 2010. *Pornland: How Porn Has Hijacked Our Sexuality*. Boston: Beacon Press. Jensen, Robert. 1998. "Pornographic Dodges and Distortions." In *Poronography: the Production and Consumption of Inequality*, edited by Gail Dines, Robert Jensen and Ann Russo, 1–8. New York: Routledge.
10 Akira, Asa. 2014. *Insatiable Porn-a Love Story*. New York: Grove Press. Miller-Young, Mireille. 2015. "Race and the Politics of Agency in Porn: A Conversation with Black BBW Performer Betty Blac." In New Views on

Pornography Sexuality, Politics, and the Law, edited by Lynn Comella and Shira Tarrant, 347–358. Oxford: Praeger.
11 Gunter, Barry. 2008. "Media violence: is there a case for causality?." *American Behavioral Scientist* 51 (8):1061–1122.
12 Croucher and Flew, "Classification-content", 99.
13 Wright, P. J., R. S. Tokunaga, and S. Bae. 2014. "Pornography Consumption and US Adults' Attitudes toward Gay Individuals' Civil Liberties, Moral Judgments of Homosexuality, and Support for Same-Sex Marriage: Mediating and Moderating Factors." *Communication Monographs* 81 (79–107).
14 McKee, "Porn as entertainment".
15 McKee, "Censorship of sexually explicit materials".
16 McKee, "Porn as entertainment".
17 McKee, Alan. 2015. "Methodological issues in defining aggression for content Analyses of sexually explicit material." *Archives of sexual behavior* 44 (1):81–87.
18 McKee, Alan, Sara Bragg, and Tristan Taormino. "Editorial Introduction"
19 McKee, ""Censorship of sexually explicit materials".
20 Gerbner, George. 1969. "Toward "cultural indicators": The analysis of mass mediated public message." *AV Communication Review* 17 (2):137–148. Gerbner, George. 1994. "The· Politics of Media Violence: Some Reflections." In *Mass Communication Research: On Problems and Policies,* edited by Cees Hamelink and Olga Linne, 133–146. Norwood, New Jersey: Ablex.
21 Gerbner, George. 1998b. "Why the Cultural Environment Movement?" *Gazette* 60 (2):133–138.
22 Gerbner, George. 1998a. "Cultivation Analysis: an Overview." *Mass Communication and Society* 1 (3–4): 175–195. Gerbner, "The Politics of Media Violence: Some Reflections.".
23 Gerbner, George, Larry Gross, Michael Morgan, and Nancy Signorelli. 1980a. "The Mainstreaming of America: Violence profile #11." *Journal of Communication* 30:10–29. Gerbner, George, Larry Gross, Michael Morgan, and Nancy Signorielli. 1980b. "Television Violence, Victimization, and Power." *American Behavioral Scientist* 5:705–16. Gerbner, George, Larry Gross, Michael Morgan, and Nancy Signorelli. 1982. "Charting the mainstream: Television's contributions to political orientations." *Journal of Communication* 32:100–27.
24 Gerbner et al., "The mainstreaming of America".
25 Gerbner et al., "The mainstreaming of America".
26 Gerbner et al., "Television Violence, Victimization, and Power".
27 Gerbner, George. 1982. "The Gospel of Instant Gratification." *Business And Society Review* (Spring):68. Gerbner, "Cultivation Analysis: an Overview." Shanahan, James, Michael Morgan, and Nancy Signorelli, eds. 2012. *Living with television now: Advances in cultivation theory and research.* New York: Peter Lang.
28 Gerbner, "Cultivation Analysis: an Overview." Morgan, Michael. 2012. *George Gerbner: A Critical Introduction to Media and Communication Theory.* New York: Peter Lang.
29 Morgan "George Gerbner: A Critical Introduction to Media and Communication Theory."
30 Ruddock, Andy. 1995. "Critical Crunching: Communication, Power and Cultivation Analysis." *CommOddities* 2 (1):22–27.
31 Gerbner, G. 1958. "The Social Anatomy of the Romance-Confession Cover Girl." *Journalism and Mass Communication Quarterly* 35 (3):299–306.

Morgan "George Gerbner: A Critical Introduction to Media and Communication Theory".

32 Innis, Harold. 2008. *The Bias of Communication, 2nd Edition.* Toronto: University of Toronto Press. Morozov, Evgeny. 2011. *The Net Delusion: How Not to Liberate the World.* London: Penguin.

33 For Innis' war experience, see Watson, Alexander. 2008. "Introduction." In *The Bias of Communication*, edited by Harold Innis. Toronto: University of Toronto Press.

34 Morgan "George Gerbner: A Critical Introduction to Media and Communication Theory".

35 Gerbner, "Why the Cultural Environment Movement?"

36 Gerbner, "The Politics of Media Violence: Some Reflections."1.

37 Gerbner, "Why the Cultural Environment Movement?", 134.

38 Newcomb, Horace. 1978. "Assessing the violence profile studies of Gerbner and Gross: A humanistic critique and suggestion." *Communication Research* 5 (3):264–282.

39 Bird, Elizabeth. 2011. "Are we all produsers now?" *Cultural Studies* 25 (4–5):502–516. Turner, Graeme. 2015. *Reinventing the Media.* London: Sage.

40 Gerbner, "Why the Cultural Environment Movement?", 137.

41 Ruddock, Andy. 2015a. "Cultural industries: a cultivation perspective." In *Routledge Companion to the Cultural Industries*, edited by Kate Oakley and Justin O'Connor, 522–534. London: Routledge.

42 Anderson, C. Nobuko Ihori, Brad J. Bushman, Hannah R. Rothstein, Akiko Shibuya, Edward L. Swing, Akira Sakamoto, and Muniba Saleem. 2010. "Violent Video Game Effects on Aggression, Empathy, and Prosocial Behavior in Eastern and Western Countries: A Meta-Analytic Review." *Psychological Bulletin* 136 (2):151–173. Bushman, Brad J., and L. Rowell Huesmann. 2014. "Twenty-Five Years of Research on Violence in Digital Games and Aggression Revisited." *European Psychologist* 19 (1):47–55.

43 Ferguson, Christopher. 2013. "Violent Video Games and the Supreme Court Lessons for the Scientific Community in the Wake of Brown v. Entertainment Merchants Association." *American Psychologist* 68 (2):57–74. Ferguson, C, and J Ivory. 2012. "A futile game: on the prevalence and causes of misguided speculation about the role of violence video games in mass school shootings." In *School Shootings: Mediatized Violence in a Global Age* edited by G Muschert and J Sumiala, 47–68. Chicago: Emerald.

44 Ferguson and Ivory, "A futile game".

45 Grayson, N. 2012. Why aren't we discussing videogame violence? *Rock, Paper, Shotgun.* Accessed January 6 2013. No page.

46 Ruddock, "Cultural Industries.

47 Comella, Lynn. 2011. "From text to context: feminist porn and the making of a market." In *The Feminist Porn Book*, edited by Tristan Taormino, Celine Parrenas Shimizu, Contance Penley and Mireille Miller-Young, 78–93. New York City: The Feminist Press CUNY.

48 Comella, "From text to context".

49 Lo, Ven-Hwei, Ran Wei, and Hsiaomei Wu. "Examining the First, Second And Third-Person Effects of Internet Pornography on Taiwanese Adolescents: Implications for the Restriction of Pornography." *Asian Journal of Communication* 20, no. 1 (2010): 90–103. McKee, "Pornography as entertainment".

3 Locating Mobile Media Audiences

In Plain View with Pokémon GO

Gerard Goggin

Introduction

Mobile media audiences have been anticipated for a fair while. Yet they have frustrated their promoters by turning up late, and not quite in the manner predicted. So, the rapturous reception of Pokémon GO in early July 2016 must have seemed like a dream come true. Launched first in the US, Australia, and New Zealand, then Japan some three weeks later, and followed by a wide range of other countries, the Pokémon GO app achieved instant popularity, outstripping sales of other mobile game apps such as Candy Crush and Clash of Clans, at comparable stages of their careers. Overnight, cities witnessed thousands of gamers and fans congregating in public places, catching Pokémon characters, seeking out PokéStops, harvesting Poké Balls and eggs, training and competing in Pokémon GO gyms, and logging kilometers travelled. As the creator company Niantic promoted it: 'Players can explore the world and play the game while keeping their attention on the people and sites around them. A walk in the park just became more fun. :-)'.[1] Regardless of your viewpoint, with Pokémon GO, mobile media audiences had arrived in droves: reconfigured, playful, fanatical, out and about, in your face, and public space. In the midst of the phenomenon, the first question that pops into someone's head when encountering and observing someone intently using a mobile device tends to be: 'are they playing Pokémon GO?'

Media coverage focused on the dangers to life and limb to and from inattentive and absorbed players, and malevolent bystanders, and others hanging out in public spaces. The unfolding reaction of communities at the epicenters of Pokémon GO gaming featured in dispatches, where Niantic was petitioned to remove unwanted PokéStops. Alongside concerned, panicked, and negative coverage came attempts to discuss the positive aspects of the Pokémon GO phenomenon. A British doctor, to give just one commentary, praised the role of Pokémon GO in encouraging children to play outside:

> Pokémon GO isn't marketed as a health app, but players still end up doing a lot of walking. The possibilities for apps to make the streets

an active, reclaimed playground in which to have interconnected fun
are boundless. Increased physical activity is a tantalizing side effect.
Game on.²

The game has been criticized for its enclosure and privatization of urban spaces, with various commentators decrying Pokémon GO as the
epitome of contemporary, commodified digital media culture.³ These
new concerns echo critiques of earlier forms of Pokémon games, such
as those popularized via the Nintendo DS console. In her critique of
'pocket capitalism', for instance, Anne Allison views the 'play structure
and commercial property of Pokémon' as a 'fantasyscape that promises
an alternative world of connectiveness but in which the logic of play
[capturing and domesticating wild monsters, in order to help them capture more monsters] also presumes, and socializes children into, a world-
view of accumulation, competition, and consumption very much aligned
with the problems of youth in millennial capitalism'.⁴

In less sweeping ways, there has been widespread debate on the revenue models for Pokémon GO, and the way its opportunities for profit-
ability rely upon sponsored content and places. In particular, the game
is premised upon the data Google has acquired over some years with
previous applications, as well as new kinds of data generated by players.
In this spirit, geographer Kurt Iveson has argued:

> Niantic is now harvesting 'geospatial data' about millions of peo-
> ple's movements: about how far they are prepared to travel as part
> of game play; about the kinds of places they stop during game play;
> about the groups they travel with; and the connections they make
> during game play, and much more. So, even gamers who never spend
> a cent on in-app purchases or promotions are effectively producing
> information that becomes a commodity owned by Niantic.⁵

Another hot topic of debate has been the efforts by users and developers
to modify, hack, and 'jailbreak' Pokémon GO, in ways that Niantic does
not wish to permit. Shades of Apple's policy on unauthorized modifi-
cation of its devices,⁶ in mid-August, 2016 Niantic announced a life
ban on players who use third-party software to find Pokémon, trick the
game's GPS and falsify location, or use game emulators (via a PC copy).⁷
In response, users have vaulted over the confines of Pokémon GO's lock-
down, rejoicing at the breaking news that a new 'cheat' requires no jail-
breaking. As one tech newsletter put it:

> ...an increasing number of Pokémon addicts take advantage of all
> the different Pokémon GO cheats and hacks out there. Don't worry,
> we won't judge you because after all, it's just a smartphone game.
> Well, if you don't mind bending the rules you're in for a serious treat

on Monday morning, because the ultimate Pokémon GO cheat ... is now available with no jailbreak required.[8]

Sooner or later the Pokémon GO craze will abate, modulating and being absorbed into the ongoing environment and repertoire of media. For the mean time, it compellingly poses the question of what we make of such irruptions of mobile audiences, and what they signify for broader questions of media and society.

As a starting point, it is important to recognize that in many ways, it has proven difficult to attract audiences to particular kinds of mobile media explicitly predicated on the affordances and uses of location. Mobile news is a case in point. In the age of the mobile internet, various kinds of mobile news have proven popular, from text messages, mobile web, and apps featured on smartphones and tablets.[9] Mobile news has also effected shifts in the production and consumption of news, and the spaces and places where this occurs.[10] Yet news that deliberately tries to gauge the location of users and customize their news (as part of 'hyperlocal' news efforts, for instance), has not yet proven especially popular, though particular small-scale ventures have had some success.[11] Many other bespoke locative media initiatives have attracted attention and audiences; though often not at scale. This is one reason why Pokémon GO is so fascinating. While diffusion is very likely restricted to particular areas, demographics, settings, and activities, where it has been taken up it has seen significant audiences turn to – or return to – mobile devices, in ways that they have not for other kinds of mobile media. At the least there are interesting lessons in Pokémon GO for the state of play of audiences. Also, if we approach it in a skeptical temper, studying the Pokémon GO moment is a rich resource for understanding and framing the present and future stakes of digital media, and media in general.[12]

In this chapter, I wish to demonstrate the benefits of approaching apparently new developments such as Pokémon GO by couching these in a broader thinking through of what mobile means in relation to digital audiences. In particular, I think there is a need to carefully dissect the context in which these kinds of development play out. Firstly then, to provide a context for understanding Pokémon GO, I discuss the emergence of mobile media audiences, and the increasingly prominent role location has played in these formations. In the second part, I turn to the emergence of Pokémon GO, placing it into the recent history of mapping, locative media, and augmented reality (AR) technology. Scholarship on mobile AR, especially the work of Tony Liao and Lee Humphreys, draws our attention to the stakes in how various interests, including users and powerful corporate actors shape places, tools, and technologies.[13] I carry this inquiry into the third part of the paper, which examines Pokémon GO against the histories of mobile gaming. Finally, I conclude with some remarks on the discursive, business, technology, and design strategies evident in Niantic's effort to configure and sustain the phenomenal success of its Pokémon GO launch.

Desperately Seeking Mobile Media Audiences

Mobile media audiences have been tricky to pin down. For some time, *mobile* audiences have been posited in audience research as a way of conceptualizing the 'interactive, multimedia, dispersed, and mobile audiences',[14] and the ways that such audience engagement and consumption might transpire and be distributed across different locations (home, shops, work, schools, and public screens); axes and modalities of mobility and immobility (transportation, waiting, recreation, leisure, work, cultural activities); media forms; media platforms; and so on.[15] The *mobilities* that constitute, contextualize, and characterize audiences have been recognized and taken up in various ways, notably in David Morley's influential 2000 book *Home Territories*,[16] as well as in a wide range of media, communication, and mobilities research.[17] The audiences associated with mobile media – that is, the media tied to cellular mobile telephones and telecommunications networks – partake of both these concepts of *mobile* and *mobilities*.

There's no doubt that such mobile phones and their successors are a very significant element of contemporary media across the world. In just over a decade, total mobile phone subscriptions have grown from 2.21 billion in 2005 to an estimated 7.38 billion in 2016.[18] Tellingly, respective share of mobile subscriptions in 'developed' versus 'developing' world (these are still the statistical categories used by the International Telecommunications Union) has changed dramatically. In 2005, there were some 992,000 subscriptions in the developed world versus 1.21 billion subscriptions in the developing world. Compare these figures to 2016, by which time the part of the world formerly known as developing really had become the mobile-using majority, with some 5.77 billion subscriptions leap-frogging the 1.6 billion subscriptions of counterparts in the developed world.[19] There are at least two major qualifications to this picture. Firstly, it is clear that patterns of access to, and affordability, literacy, and use of, mobile technologies, especially advanced technologies, remains very different and highly unequal around the world. This is especially the case when we consider the many ways in which Internet is accessed on mobile devices, software, and networks. Figures show that much of the world's population experiences significant shortfall. As the International Telecommunications Union (ITU) notes concerning its 2016 figures:

> ...developing countries now account for the vast majority of Internet users, with 2.5 billion users compared with one billion in developed countries. But Internet penetration rates tell a different story,

with 81% in developed countries, compared with 40% in developing countries and 15% in the Least Developed Countries.[20]

Add to which, ITU 2016 estimates indicate that mobile broadband networks reach 87% of the world's population, but only 67% of the rural population.[21] Second, the best available research indicates that we lack a good sense of how these issues of inclusion, exclusion, infrastructure, pricing and affordability, disability accessibility, and so on, play out in relation to mobile take-up and gradations and modalities of use (a key threshold of mobile audiences). The Internet itself is clearly shifting across a range of devices, platforms, software, and media forms, but the *mobile* element of this is entangled in various dynamics.

Hence Jonathon Donner in his authoritative conceptualization of the 'more-mobile Internet' posits the need to understand the 'digital repertoires' of users, as they toggle among parts of the transforming media ecologies.[22] From another perspective, Adrian Athique, discussing the mobile media involvement in the increasingly transnational character of online audiences, rightly suggests that '[a]cross this vast canvass, the combination of 'multimedia' performance, the 'many to many' potentials of networked computing, and the rise of mobile and locative media has engendered a bewildering array of audience configurations that are yet to be adequately described'.[23] The sheer number of mobile devices goes hand in hand with the expansion of mobile media as a platform for a wide array of remediated and new media forms, formats, and technologies, and associated cultures of use and social practices.[24] The definition of mobile media is no longer clear-cut, if it ever was, because mobile phones and telecommunications have been extensively crossing over with a wide range of previous media, internet, and, increasingly, emerging media as various as sensors, wearable computers, internet of things, everyday material culture (including clothing, watches, fashion). This continuing evolution and complexity of mobile media goes hand in hand with revisions and inventions of the audiences that belong to, and in many ways, create these technologies.

The study of the mobile elements and inflections of media audiences also depends a great deal on what you think mobile media is, and, in a particular media environment, what takes your interest. Early on, scholars felt a need to make a case for mobile phone users (like their Internet-wielding counterparts) as audience-like or audience-forming.[25] Thus, in their study of mobile phone as fashion statements, James E. Katz and Satomi Sugiyama liken mobile phone users to 'audiences of various mass media texts, creating, interpreting, appropriating material, to develop meaningful, personalized, and culturally appropriate new texts'.[26] As the technology and its social coordinates co-evolved, the technology was explicitly recognized as a medium in its own right. The mobile phone also shifted center-stage into contemporary media, prompting researchers to consider how to place it into media and cultural-historical context. For instance, researchers placed mobile media in the broad currents of social transformation, especially concerning the relationships between public and private spheres, deeply entwined in the changing distinctions between mass communications and media, on the one hand, and personal systems and forms, on the other hand. Thus Sonia Livingstone draws attention to the rise of personal media, as media goods reduce in price and mobile media – such as the Walkman and mobile phone – become more prevalent. Livingstone see this as 'primarily to do with the social contexts of use rather than the technologies themselves'.[27] She notes that these 'social contexts of use are themselves part of a wider reformulation of the relation between public and private', as in the paradigmatic case of 'family television', and the way in which its 'associated hierarchies of gender and generation' are being transformed with households with multiple devices. Another way to proceed is to place histories of mobile phones and their nascent audiences against the *longue durée* of structures of culture, art, space, artifacts as they are imbricated in everyday life. For instance, the first volume explicitly devoted to the subject, Martin Rieser's 2011 *The Mobile Audience* traces a trajectory across mobile media from media art, and includes studies of audience mobility (and hybridity), public spatiality, creative users, everyday life, and wearable computing.[28] An allied line of inquiry is the recovery and reinterpretation of obscured histories of telephones as media.[29]

Overall, there is a growing research literature on mobile media audiences, in addition to burgeoning scholarship on the mobile component of a wide array of audiences.[30] Location has figured heavily in two closely related areas of this research. Firstly, location has been an important facet of the research in mobile games, explicitly so when it comes urban games and play, and perforce so, in relation to mobile location gaming.[31] Secondly, location has been an inescapable and closely studied aspect of research on location-based technology and media.[32] The research shows the important ways in which location information and media are often very deeply and affectively part of people's lived experience, attachment to, and construction of place.[33] From the pioneering work of scholars working on mobile games in Asia, in particular, location has been framed in a broader sense. In particular, Larissa Hjorth and Ingrid Richardson have reminded us:

> …mobile gaming has many histories subject to intersecting contextual trajectories—socio-linguistic, geographical, technocultural, medium, and platform specific. That is, the definition and constitution of 'mobile gaming' depends largely upon one's historical epoch and cultural region, in terms of broader technological, economic and transnational flows, the collective gaming habits, attitudes and

uptake within one's cultural milieu, and more narrowly upon one's individual game experiences and preferences within these contexts.[34]

This is especially important in considering the Pokémon GO 'moment', where, as it was rolled out, the game was presented as an avidly awaited global phenomenon. As is often the case, the staging of the rollout was hampered by server capacity issues and challenges in particular markets (the restrictions on mapping functions in South Korea were cited, for example, due to security tensions with North Korea).[35] Here Larissa Hjorth and Dean Chan's earlier, pioneering work on gaming cultures in the Asia-Pacific region provides a salutary reminder, as they note 'many American online games like *EverQuest* would fail at launch in East Asian gaming territories [in the 1990s] due to a failure to recognize and negotiate myriad culturally specific protocols informing the seemingly 'neutral' aspects of local business practices and game play preferences'.[36] The importance of this nuanced geopolitical, transnational, regional, national, intercultural, cross-generational, and translocal framing of locations of audience, with attention paid to these kind of scales of audiences, and their interplay, is something that has been recently emphasized across other areas of media, such as television and internet.[37] When it comes to the Pokémon GO experience, acknowledging and thinking carefully about location is important, precisely because of the complex terrain of contemporary media audiences. As Tama Leaver and Michele Willson note: 'One of the most immediately obvious challenges when talking about the contemporary gaming landscape is how to situate the type of games and game practices being enacted through [the] multiplicity of devices'.[38] Leaver and Willson contend that '[w]hat is undeniable is that social, casual and mobile games in all of their forms are being adopted by increasing numbers of the population, being played in multiple locations and being adopted in multifaceted ways into people's lives'.[39]

A helpful starting point in provided by Jordan Frith's theorization of smartphones as media, in which he muses that future media might be characterized by a type of 'seamlessness' in which 'location awareness will be incorporated into most networked interactions, operating invisibly in the background',[40] a scenario he invokes with the example of Spike Jonze's 2013 film *Her*, in which, as Frith nicely puts it, 'a man falls in love with a sentient mobile operating system'.[41] Frith imagines a likely future in which 'smartphones are even more closely interwoven with everyday interactions and location information is passively present in most interactions with mobile devices'.[42] However, for the present he believes that 'people will continue to use their individual location-based services, and physical spaces will continue to be filled with even denser layers of digital spatial information'.[43] For Frith, the continuing situation is that the 'most significant social impact of the growth of smartphones as locative media involves the new ways in which the merging of the digital and physical have impacted people's experience of place'.[44] This is something that mobile games scholar Kyle Moore points out, in his intervention into the early phase of Pokémon GO diffusion:

> The popularity of the game means we need to rethink our engagement with traditional spaces of play and leisure, such as parks and playgrounds, as well as spaces where play has traditionally been seen as subversive – city spaces in general. It's also important to consider the implications this has for spaces outside the city, for those in rural or suburban spaces, who will have difficulty playing in these familiar spaces, and the impact traveling to play will have on these groups.[45]

Building on Moore's prompt, I would argue that, while clearly a highly commercial and commodified popular culture form, offered by a striking alliance of three global media giants, nonetheless Pokémon GO is a significant development for how we understand the social function of media. The distinctiveness of Pokémon GO lies in the way that it brings together a number of elements in the development of digital media, especially mobile and location media, a conjunction I explore in the next parts of the chapter.

Mapping Pokémon GO

Pokémon GO draws upon developments and investments mapping, spatialization, and visualization technology spanning decades.[46] Google has been an especially interesting player in this area, as its Google Maps product is what it is best known, and used, for next to its original and enduring search technology.[47] Google's investment and capabilities in location and mapping technology saw the creation of a global dataset that underpins the development of Pokémon GO. Niantic's John Hanke co-founded Keyhole Corp, Mountain View, California, a digital mapping company, in 2001. Google acquired it in 2004. At the time, Vice President Product Management, Jonathan Rosenberg declared: 'With Keyhole, you can fly like a superhero from your computer at home to a street corner somewhere else in the world – or find a local hospital, map a road trip or measure the distance between two points'.[48] As Rosenberg put it:

> This acquisition gives Google users a powerful new search tool, enabling users to view 3D images of any place on earth as well as tap a rich database of roads, businesses and many other points of interest. Keyhole is a valuable addition to Google's efforts to organize the world's information and make it universally accessible and useful.[49]

As press noted at the time, Keyhole's financial backers included the Central Intelligence Agency (CIA) 'venture spatial' unit, as well as Sony Corp and graphics-chip manufacturer Nvidia Corp.[50] Keyhole's military connections attracted widespread interest, underscoring the military-industrial-entertainment complex in which Google was increasingly involved: 'The three-year-old company made a name for itself during the war in Iraq when news outlets, including CNN, used its maps to 'fly' over the Iraqi landscape and cities to show viewers where battles were being fought'.[51] Within a year, Google had integrated Keyhole's service into Google Maps.[52] Hanke headed Google Maps for several years, and, when he wished to leave Google, was reportedly persuaded by CEO Larry Page to stay and start up the lab that became Niantic instead.[53] Niantic's first product was the Field Trip app,[54] offering users 'facts about the places around them – unprompted, without the need to even ask for the information' (as the *New York Times* put it).[55] According-ing to Hanke:

> The idea behind the app was to build something that would help people connect with the real, physical world around them ... It's always running in the background, so it knows where you are and is always looking to see if something interesting is in your immediate physical environment.[56]

Atlantic writer Alexis C. Madrigal suggested that 'the app is Google's probe into the soft side of augmented reality'. Ultimately, having tested the app, she felt its main shortcomings were to do with content: 'Google's great with structured data – flight times, baseball box scores – but it's not good with the soft, squishy, wordy stuff'.[57] She contended that what was needed was a 'new kind of media', of 'awesome 'digital notes', out there in the real world', rather than building on legacy print media, or computer and database media, where 'everyone is still fundamentally writing for an audience made up of people who they expect are at their computers or curled up on the couch'.[58] Since these high hopes, the Field Trip app has been eclipsed by a variety of applications, not least Yelp!, Foursquare, and many specific apps providing location-based information and interaction. The deployment of augmented reality (AR) has featured heavily in quite a number of these efforts. In 2009, Yelp! released an augmented reality extension called Monocle, which briefly was pre-dicted to 'murder all other iPhone restaurant apps',[59] but subsequently faded away. A dedicated and for a time widely used AR application was Layar. Liao and Humphreys' important study of Layar discussed the way it allowed users to create their own content, annotations, and rep-resentations of space, 'using the technology to heighten their connec-tions with their surroundings, changing the augmented representation and meaning of places, and questioning people's authority to construct place'.[60] These user-driven, proto-democratic possibilities of AR were counterbalanced in Liao and Humphreys' analysis against the forces of 'many powerful and strategic actors': 'As AR's potential for tactical reproduction and reinterpretation of space is realized, it is possible that strategic forces will seek to reclaim, limit, and possibly censor some of that tactical production'.[61] This is precisely the scenario many fear is playing out with the implementation of AR in Pokémon GO. To understand this issue, we need to shift from mapping to mobile games.

Pokémon GO's World of Mobile Games

More than anything, Pokémon GO is a legatee of the traditions of mobile location gaming. Mobile games have a history stretching back to early handset-based and installed games such as the Nokia Snake game. As mobile handsets became increasingly portable, and especially after the advent of consumer Global Positioning Technology (GPS), a distinct strand of location-based mobile games developed. These included BotFighter, a mobile location game launched in Sweden in 2001. The development of mobile location gaming also fits into the broader sweep of innovation in locative art and urban culture, and the specific social configuration and coordination they require. At roughly the same time, we also see the emergence of mobile social networking ('MoSoSo'), with location being used to enable and encourage serendipitous or planned urban encounters between friends, acquaintances, and strangers.[62] Mobile social networking applications were forerunners of a wide range of location-based applications such as Foursquare, but also the later 'dating' and 'hook-up' apps such as Grindr and Tinder. In different parts of the world, notably East Asia (especially Japan and Korea), and the US, a range of location-based mobile games developed, with a few achieving dedicated, 'cult' following, though with only relatively small numbers. After a relatively slow start, due to the limitations of handsets and data capacity speeds of first and second generation mobiles, mobile gaming finally began to rival its console, Internet, and other online gaming counterparts with the advent of smartphones. Here the capabilities of the devices were important, because of the processing power, but also incorporation of sensors, location, multimedia, and other technology, as various scholars have noted.[63]

These location-inflected and leveraged mobile technologies and cultures fed into the mobile location game, Ingress, created by Niantic Labs. Ingress is a mobile augmented reality 'capture the flag' style of game in which players are assigned to one of two factions, Enlightenment (green team) or Resistance (blue team). They range across the city, vying to capture 'portals'. The portals are associated with nearby landmarks, so players need to travel to that location to secure them. Ingress launched in late 2012 and has a dedicated international player base. Exact figures are difficult to pin down; however, Niantic founder John Hanke in his January 2016 'Three Year Impact Report', claimed 14 million downloads of Ingress, 5.39 million portals created with 729 million visits by players, and 254,184 playing attending live events.[64] In August 2016, Ingress's Google+ page passed 4.5 million followers. Ingress has generated a body of scholarship in its own right.[65] Erin Stark argues that the game represents an intervention into 'everyday mobilities', because Ingress:

> invites individuals to engage with third places by transforming everyday spaces into playful places. Motivated by in-game achievements and community membership, Ingress players diverge from everyday mobilities by reframing familiar locations as hybrid digital–physical landscapes.[66]

Discussing the potential for players to nominate their own 'portals', Stark argues that 'Ingress capitalizes upon the extraordinary in the everyday', with players able to draw attention to 'sites, structures and spaces that would otherwise, by virtue of their familiarity or location go unseen' – and thus contributing to 'community-led curation of cultural heritage' of vast scope.[67] While supporting such possibilities, Ingress also provided the opportunity for Google to experiment with augmented reality technology in mobile gaming, in tandem with its various other AR and location technology product developments such as Google Glass.

In 2015, Google reorganized and relaunched under the newly formed umbrella company Alphabet, spinning off Niantic Labs at the same time. Niantic's announcement and the press and tech blog discussion focused on the newly independent enterprise taking an 'entertainment turn': 'Niantic Labs may be looking to move into the entertainment industry and work more closely with Hollywood'.[68] Three months later, Hanke announced

> ...we are thrilled to disclose that our mission will be backed by global giants in the game, entertainment and technology sectors. The Pokémon Company, Google and Nintendo are investing up to $30 million in Niantic, Inc., which includes an initial $20 million upfront and an additional $10 million in financing conditioned upon the company achieving certain milestones. We will be using this capital to continue the development of Pokémon GO, to evolve and grow Ingress and its thriving global community, and to build out our realworld gaming platform.[69]

This 'entertainment turn' does seem to have worked so far for Niantic and its partners. Certainly, Pokémon GO builds directly on the player community, features, reputation, and, especially, database of Ingress.

However, many players have been critical of the shortcomings of Pokémon GO, compared to its much beloved predecessor.

Various Ingress adherents maintain its superiority to Pokémon GO, with player and journalist Beth Winegarner suggesting: 'While Pokémon Go is a watered down version of the original Pokémon empire, Ingress has a complicated and social-minded narrative structure'.[70] That Ingress is a much more thoroughly 'social' game than Pokémon GO is a theme Winegarner pursues, suggesting that 'Ingress ... has many levels of so-cial cooperation baked into the game', requiring sustained, complex, on-going, and cumulative teamwork'.[71] Winegarner also draws attention to the contrasting ethics of care for place that the two games entail. She argues that Pokémon GO's PokéStops are based on its predecessor's concept of portals, however 'its players can't capture, build or maintain them', whereas Ingress 'offers more and richer opportunities for players to feel like caretakers of neighborhood sites'.[72] The topic of exactly how Pokémon GO adapts, departs from, or traduces Ingress is generating significant research, and forms part of a larger discussion of game design, game play, narratives, imaginaries, and materialities. However, it is the combination of Ingress (even with some of its more expansive affor-dances curtailed) with the brand name, fan base, and characters of the immensely popular Pokémon franchise that provides a transformative edge in terms of audience size and reach.[73]

With the Pokémon cachet and inventory, Niantic is able to take mobile locative gaming far beyond the footprint of Ingress to potentially vast global audience. While Nintendo has not featured prominently in the Pokémon GO launch, its entry into the mobile games arena in March 2015 was a hotly discussed issue, and seen as a turning point in the games industry. What is very interesting about the Niantic spinoff, and Pokémon launch, is the way that Google turns to two major Japanese corporations, as a way to incubate games. As scholars have discussed, the East Asian region was an early mover in mobile gaming, functioning as a test bed, but, especially in countries like Korea and Japan, establish-ing the largest and most profitable markets.[74]

What also makes the shift from Ingress to Pokémon GO possible is the belated mass take-up of mobile gaming enabled the transformation in mobile data and software, represented by the emergence of apps and apps stores associated with smart phones and tablets. These new mobile media platforms from 2007 onwards supported the widespread diffu-sion and popularity of highly successful mobile games in the form of apps, such as Candy Crush, Angry Birds, and Clash of Clans. This was a point of comparison not lost on the apps industry and its pundits, quickly recorded in websites that reported, for instance, 'Pokémon Go App Downloads and Revenue in Real Time', showing 'Daily Time Spent in Pokémon GO by Average iOS User, Compared to Top Mobile Apps'.[75] With the popularity of such mobile apps, 'casual gaming' arrived as a real force in gaming that could no longer be ignored or slighted in favor of more 'hard-core' or 'serious' gaming. These casual mobile games and their associated social practices – easy to play in all sorts of locales, and in short periods of time – paved the way for the reception of Pokémon. Significant audiences have emerged who are accustomed to attractive, relatively simple to play mobile games, with relatively straightforward narrative, characters, and game play. Added to which, as Dal Yong Jin points out, the dichotomy between console-based, 'hard-core' gamers, and casual, mobile gamers no longer holds: 'the dichotomy of console and mobile games based on game genres cannot explain the new trend because mobile gamers also enjoy role playing games on their smart-phones'. Thus he argues that:

> Enhanced 3D techniques, bigger and better screens, and visual effects developed in recent years have become major dimensions for the growth of mobile role playing games ... Mobile gaming has consequently become the most significant video game sector that many players, either role playing gamers or casual gamers, enjoy.[76]

As a central force in games and culture generally, mobile games also offer a flexible architecture, set of forms, platforms, and, above all, habitus, to support the packaging of different aspects of convergent digital media. This kind of flexibility of mobile games and the power it offers when harnessed by major media giants is an impressive part of the story of Pokémon GO. Yet how we precisely identify its scope and capabilities, as well as limits and potential dangers, is the subject of furious debate.

Conclusion: The Powers and Perils of Pokémon GO

Writing about Pokémon GO at a relatively early time in its adoption and development is fraught with shortcomings. Yet it also provides an irresistible opportunity, because it is such a striking test case of what happens when a digital technology moves beyond the early adopters (such as those of mobile AR technologies in the 2005–2015 period, or locative technology from a longer timeframe of early 2000s until 2015) to go mainstream fast. Rightly so, users, gamers, researchers, urban planners and designers (especially those in city and municipal government), are thinking about the implications for Pokémon GO in terms of rights to the city, and other claims of 'spatial justice',[77] as well as the interventions the game represents into the mediascapes of contemporary culture, networks, and platforms.

In addition, among scholars and public alike, there has been a reflex response to perceive Pokémon GO as precipating people, especially as publics, to become mobile fixated. Not for the first time, mind you, but in calling contemporary digital audiences back to mobile media, when many had been well habituated to integrating mobiles into their media habits, social practices, and cultural horizons. So research must need follow to pin down the specific coordinates and implications of Pokémon GO, given it is clearly limited in its rollout, takeup, interest, and implications.[78] Niantic itself has played with the unevenness of internationalization of Pokémon GO, with its rules on international availability of characters, and its release of 'regional exclusives' (Kangaskhan available solely in Australia and New Zealand, for example).[79] In terms of significance, it probably falls somewhere among the field of original Pokémon franchise, Candy Crush, and Facebook's social games (like FarmVille, for instance) – but it certainly takes locative mobile games mainstream, and, for a time, brings audiences back to their mobile devices and heading outside, with mainstream media avidly reporting developments.

In interpreting Niantic's efforts to crest the wave of enthusiasm for Pokémon GO, expanding it wider into new markets and deepening its take-up and use in markets where it is already popularly, we can detect a fair bit of juggling of the various moving parts of the phenomenon, and the claims these elements represent against particular constituencies, such as game players, businesses with a geo-location stake in the game, affected communities, investors, software developers, and so on. Here we need to grasp and interrogate Niantic's effort to create Pokémon GO as a platform. In this endeavor, it is useful to look at the way that another mobile location-based technology, with gaming aspects, has also conjured with different media affordances and discourses. In his study of Foursquare's strategy deployment and withdrawal from 'gamification' talk, Wilken looks at how Foursquare moved, over the space of a few years, 'from a stand-alone mobile social software (check-in based) application to a more overtly commercially focused location platform', flying a flag to become the 'location layer of the internet'.[80] Wilken finds that: 'Attempting to reinvent the company in this way requires the performance of a delicate balancing act, one that aims to satisfy multiple competing desires and demands with the need for richer end-user-generated data and commercialization opportunities than cannot be achieved through game driven interactions alone'.[81] Rather, Foursquare has to carefully use language to strategically engage via discourses its various audiences and interest groups comprehend. Wilken's approach provides a useful way to cut down to size and analyze the grander claims at play in the Pokémon GO moment, that variously feed into affirmative imaginaries of great civil, child and youth participation in life and the city; the dystopia of public space colonized in new, heightened systems of commodification and surveillance; and the market celebration of a new wave of ubiquitous, commercial media supporting fun activity and popular culture.

In his puff piece heralding Pokémon GO, Hanke cautioned against seeing one kind of device as encapsulating the future of online media, instead suggesting that:

> At one level you could say that all of it is an outgrowth of the smartphone revolution – tiny powerful processors, amazing displays, sensors of all kinds, robust location and mapping technology – all now made cheap, reliable and ubiquitous. I think we are going to see those basic building blocks refactored into all kinds of new hardware that will be exploited to blur the lines between games, cinema, apps, fitness and even navigation and commerce.[82]

It turns out that Hanke does 'bet on things that are more phone-like than PC-like', musing that the 'future of technology will be one where it accompanies us everywhere and is there to enhance, enrich, and sometimes transform our lives on demand'.[83] Thus, while based on mobile locative technology, games, and entertainment media, Pokémon GO also gestures towards other themes of the 'connected' and 'digital' life discourses of the present conjuncture – especially fitness and health. Contemporary media audiences need to govern themselves, tracking their activity, and monitoring their health, as they entertain themselves, inhabit, occupy, represent, and engage with urban space. Pokémon GO's capability to record and require distance travelled is a fairly superficial 'add on', rather than a serious point of competition for Fitbits, health apps, and other digital health technologies. However, like the discursive, technology, and business strategies of Foursquare identified by Wilken, such a balancing act seeks to put Niantic in the driver's seat for what the future mobile media audiences desire, once the initial fuss dies down.

Acknowledgments

An Australian Research Council (ARC) Future Fellowship awarded to Gerard Goggin (FT130100097) supported the research presented in this chapter. My thanks to Kyle Moore and the editors for their helpful comments.

Notes

1 Niantic, "Break Out the Sneakers and Poké Balls!" July 6, 2016, https://www.nianticlabs.com/blog/launch/.
2 Margaret McCartney, "Game on for Pokémon GO," *British Medical Journal*, 354 (2016), i4306,
3 For instance, in Graham Murdock's keynote address to the 2016 International Association of Media Communication Research (IAMCR) conference, entitled "Communication and Crisis: Economies, Polities, Ecologies." For a useful response, see Katherine Howell's blog post, "Use and Misuse of Digital

Cultural Examples: Pokémon GO and the Rijksmuseum Teenagers," 28 July, 2016, "http://www.lovelyoldtree.com/examples-digital-culture-misuse/.

4 Anne Allison, "Pocket Capitalism and Virtual Intimacy: Pokémon as a Symptom of Post-Industrial Youth Culture," in Anthony Y.H. Fung (ed.), *Asian Popular Culture: The Global (Dis)Continuity* (New York: Routledge, 2013), 200.

5 Kurt Iveson, "Pokémon GO and the Business of Free Play," *The Age*, 4 August, 2015, 19.

6 On jail-breaking of mobile technology, see: Adriana Amaral and Rosana Vieira de Souza, "User Resistance and Repurposing: A Look at the iOS "Jailbreaking" Scene in Brazil," *Selected Papers of Internet Research 14.0*, Denver, USA, 23–26 October, 2013, http://spir.aoir.org/index.php/spir/article/view/686; Gerard Goggin, "Ubiquitous Apps: Politics of Openness in Global Mobile Cultures," *Digital Creativity* 22 (2011): 147–157; Thomas Fox-Brewster, "Of Ma And Malware: Inside China's iPhone Jailbreaking Industrial Complex," *Forbes*, 26 June, 2015, http://www.forbes.com/sites/thomasbrewster/2015/06/26/china-iphone-jailbreak-industry/#3464349b7fa5.

7 Helena Horton, "Pokémon GO Update Means Cheats Get a Life Ban — Here's How to Avoid Getting Banned," *The Telegraph*, 15 August, 2015, http://www.telegraph.co.uk/technology/2016/08/15/pokemon-go-update-means-cheats-get-a-life-ban---heres-how-to-avo/.

8 Zach Epstein, "The Holy Grail: Hack Pokémon GO So You Can Walk Anywhere, No Jailbreak Required," *BGR*, 22 August, 2016, http://bgr.com/2016/08/22/pokemon-go-cheats-ios-no-jailbreak-gps-hack/.

9 Gerard Goggin, "The Intimate Turn of News: Mobile News," in Graham Meikle and Guy Redden (eds.), *News Online: Transformation and Continuity* (London: Palgrave Macmillan, 2011), 99–114.

10 Oscar Westlund, "News Consumption in an Age of Mobile Media: Patterns, People, Place, and Participation," *Mobile Media & Communication* 3.2 (2015), 151–159.

11 See, for instance: Kjetil Vaage Øie, "Sensing the News: User Experiences when Reading Locative News," *Future Internet* 4.4 (2012), 161–178; Gerard Goggin, Fiona Martin, and Tim Dwyer, "Locative News: Mobile Media, Place Informatics, and Digital News," *Journalism Studies* 15.2 (2014): 41–59; Brett Oppegaard and Michael K. Rabby, "Proximity: Revealing New Mobile Meanings of a Traditional News Concept," *Digital Journalism* 4.5 (2016): 621–638.

12 On digital and media futures, see variously: Paul Dourish and Genevieve Bell, *Divining a Digital Future* (Cambridge, MA: MIT Press, 2011); Graeme Turner, *Reinventing the Media* (London and New York: Routledge, 2015).

13 Tony Liao and Lee Humphreys, "Layar-ed Places: Using Mobile Augmented Reality to Tactically Reengage, Reproduce, and Reappropriate Public Space," *New Media & Society* 17.9 (2015): 1418–1435.

14 Sonia Livingstone, "Engaging with Media — A Matter of Literacy?", *Communication, Culture & Critique* 1 (2008), 59.

15 Michel Sorice, *Mobile Audiences: Methodological Problems and New Perspectives in Audience Studies*, Centre for Media and Communication Studies (CMCS) Working Papers (Rome: CMCS, LUISS University); http://eprints.luiss.it/448/1/CMCSWP_0209M.pdf.

16 David Morley, *Home Territories: Media, Mobility and Identity* (London and New York: Routledge, 2000).

17 For example, see: Mimi Sheller and John Urry (eds)., *Tourism Mobilities: Places to Play, Places to Stay* (London and New York: Routledge, 2004); Nick

Couldry and Anna (eds), *MediaSpace: Place, Scale and Culture in a Media Age* (London: Routledge, 2004); Peter Adey, " 'May I Have Your Attention': Airport Geographies of Spectatorship, Position, and (im)Mobility," *Environment & Planning D* 25 (2007), 3515–3536; Ole J. Mjøs, *Music, Social Media and Global Mobility: MySpace, Facebook, YouTube* (New York: Routledge, 2012); and, especially, Shaun Moores, *Interpreting Audiences* (London: Sage, 2003), and *Media, Place and Mobility* (Basingstoke, UK: Macmillan, 2012).
18 International Telecommunications Union (ITU), "Key ICT Indicators for Developed and Developing Countries and the World", 12 July 2016, http://www.itu.int/en/ITU-D/Statistics/Documents/statistics/2016/ITU_Key_2005–2016_ICT_data.xls.
19 ITU, "Key ICT indicators."
20 "ITU releases 2016 ICT figures: ICT services getting more affordable – but more than half the world's population still not using the Internet," media release, 22 July, 2016, http://www.itu.int/en/mediacentre/pages/2016-PR30.aspx.
21 ITU, "Facts and Figures 2016," 22 July, 2016, http://www.itu.int/en/ITU-D/Statistics/Documents/facts/ICTFactsFigures2016.pdf.
22 Jonathon Donner, *After Access: Inclusion, Development, and A More Mobile Internet* (Cambridge, MA: MIT Press, 2015).
23 Adrian Athique, *Transnational Audiences: Media Reception on a Global Scale* (Cambridge, UK, and Malden, MA: Polity Press, 2016), 9.
24 See, for instance: Mizuko Ito, Daisuke Okabe, and Misa Matsuda, eds., *Personal, Portable, Pedestrian, Mobile Phones in Japanese Life* (Cambridge, MA: MIT Press, 2005); Gerard Goggin, *Global Mobile Media* (New York: Routledge, 2011); Larissa Hjorth and Jean Burgess, eds., *Studying Mobile Media: Cultural Technologies, Mobile Communication, and the iPhone* (New York: Routledge, 2012); Barbara Crow, Michael Longford, and Kim Sawchuk, eds., *The Wireless Spectrum: The Politics, Practices, and Poetics of Mobile Media* (Toronto: University of Toronto Press, 2013); Gerard Goggin and Larissa Hjorth, eds., *Routledge Companion to Mobile Media* (New York: Routledge, 2014); Hidenori Tomita, ed., *The Post-Mobile Society: From the Smart/Mobile to Second Offline* (London and New York: Routledge, 2016); and Ulrik Ekman, Jay David Bolter, Lily Díaz, Morten Søndergaard, and Maria Engberg, eds., *Ubiquitous Computing, Complexity, and Culture* (New York: Routledge, 2016).
25 On users, Sonia Livingstone that those "who use the Internet, mobile phones, digital games, and even those who engage with traditional media (radio, print, and television) via the Internet, are not easily labeled an audience. The term "user" is, it seems, becoming commonplace in ordinary discourse, but this is equally unsatisfactory, for it lacks any direct relation to communication in particular, and it implies an instrumental individualism ..." ("Engaging with Media," 52).
26 James E. Katz and Satomi Sugiyama, "Mobile Phones as Fashion Statements: The Co-Creation of Mobile Communication's Public Meaning," in Rich Ling and Per E. Pedersen (eds.), *Mobile Communications: Re-Negotiation of the Public Sphere* (London: Springer-Verlag, 2005), 79.
27 Sonia Livingstone, "New Media, New Audiences?", *New Media & Society* 1 (1999), 62.
28 Martin Rieser, ed., *The Mobile Audience: Media Art and Mobile Technologies* (Amsterdam and New York: Rodopi, 2011).
29 On the histories of telephones as media and their audiences, see: Ithiel de Sola Pool (ed.), *The Social Impact of the Telephone* (Cambridge, MA: MIT Press,

1977); Carolyn Marvin, *When Old Technologies Were New: Thinking about Electric Communication in the Late Nineteenth Century* (New York: Oxford University Press, 1988); Adriana de Souza e Silva, "Art by Telephone: From Static to Mobile Interfaces," in *The Mobile Audience: Media Art and Mobile Technologies*, ed. Martin Rieser (Amsterdam: Rodopi, 2011), 67–80; Gerard Goggin, "Telephone Media: An Old Story," in *The Long History of New Media: Technology, Historiography, and Newness in Context*, ed. David W. Park, Nicholas W. Jankowski, and Steve Jones (New York: Peter Lang, 2011), 231–252.

30 Gerard Goggin, "Going Mobile," in Virginia Nightingale (ed.), *The Handbook of Media Audiences* (Malden, MA, and Oxford, UK: Wiley-Blackwell, 2011), 128–146.

31 For example, see: Adriana de Souza e Silva and Daniel M. Sutko (eds), *Digital Cityspaces: Merging Digital and Urban Playspaces* (New York: Peter Lang, 2009); Samuel Tobin, *Portable Play in Everyday Life: The Nintendo NS* (Basingstoke, UK: Palgrave Macmillan, 2013); Sam Hinton and Larissa Hjorth, *Understanding Social Media* (London: Sage, 2013); Larissa Hjorth and Ingrid Richardson, *Gaming in Social, Locative, and Mobile Media* (Basingstoke, UK: Palgrave Macmillan, 2014); Tama Leaver and Michele Willson (eds), *Social, Casual, and Mobile Games: The Changing Gaming Landscape* (London and New York: Bloomsbury, 2016).

32 For instance, see: Eric Gordon and Adriana de Souza e Silva, *Net Locality: Why Location Matters in a Networked World* (Chichester, UK, and Malden, MA: Wiley-Blackwell, 2011); Adriana de Souza e Silva and Jordan Frith, *Mobile Interfaces in Public Spaces: Locational Privacy, Control, and Urban Sociability* (London and New York: Routledge, 2012); Rowan Wilken and Gerard Goggin (eds), *Mobile Technology and Place* (New York: Routledge, 2012), and *Locative Media* (New York: Routledge, 2015); Jason Farman, *Mobile Interface Theory: Embodied Space and Locative Media* (London and New York: Routledge, 2012); Jason Farman (ed.), *The Mobile Story: Narrative Practices with Locative Technologies* (New York: Routledge, 2014); Adriana de Souza e Silva and Mimi Sheller (eds.), *Mobility and Locative Media: Mobile Communication in Hybrid Spaces* (London and New York: Routledge, 2015).

33 See, for instance, Didem Özkul, "Location as a Sense of Place: Everyday Life, Mobile, and Spatial Practices in Urban Places," in de Souza e Silva and Sheller (eds.), *Mobility and Locative Media*, 101–116. Also: Raz Schwartz and Germaine R. Halegoua, "The Spatial Self: Location-Based Identity Performance on Social Media," *New Media & Society* 17.10 (2015), 1643–1660.

34 Larissa Hjorth and Ingrid Richardson, "Games of Being Mobile: The Unruly Rise of Mobile Gaming in Japan," in Dal Yong Jin (ed.), *Mobile Gaming in Asia: Politics, Culture, and Emerging Technologies* (Dordrecht: Springer, 2017), 21.

35 Makiko Yamazaki, "Developer of Nintendo's Pokémon GO Aiming for Rollout to 200 Markets Soon," *Reuters*, 15 July, 2015, http://www.reuters.com/article/us-nintendo-pokemon-niantic-idUSKCN0ZV0I2.

36 Larissa Hjorth and Dean Chan, "Locating the Game: Gaming Cultures In/And the Asia-Pacific," in Larissa Hjorth and Dean Chan (eds), *Gaming Cultures and Place in Asia-Pacific* (London and New York: Routledge, 2009), 4.

37 For instance: Anna Cristina Pertierra and Graeme Turner, *Locating Television: Zones of Consumption* (London and New York: Routledge, 2012); Gerard Goggin and Mark McLelland (eds), *Routledge Companion to Global Internet Histories* (New York: Routledge, 2017).

38 Tama Leaver and Michele Willson, "Social Networks, Casual Games and Mobile Devices: The Shifting Contexts of Gamers and Gaming," in Leaver and Willson (eds), *Social, Casual and Mobile Games*, 2.
39 Leaver and Michele Willson, "Social Networks, Casual Games and Mobile Devices," 3.
40 Jordan Frith, *Smartphones as Locative Media* (Cambridge: Polity; Hoboken, NJ: Wiley, 2015), 144.
41 Frith, *Smartphones as Locative Media*, 144.
42 Frith, *Smartphones as Locative Media*, 145.
43 Frith, *Smartphones as Locative Media*, 145.
44 Frith, *Smartphones as Locative Media*, 145.
45 Kyle Moore, quoted in Luke O'Neill, "Why Augmented Reality in Public Spaces is a Game Changer ... An urban mobile gaming researcher explains what Pokémon GO and Ingress can tell us about augmented reality experiences," 20 July, 2016, http://sydney.edu.au/news-opinion/news/2016/07/20/why-augmented-reality-in-public-spaces-is-a-game-changer.html.
46 Inter alia, see: Arno Scharl and Klaus Tochtermann (eds.), *The Geospatial Web: How Geobrowsers, Social Software and the Web 2.0 are shaping the Network Society* (London: Springer, 2007); Alice Crawford and Gerard Goggin, "Geomobile Web: Locative Technologies and Mobile Media," *Australian Journal of Communication* 36.1 (2009), 97–109; Gretchen Wilken (ed.), *Distributed Urbanism: Cities after Google Earth* (London and New York: Routledge, 2010); Nicholas Mirzoeff, *How to See the World* (London: Pelican, 2015).
47 Ken Hillis, Michael Petit, and Kylie Jarrett, *Google and the Culture of Search* (New York and London: Routledge, 2013).
48 Google, "Google Acquires Keyhole Corp," media release, 27 October, 2004, http://googlepress.blogspot.com.au/2004/10/google-acquires-keyhole-corp.html.
49 Google, "Google Acquires Keyhole Corp."
50 *Wall Street Journal*, "Google Acquires Keyhole: Digital-Mapping Software Used by CNN in Iraq War," *Wall Street Journal*, 27 October, 2004, http://www.wsj.com/articles/SB109888284313557107. On Keynote, see an interview with its other founder, Avi Bar-Zeev: Jeremy Crampton, "Keyhole, Google Earth, and 3D Worlds: An Interview with Avi-Bar-Zeev," *Cartographica*, 43.2 (2008), 85–93.
51 *Wall Street Journal*, "Google Acquires Keyhole." For analysis, see: Micky Lee, "A Political Economic Critique of Google Maps and Google Earth," *Information, Communication & Society* 13.6 (2010), 909–928; and Jeremy Crampton, "Mappings," in *The Wiley-Blackwell Companion to Cultural Geography*, ed. Nuala C. Johnson, Richard H. Schein, and Jamie Winders (New York: Wiley-Blackwell, 2013), 423–436.
52 Google, "Google Maps and Keyhole Integration," media release, 3 April, 2005, http://googlepress.blogspot.com.au/2005/04/google-maps-and-keyhole-integration_03.html.
53 Claire Cain Miller, "A New Google App Gives You Local Information — Before You Ask For It," *Bits, New York Times* Blog, 27 September, 2012, http://bits.blogs.nytimes.com/2012/09/27/a-new-google-app-gives-you-local-information-before-you-ask-for-it/.
54 "Field Trip," Niantic Inc., *App Store*, https://itunes.apple.com/us/app/field-trip/id567841460?ls=1&mt=8.
55 Claire Cain Miller, "A New Google App ..."
56 John Hanke, quoted in Claire Cain Miller, "A New Google App."

57 Alexis C. Madrigal, "The World is Not Enough: Google and the Future of Augmented Reality," *The Atlantic*, 25 October, 2012, http://www.theatlantic.com/technology/archive/2012/10/the-world-is-not-enough-google-and-the-future-of-augmented-reality/264059/.
58 Alexis C. Madrigal, "The World is Not Enough."
59 John Herrman, "Augmented Reality Yelp Will Murder All Other iPhone Restaurant Apps," *Gizmodo*, 27 August, 2009, http://gizmodo.com/5347194/augmented-reality-yelp-will-murder-all-other-iphone-restaurant-apps-my-health. For a very helpful critical discussion of the differences between a location-based service such as *Yelp!* and the specific augmented reality aspect of *Monocle*, see Liao and Humphreys, "Layar-ed Places."
60 Liao and Humphreys, "Layar-ed Places," 1432.
61 Liao and Humphreys, "Layar-ed Places," 1432.
62 Among others, see: Alice Crawford, "Taking Social Software to the Streets: Mobile Cocooning and the (An)Erotic City," *Journal of Urban Technology* 15.3 (2007), 79–97; Lee Humphreys, "Mobile Social Networks and Urban Public Space," *New Media & Society* 12 (2010), 763–778; Adriana de Souza e Silva and Jordan Frith, "Locative Mobile Social Networks: Mapping Communication and Location in Urban Spaces," *Mobilities* 5.4 (2010), 485–505.
63 Frith, *Smartphones as Locative Media*.
64 John Hanke, "Three Years of Ingress and the Road for Niantic: VR vs. AR and What It Means for Games Like Pokémon GO," *Medium*, 28 January, 2016, https://medium.com/@johnhanke/three-years-of-ingress-and-the-road-for-niantic-a991a2d6587#.evu82qyoa.
65 Stacey Blasiola, Miao Feng, and Adrienne Massanari, "Riding in Cars with Strangers: A Cross-Cultural Comparison of Privacy and Safety in *Ingress*," in Leaver and Willson, *Social, Casual and Mobile Games*, 135–148.
66 Erin Stark, "Playful Places: Uncovering Hidden Heritage with Ingress," in Leaver and Willson (eds), *Social, Casual and Mobile Games*, 150.
67 Stark, "Playful Places," 161–162.
68 Claire Groden, "Google's Internal Start-Up Niantic Labs Spins Off," 13 August, 2015, http://fortune.com/2015/08/13/googles-niantic-labs-spins-off/. See also: Janko Roettgers, "Google Spins Out Location-Based Game Company NianticLabs," 12 August, 2015, *Variety*, http://variety.com/2015/digital/news/google-spins-out-location-based-game-company-niantic-labs-1201569016/.
69 John Hanke, "Niantic Inc. Raises $20 Million in Financing from The Pokémon Company, Google and Nintendo," 15 October, 2015, https://www.nianticlabs.com/blog/niantic-tpc-nintendo/.
70 Beth Winegarner, "Forget Pokémon GO, There's Another Augmented Reality Game That's Way Better," *Quartz*, 15 July 2016, http://qz.com/732809/forget-pokemon-go-theres-another-augmented-reality-game-thats-way-better/.
71 Winegarner, "Forget Pokémon GO."
72 Winegarner, "Forget Pokémon GO."
73 See, for instance: Joseph Tobin (ed.), *Pikachu's Global Adventure: The Rise and Fall of Pokémon* (Durham, NC: Duke University Press, 2004). Of interest for their arguments about the potential uses of Pokémon and the ways in which power circulates around it, especially in relation to children and young people, see: Mark Gibson, "The Powers of the Pokémon: Histories of Television, Histories of the Concept of Power," *Media International Australia* 104 (2002): 107–115; David Buckingham and Julian Sefton-Green, "Gotta Catch 'Em All: Structure, Agency and Pedagogy in Children's Media Culture," *Media Culture & Society* 25. 3 (2003),

379–399l; Maya Gotz, Dafna Lemish, Hyesung Moon, and Amy Aidman, *Media and the Make-Believe Worlds of Children: When Harry Potter Meets Pokémon in Disneyland* (New York and London: Routledge, 2005); Mimo Ito, "Mobilizing the Imagination in Everyday Play: The Case of Japanese Media Mixes," in Stefan Sonvilla-Weiss (ed.), *Mashup Cultures* (Vienna: Springer, 2010), 79–97; Jason Bainbridge, " 'It is a Pokémon World': The *Pokémon* Franchise and the Environment," *International Journal of Cultural Studies* 17.4 (2014): 399–414.

74 Dal Yong Jin, "The Emergence of Asian Mobile Games: Definitions, Industries, and Trajectories," in Dal Yong Jin (ed.), *Mobile Gaming in Asia: Politics, Culture, and Emerging Technologies* (Dordrecht: Springer, 2017), 4–5.

75 See the App Institute's "Pokemon GO App Downloads and Revenue in Real Time," with the takeaway message spelt out clearly: "While you've been on this page Pokemon GO has taken over the world" (12 August, 2015, http://appinstitute.com/pokemongo-realtime-stats/#sthash.p5ryt5dv.dpuf).

76 Dal Yong Jin, "The Emergence of Asian Mobile Games," 8.

77 Edward W. Soja, *Seeking Spatial Justice* (Minneapolis, MN: University of Minnesota Press, 2010).

78 As well as the model of the excellent Tobin 2004 collection, *Pikachu's Global Adventure*, and the scholarship on Asian Pacific gaming cultures, pioneered by Hjorth, Chan, Jin, and others, there is also burgeoning work offering international perspectives on location technology, including Rowan Wilken, Gerard Goggin, and Heather Horst (eds), *Location Technologies in International Contexts* (New York: Routledge, 2017).

79 Sean Gibson, "Full List of Pokémon Available to Catch Including Region-Exclusives ...", *Daily Telegraph*, 16 August, 2016, http://www.telegraph.co.uk/gaming/what-to-play/pokemon-go-full-list-of-original-151-pokemon-available-to-catch/.

80 Rowan Wilken, "The De-Gamification of Foursquare?" in Leaver and Willson (eds), *Social, Casual and Mobile Games*, 186–188.

81 Wilken, "The De-Gamification of Foursquare?" 187.

82 Hanke, "Three Years of Ingress ..."

83 Hanke, "Three Years of Ingress ..."

4   Social Media, Radicalization and Extremist Violence

Challenges for Research

Ramaswami Harindranath

Introduction

At the time of writing (late 2016) there have been several attacks and mass killings in the first half of this year alone, in countries as diverse as France, Iraq, Syria, Turkey, Pakistan, Germany, Afghanistan, Egypt, and the United States, resulting in scores of deaths. Each such event is followed by the inevitable search for explanations - an almost impossible demand, for what possible framework could offer a reason for the intrinsically inexplicable? Discussions of possible solutions, more often than not based on explanations and interpretations of such events are, at best, partial. Of the terms that have gained near-universal currency as offering a shared understanding of such acts of extremist violence, two of the most significant are 'terrorism' and 'radicalization', which share an alleged explanatory force that, on closer examination, appears shaky. Regardless, 'terrorism' and 'radicalization' have, in turn, come to be connected through a perception of the role of social and digital media as a means to recruit young men and women to carry out acts of terror and mass-murder.

Digital media and terrorism – two of the more recent global developments that continue to generate public interest, media scrutiny, and academic research – have been brought together recently in the context of growing concerns about the use of social media and the internet by extremists to radicalize and recruit individuals and groups across the globe. Using al-Qaeda as a particularly vicious example of cyber-insurgency, a 'networked social movement' that used 'resource mobilization via propaganda and propaganda by deed, "flattened" hierarchy, decentralization and self-organization, all of which depend on networks', David Betz and Tim Stevens[1] highlight the perceived links between digital technologies and violent extremism. They see cyberspace as presenting 'something of a paradox in its tendency to foster great opportunity and significant threat'.[2] On one level, this is a legitimate worry, particularly given the proliferation online of images of grisly violence and proclamations purportedly on behalf of extremists groups carrying out acts of terror. A recent article in the online news outlet *The Intercept* provides an indication of this growing concern:

'Since 2004, the group [Islamic State], also known as ISIS, has managed to attract as many as 30,000 recruits from around the world, including several thousand men and women from Europe and North America. A significant number of these individuals are believed to have been recruited online using social media'.[3]

The very affordances of new media technologies that have given rise to grassroots movements for social and political change, including the much celebrated but all too brief Arab Spring, are the very ones being exploited by extremist groups such as ISIS. Cora Kaplan's observation that '[a]ny emancipatory qualities of digital information technologies and new media long touted by theorists, politicians and journalists are destabilized by the rapid incorporation of such technologies into the standing militaries of the Western superpowers and their allies via various 'revolutions' in tactics and strategies, as well as their newly apparent adoption by so-called 'jihadi' and other non-state networks'[4] has now become commonplace among scholars, security experts and commentators. It is now widely accepted that intrinsic to contemporary technoculture are contradictory impulses, offering both promises and threats.

As Jason Burke recently observed in a report on how changes in media technologies have changed terrorism, published in *The Guardian*, '[n]ew technologies have not only made it possible to produce propaganda with astonishing ease – they have also made it far easier to disseminate these films and images'.[5] Groups such as ISIS have been able to exploit the new technologies, including lightweight digital cameras, editing software, and advances in mobile and social media hardware and software: '[t]he group's use of social media marks it out from predecessors such as al-Qaeda. So, too, do the high production values and visual images derived from video games and Hollywood blockbusters'.[6] Implied in such arguments about the use of digital and social media for propaganda are assumptions about the audiences or users that have not been adequately explored or justified. While, on the one hand, such propaganda material does evidently exist on digital and social media, and concerns about the potential radicalization of Muslim youth are, to a large extent, justified, such arguments reiterate older assumptions with regard to audiences, basing their assertions on links between online content and radicalization that are largely unsupported by empirical research, and consequently reading off perceived 'effects' from the text and from the possibilities afforded by the technology. There is an urgent need for a new framework that builds on relatively recent and new theorizations on new media technologies, in particular, on mediation and materiality. Without such a framework, exploring and making any link between radicalization and digital media risks repeating generalizations about vulnerable audiences and thereby contributing to public anxieties and fear.

Digital Media, Terrorism, Audiences

It is difficult to disagree with assessments such as Maura Conway's[7] that the affordances of new media technologies, the accessibility of global portals, and their multimedia content hold specific kinds of appeal to young people. As she has argued, the 'violent jihadi online milieu', or 'the jihadisphere' was made possible by the technological possibilities offered by Web 2.0, including online social networking, user-generated content and multimedia platforms. Concerns regarding the links between this online jihadi milieu and enactments of extremist violence in the 'real world' underpin counter-terrorism measures adopted by multiple national and transnational agencies. I have explored elsewhere the damaging consequences of the performativity of terrorism and counter-terrorism.[8] The main focus of this essay is on current accounts of the links between digital media and terrorism, and the need, empirically and analytically, to go beyond assumptions that uncritically position dispersed, networked digital and mobile audiences and social media users as being manipulated by overtures from extremists located elsewhere.

In her commentary on terrorism and the internet, Conway identifies five 'core terrorist uses of the Net: information provision, financing, networking, recruitment and information gathering'.[9] Information provision, according to Conway, enables extremists to participate in 'publicity, propaganda and, ultimately, psychological warfare',[10] and to circumvent the editorial control and gatekeeping that are prevalent in traditional media. 'The Internet', she argues, 'offers terrorist groups an unprecedented level of direct control over the content of their message(s). It considerably extends their ability to shape how different target audiences perceive them and to manipulate not only their own image, but also the image of their enemies'.[11] While her argument regarding the ability of the internet to largely bypass editorial control is well taken, the premises on which this statement is based include a conception of the audience that appears to merely extend that from television and cinema studies from the late twentieth century. It recalls earlier debates on the 'effects' tradition, and on conceiving audiences as uncritical 'dupes', easily manipulated and/or influenced by film and television texts, or as 'vulnerable' groups with a strong predilection towards succumbing to the attractions and influences of the text. Such debates preceded and contributed to the emergence of reception studies, which emphasized sense-making and enjoyment as arising from interpretive practice, on the interaction and dialogue between the text and an 'active' audience.

From a different perspective, and aiming to introduce some academic rigor from the field of media studies into this issue, Anne Aly tackles the question of a 'terrorist audience' much more centrally. Claiming that 'the internet has surfaced as an important and critical tool in the extremists' repertoire', and that [f]or those individuals and groups who seek to spread the message of violent Islamism and indoctrinate the vulnerable to violent action, the internet presents as a one stop shop where they can identify, inform, influence and indoctrinate', she argues for an analytical framework with which to understand 'the appeal and functionality of the internet to users: the terrorist audience.[12]

Aly's model adapts the users and gratifications theory for a digital audience in order to

> explain the nexus between user needs and extremist content. Understanding what motivates people to turn to the internet for inspiration and guidance and in turn how extremist content on the internet might fulfill their needs can assist in the development of counter terrorism and security measures to tackle the growing challenge of internet radicalization.[13]

Building on David Romano's identification of the factors that contributed to the use of digital media technologies among Kurdish refugees[14], Aly's model rests on two important arguments: firstly, the context, including Muslim diaspora and transnationalism and the identity that is perceived to be shared among Muslim communities globally, including the apparent perception among these communities of the complicity of Western media in attempts to undermine and stereotype Islam and Muslims; and secondly, the specific technological attributes and the affordances of the internet. These, together with the consequent needs of the Muslim diaspora, she argues, are exploited by extremists:

> the social situation of Muslims around the globe generates media needs that, for those who are predisposed to radicalization, are gratified by the content and functions of the internet which in turn is generated by the aims of terrorist organizations to identify, inform, influence and indoctrinate potential members. *The role of the internet in radicalization lies in its ability to present alternative realities and truths that invite people to be part of the social network where the boundaries of belonging are set by terrorists.*[15] (my emphasis)

In her view, then, the need experienced by young Muslims for interpretations of global events by sources other than mainstream media outlets leaves them open for manipulation by 'terrorist organizations'.

By distinguishing between four inter-related aspects of 'internet radicalization': the context and needs of the audience, the affordances of the internet, and extremists' goals, this model offers an intriguing framework for examining the 'terrorist audience'. The internet's ability to present an alternative narrative to that available in mainstream national and global news networks can justifiably be seen as making it attractive to groups who feel marginalized in host communities and who look for explanations of world events from sources other than mainstream news of which they are wary. The redrawing of 'the boundaries of belonging', the attractiveness of, and therefore allegiance to, social networks that transcend local and national borders and based on a shared sense of dispossession too, is plausible. However, this model retains a conception of the audience – in this case digital – that approximates outmoded notions of certain sections of the community being affected by media content. In addition, it leaves little room for a deeper examination of *context*. For instance, the question of what is 'the social situation of Muslims around the globe' that prompts their search for alternative explanations and interpretations? What is the connection between the lived experience of these communities and their suspicion of mainstream media worlds and realities? Does the belief in the complicity of Western media spring only, or even mainly, from what they perceive as stereotyping? In other words, what is the political, cultural, historical, and social context in which the 'target audience' encounters this online propaganda, and what relevance does this context have to the ways in which digital content is received and used, both in terms of potential recruitment by extremist groups and also more generally? And how do we conceive the *digital* audience?

Arguing that

> propaganda is especially important in recruiting individuals and organizations who might never come into physical contact with Islamic State fighters, and who instead judge the group largely based on the image it has cultivated through social media and online strategic messaging, and on the mainstream media's reporting on IS's gains and overall health[16]

Daveed Gartenstein-Ross identifies four types of messages that together constitute 'a multifaceted narrative that appeals to its various target audiences in several ways': 'religious obligation, political grievance, and sense of adventure', which make up the bottom of the pyramid, and which are 'some of the most difficult for IS's foes to counter', and 'success: IS is winning' message at the top of the pyramid.[17]

> Foreign fighter recruitment videos blend narrative about religious obligation with themes depicting jihad as an action-packed adventure, replete with symbols of masculinity to attract young men.

IS's cutting-edge special effects also help life on the battlefield to seem both exciting and "cool".[18]

There is little acknowledgment of the affordances characteristic of digital media. With the emphasis placed more centrally on the *content* of the videos and its potential for propaganda and recruitment, the technology itself becomes incidental. Scott Gates and Sukanya Podder make a similar case on the use of social media by IS to recruit foreign fighters. 'IS has developed an effective virtual propaganda machinery', they argue. 'The vast global social media presence of IS is sustained by significant manpower. Linguistic and technical skills are clearly evident. Obviously some effort is being made not only to recruit foot soldiers, but also to enlist technically proficient and talented users of social media to sustain the machinery of recruitment'.[19] Implicit in such commentary are assumptions about digital media technologies that are seen to afford IS and other extremist groups a 'vast global social media presence', predicated on capacities of the technologies. The unique characteristics of digital and social media are not sufficiently interrogated, and what the 'technically proficient' actually engage with is left unexplored.

Two inter-linked but analytically separate issues are critical here – a reconsideration of the ways in which we conceptualize new media and digital technologies, and of the ways in which we understand and frame the context of radicalization and extremist violence. The near-global adoption and use of social media and, in particular, its ongoing technological developments have amplified scholarly interest. Most pertinent among these, for our purposes, are, firstly, conceptualizations of the human or social relations with technologies by sociologists, geographers and anthropologists, and secondly, elaborations on the materiality of the technologies, conceived differently by different media philosophers, that delve into what are considered to be the material foundations of the technologies themselves as well as their broader, socio-cultural consequences. While, in this instance, the latter is specific to the issue of terrorism, 'context' – both in the abstract and in the empirical senses – has been a term about which audience researchers have been constantly reminded since at least the 1990s, in terms of culture, ethnicity, class, economic and cultural capital, and so on. As has been demonstrated repeatedly in the history of media research, context *matters* in studies of audience.

Mediology, Materiality, Mediation

The analytical links between technology and culture are most evident in Régis Debray's mediology. What he refers to as cultural mediation includes, for Debray, both technology, which comprises 'the intimate prosthetics of cultural life'[20] – technology makes culture – and the socio-cultural dimension, without which technological advances will not function. As noted by Constantina Papoulias, Debray's work 'demonstrates the difficulty of rendering an analytics of technoculture compatible with an analytics of the social imaginary or, in his words, of crossing the "story of our tools" with that of "our hopes and dreams"'.[21] He makes a sharp distinction between 'communication' and 'transmission' in his '*Introduction à la Médiologie*: To communicate', he argues,

> is to transport information through space; to transmit is to transform information through time. ... In the first case, by relating a here with an elsewhere, we will make connections (and thus a society); in the other case, by relating a now and a then, we will make continuity (and thus culture).[22]

Is it possible then, to argue that extremist strategies on the social media include aspects of both communication and transmission, as conceived by Debray, making spatial and historical connections, seeking allegiances and alliances across sections of the global population sympathetic to their claims of victimhood, particularly in terms of European and American imperialist adventures? What historical grievances echo in the pronouncements of extremist leaders and the responses to them? Which of these are clearly articulated, which are implied, and which left unsaid but largely agreed on, a sedimentation of accepted knowledge that forms links between dispersed networks? And, most significantly for our present purposes, how are these implicated and in turn affected, consolidated, strengthened, by the technology of social media? How does the experience of being part of an alternative network, a member of an audience group, which transgresses national boundaries and forms alliances and affiliations while resisting that of national or more conventional cultures, sanction the emergence of values and beliefs specific to the technoculture of extremism? These are important questions, the explorations of which require taking into account recent attempts to reformulate notions of mediation and materiality.

Michael Jackson, arguing for a phenomenology of the human-technology interface, points out that, in their evaluations of new technologies, on-going debates

> often leave unexplored the more immediately empirical issue of how we actually experience and interact with technologies, and how our attitudes towards them are linked to perennial human anxieties about the strange, the new, and the other.[23]

His builds on the contributions, inspired by Heidegger's commentary on technology – Don Ihde's approach to the technology-human interaction as existential relations embedded in the life-world, an insight empirically investigated by Tim Ingold, for whom the technological and the social are inextricably intertwined and form one dimension of human sociality, and Bryan Pfaffenberger's notion of the 'sociotechnical system', which argues against the idea of technology 'as a body of techniques and material objects that answer human needs yet remain separate from ourselves', focusing instead on 'the intimate and complex interactions that bind technology, human labor, and social relationships'.[24] Jackson's goal is to explore further 'the existential-phenomenological threads in this body of work'[25], hypothesizing that 'our human ambivalence towards new technologies must be understood against the background of our ambivalence towards others' and that how we experience both these sets of relationships 'will depend upon the degree to which we feel in control' of them, and the extent to which they 'are felt to augment rather than diminish our sense of well-being'.[26]

Reading a little against the grain, it is possible to re-position Jackson's hypotheses and see how our discomfiture with both technologies as well as our others – racial, ethnic, sexual, or religious Others – diminish rather than augment our sense of well-being, and it is possible to see how misgivings about one lead to wariness about how it relates with the other, and the broader repercussions of those relations. When public anxieties about digital audiences and users of social media intersect with those involving racial and/or religious Others, as in the case of digital and mobile media and radicalization, the ambivalences to which Jackson refers assume disturbing proportions, including fear, insecurity and xenophobia. This, in turn, has wider implications for the public sphere and for civil society.

Writing a little earlier than Jackson, Paolo Carpignano advanced the conception of 'media *as* public sphere or, conversely, ... the public sphere *as* a medium', for heuristic purposes. 'Thus, the media can be studied not simply as a technology of communication or as institution that regulates communication, but as *itself* a social relation of communication'. This will allow the study of the public sphere not so much as discourse and action,

> but also as the location where material articulations, the technological mediations of social communication, take place. In sum, adopting this kind of perspective would mean investigating not only what is public in the public sphere, but also how publicity is materially constituted.[27]

This is particularly pertinent in the context of global terrorism, given Habermas's view of global terrorism as a form of communicative pathology, inaugurated by the 9/11 attacks that constituted the 'first historic world event' that 'took place in front of the "universal eyewitness" of a global public'.[28]

Alongside this re-emphasis on materiality there has been a renewed interest in mediation, with reconceptualizations of the term often making overt or subtler connections with Marshall McLuhan's formulations. Thus, Arjun Appadurai has recently made a plea for shifting the focus from the material and materiality to an examination of the relations between materiality and mediation:

> My view of the relationship between mediation and materiality, put briefly, is as follows: mediation and materiality cannot be usefully defined except in relationship to each other. Mediation, as an operation or embodied practice, produces materiality as the effect of its operations. Materiality is the site of what mediation – as an embodied practice – reveals. Thus speech is the materiality from which language – as mediation – takes its meaning. Pictures are the materiality ... from which images, as practices of mediation, take their meaning. The eye (and its sensory-neutral infrastructure) is the materiality through which seeing – as a practice of mediation – takes its effect.[29]

Although mediation could be perceived 'as effect, of which some sort of materiality is always the condition of possibility', it would be incorrect to conclude that materiality pre-exists mediation 'any more than speech pre-exists language, pictures pre-exist images, or the eye pre-exists vision. The two sides of this relationship always exist and work together as two sides of the same thing'.[30]

If mediation and materiality are inextricably intertwined, or to be seen as two sides of the same thing, and if mediation is 'an operation or embodied practice' and materiality its 'effects', how are we to re-construe the links between extremist content on digital media, young Muslims, and extremist violence? It is possible to argue that enactments of terror are the *mediation* and radicalization the *material* consequences of both the terrorist acts as well as the depiction on social media of gruesome images from such events. The terrorist incidents themselves, which constitute Jurgen Habermas's 'communicative pathology', the images from which are circulated in the media, thus have both a mediational and a material existence, and contribute to a circularity of signification and re-enactment. It is this, mainly, that contributes to what Nigel Thrift refers to as 'affective contagion'[31], in this case a contagion of fear and vulnerability. As Richard Grusin has argued,

> although media and media technologies have operated and continue to operate epistemologically as modes of knowledge production, they also function technically, bodily, and materially to generate and modulate individual and collective affective moods or structures of feeling among assemblages of humans and nonhumans. ... Like the

way media operate affectively, mediation must be understood onto-
logically as a process or event prior to and ultimately not reducible
to particular media technologies.[32]

This, for Grusin, constitutes 'radical mediation'. Such re-consideration
of the human-technology interface, and of the links between technology
and society/culture are critical to any theoretically sophisticated investigation and analysis of digital audience practice.

Digital Audiences and Radicalization

From a more sociological perspective, Saskia Sassen distinguishes between two kinds of 'socio-technical formations' comprising 'global
ICT-mediated financial markets' and 'local social actors geographically
dispersed yet increasingly part of a globally articulated space even though
they mostly are not in direct communication with each other'.[33] Her emphasis is on the interactive nature of these domains, which, she argues,
contributes to the capacities of such 'socio-digital formations' enabled
by 'digital technologies to override existing relations of law to territory.
One notable emergent trend is the possibility even for resource-poor actors partially to exit national encasements and emerge as global political
actors'. More significantly for her, such cases 'also illuminate the specific
conditions under which this takes place: the fact that there is both a
digital and a non-digital moment in the often complex process wherein
these new technologies are deployed'.[34]

The process of radicalization of young Muslims living in Europe and
North America could perhaps be seen as an instance of such socio-
digital formations, comprising a network of actors and technologies
that link terrorist leaders and strategists, locally dispersed extremists,
as well as the acts of terror. Uniquely, such acts themselves, and the
images of their aftermath that circulate on the news and on extremist digital networks, become currency of signification, gaining affective
weight while contributing to the continual destabilization of security,
both personal and public. Together, these constitute both the 'assemblage of the human and the non-human' described by Grusin, generating
public moods and structures of feeling, and their deployment instanti-
ates, in a particularly deadly fashion, Sassen's observation regarding the
digital and non-digital moments that allow actors to transcend national
and territorial laws. Furthermore, the complexity of this relationship
comprising extremist leaders, radicalized local actors, terrorist events
and the coverage of them as well as the responses from political leaders
to such events – all these aspects illustrate the intricate entanglements
that constitute what Appadurai understands as 'mediation' and 'materiality', and what Debray designates 'communication' and 'transmission'. Isolating the category of 'audience' in this complex mix therefore

requires a new understanding of 'audience', and a new approach to the study of digital audiences.

The term 'radicalization', which, as Gessen concludes towards the end of an investigation of the Boston bombers[35], has influenced both media coverage of terrorist incidents as well as law enforcement, suggests a theory according to which

> a person becomes a terrorist by way of identifiable stages of adopting increasingly radical ideas, until he or she is finally radicalized into terrorist action. This theory has shaped behaviour, and lives, though it remains highly controversial among terrorism scholars.[36]

Despite studies demonstrating that, not only do all those engaging in extremist violence not hold radical views, but that only a miniscule proportion of those who hold radical views actually carry out acts of violence, the 'radicalization hypothesis itself ... has held steady in the face of a glaring lack of evidence'.[37] And in instances where there is no indication of any connection with a network, the hypothesis has been that such 'lone wolf' operatives had become 'self-radicalized'. As Arun Kundnani has observed, although the concept of radicalization appears to offer the possibility of interrogating and understanding the causes of terrorism, its value is limited by the various assumptions that accompany it. This includes emphasizing 'individual psychological or theological journeys, largely removed from social or political circumstances, [which] are claimed to be the root causes of the radicalization process'.[38] Implicit in this is the idea of contemporary terrorism as a result of a particular interpretation of Islam, which 'renders irrelevant consideration of terrorism not carried out by Muslims. An a priori distinction is drawn between the new terrorism, seen as originating in Islamic theology, and the old terrorism of nationalist or Leftist political violence, for which the question of radicalization is rarely posed'.[39]

Engaging with the issue of social media, radicalization and extremism also involves the question of socio-cultural and political context. As mentioned earlier, the significance of 'context', broadly and variously considered, has been emphasized in audience research for at least the last thirty years. However, as Lawrence Grossberg has recently pointed out, context is 'almost never defined, and even more rarely theorized'.[40] He presents a theory of context 'as a singularity that is also a multiplicity, an active, organized and organizing assemblage of relationalities'.[41] While this statement is a prologue to Grossberg's proposal of three 'modes of contextualization': milieu, territory or place, and region, it is worth noting how his account of context could also adequately describe the complex networks that together constitute both the contemporary digital world and also the world of extremist violence. At the very least, the kinds of, as well as the reasons for, radicalization might differ from person to person, group to group; while not everyone who is radicalized turns to violence, what propels a few of these individuals to perform acts of violence? One of the main contentions of this essay is that investigating the multiple dimensions of the context and of the motivations behind digital media and radicalization requires taking into account the broader context in which encounters – between extremist groups and between individuals, as well as between digital, social and mobile media and audiences/users – occur.

The events of 9/11 inaugurated new ways of perceiving the world that included a novel configuration of a Manichean divide that splits the putative 'West' from the alleged 'Islamic world', with attendant notions of victims and perpetrators of extremist violence, and, more importantly, it contributed to a redefinition of terrorism and of the role of extra-state actors in new forms of conflict, making a close link between acts of terror and their witnessing by media audiences. They were globally available 'live' events – Habermas's idea, mentioned earlier, of 9/11 being the first world historic event. Commenting on the live coverage of the events, Jacques Derrida claims that what was most significant was 'that we do not *know* what it is and so do not know how to describe, identify, or even name it'.[42] It is possible to see how this ignorance led to the uncritical adoption of concepts, vocabulary, and frames of interpretation, which subsequently contributed to the emergence of policies that many have identified as counter-productive. For Derrida, the 'real "terror" consisted of and, in fact, began by espousing and exploiting, having espoused and exploited, the image of this terror by the target itself'.[43] This, in turn, has led to what he calls an '*autoimmunitary* process', which is 'that strange behavior where a living being, in quasi-*suicidal* fashion, "itself" works to destroy its protection, to immunize itself *against* its "own" immunity'.[44]

Derrida's diagnosis of the autoimmune disorder that followed 9/11 and which was further escalated after subsequent acts of terror, is an important aspect of the 'context' in which radicalization occurs. Studies by researchers such as Ben O'Loughlin, Carole Boudeau, and Andrew Hoskins as well as Marie Gillespie[45] that have examined the connections between media audiences and radicalization have alerted us to the ongoing risk of media discourses and security policies themselves potentially contributing to marginalization of minorities in multicultural societies, and how this, in turn, could result in radicalization. Other than 'the "modulation of terror" that contains fear and amplifies threat', the other logic 'amplifying notions of emergence and catastrophic risk is the interacting logic of *re*mediation and *pre*mediation'[46], in which 'remediation' implies the creation of reports through a process of re-appropriation of news materials from different sources, and 'premediation' refers to the speculation and forecasting of future risks and threats. For Gillespie, 'The term mediation, in this context, refers to the multiple, interacting sets of relationships between news media production and consumption, within the framework of political debates, policy formation processes, and other dimensions of "public affairs" which may or may not be "visible" in media texts'.[47] The '"battlespace" of mutual disrespect and suspicion' that comprises the forum of interactions between journalists and policy makers, she argues, increases feelings of marginalization among ethnic minorities, in particular Muslim minorities. As a consequence, mediation 'is an irreducibly political process'.

Jeffrey Di Leo and Uppinder Mehan have pointed out that, 'post 9/11, it no longer seems responsible for theorists to engage in *a*political analysis; to dwell on the concept at the expense of the empirical; to ignore the social while reveling in the ideal'.[48] They have in mind the difficulties of scholars in expressing dissent without fear of retaliation in the wake of 9/11, but concerns about how post-9/11 responses to terrorist incidents and subsequent security policies have continued to affect the lives of racial and ethnic minorities are also factors that need to be taken into account while considering the context in which extremist content on social media is received and re-circulated. Racialized perceptions of minorities as potential threats to security add to and worsen marginalization and feelings of disenfranchisement in such communities in Europe, North America, and Australia. This is the other side of the 'affective contagion', through which minority communities find themselves as victims twice-over – possible victims of indiscriminate extremist violence, and victims of subsequent reprisals by security forces and the public. This too, is part of the context. As David Altheide has noted, 'terrorism plays well with audiences accustomed to the discourse of fear'.[49]

In his essay on Palestinian extremists Ghassan Hage introduces the terms 'exighophobia (from the Greek *exigho*, to explain) and homoiophobia (from the Greek *homoio*, the same)' (p. 87) to understand the exclusionary ethics that underlies the process of 'Othering' that prefigures inter-ethnic conflict:

> In this homoio-exighophobic culture anyone wishing to *know* and to inquire about the social conditions that might explain a possible rise in criminal offenses, for example, or about the social background of asylum seekers, is perceived as an inherent suspect, a nuisance if not a traitor. Recently, it was revealed that the Australian government directed its bureaucrats against issuing photos that would "humanize" the refugees seeking entry to Australia. Note that while people refer to such an attitude towards refugees as xenophobia, what is really feared here is not the otherness of the other but the other's human sameness – not xenophobia but homoiophobia.[50]

This is a crucial argument, as it underlines the significance of ethical positions that inform public attitudes to asylum-seekers and public fears about potential terror attacks and the consequent affective contagion of vulnera-bility and suspicion. As I have argued elsewhere[51], lost in the anxiety about media, radicalization, terrorism and counterterrorism is the consideration of how, as victims twice-over of acts of terror – once as innocent victims of the violent acts and again as victims of public and state suspicion – the racial and/or religious Other could feel more marginalized.

Conclusion

The example of digital/mobile media and radicalization highlights the contextually complex considerations of the socio-cultural and historico-political contexts in which the encounters between audience/user and mobile digital technology occur. Underlining the significance of context in the study of audiences is by no means novel or startling. How-ever, while context has been recognized as a significant factor in audience research for several decades, the novel considerations and conceptual-izations of mediation, materiality and the human-technology interface that have been developed alongside the changes in digital technologies are also critical. Not only do these theoretical interventions usefully problematize the nature of 'audiencing' and audience activity, they also reconfigure the notion of context. Considered together, these raise im-portant methodological considerations with regard to small-scale quali-tative analyses that adopt a range of mixed-methodologies and methods that acknowledge the profound entanglements that together constitute the issue of digital audience studies.

Notes

1 David J. Betz and Tim Stevens, *Cyberspace and the State: Toward a Strategy for Cyber-Power*, Routledge,(2011) 122.
2 Betz and Stevens, 125.
3 Murtaza Hussain in *The Intercept*, https://theintercept.com/2016/07/11/islamic-state-defectors-hold-key-to-countering-groups-recruitment/ - downloaded on 12 July 2016.
4 Cora Kaplan, "The biopolitics of technoculture in the Mumbai attacks", *Theory, Culture & Society*, 26 (7–8) (2009), 302.
5 http://www.theguardian.com/world/2016/feb/25/how-changing-media-changing-terrorism.
6 ibid.
7 Maura Conway "From al-Zarqawi to al-Awlaki: the emergence and deve-lopment of an online radical milieu", *CTX: Combating Terrorism Exchange*, Special Issue on 'Social Media in Jihad and Counterterrorism', 2 (4) (2012), 1–10.
8 See R. Harindranath "Counterterrorism as a contested terrain: performative contradictions and 'autoimmune disorder'", in Daniela Pisoiu (ed) *Arguing Counterterrorism: New Perspectives*. Routledge (2014) 181–198.
9 Maura Conway "Terrorism and the Internet: new media – new threat?" *Parliamentary Affairs*, 59. 2 (2006), 283.

10 ibid.
11 Conway, "Terrorism and the Internet", p. 284.
12 Anne Aly, "The terrorist audience: a model of internet radicalization", *Journal of the Australian Institute of Professional Intelligence Officers*, 17.1 (2009), 3.
13 ibid.
14 David Romano, "Modern communication technology in ethnic nationalist hands: the case of the Kurds", *Canadian Journal of Political Science*, 35 (2002), 127–149.
15 Aly, "The terrorist audience", 12–13.
16 Daveed Gartenstein-Ross, 'Jihad 2.0: social media in the next evolution of terrorist recruitment', Senate Testimony, Hearing before the Senate Committee on homeland security & governmental affairs, *Foundation for Defense of Democracies*, May 2015, www.defenddemocracy.org downloaded on 15 May 2016, p. 5.
17 ibid., p. 6.
18 ibid., p. 7.
19 Scott Gates and Sukanya Podder, (2015) "Social media, recruitment, allegiance and the Islamic State", *Perspectives on Terrorism*, 9.4 (2015),109.
20 Régis Debray *Transmitting Culture*, trans. Eric Rauth, New York: Columbia University Press (2000), 52.
21 Constantina Papoulias "Of tools and angels: Régis Debray's mediology" *Theory, Culture & Society*, 21 (3) (2004), 165.
22 Cited in 'Frédéric Vandenberghe "Régis Debray and mediation studies, or how does an idea become a material force?" *Thesis Eleven*, no:89 (2007), 26.
23 Michael Jackson, "Familiar and foreign bodies: a phenomenological exploration of the human-technology interface", Journal Royal Anthropological Institute, 8 (2002), 333.
24 Jackson, 334.
25 ibid.
26 Jackson, 336.
27 Paolo Carpignano "The shape of the sphere: the public sphere and the materiality of communication", *Constellations*, 6 (2) (1999), 177; emphasis in the original.
28 Jurgen Habermas and Giovanna Borradori "A dialogue with Jurgen Habermas", in Giovanna Borradori (ed.) *Philosophy in a Time of Terror: Dialogues with Jurgen Habermas and Jacques Derrida*, Chicago University Press (2003), 28.
29 Arjun Appadurai "Mediants, materiality, normativity", *Public Culture*, 27:2 (2015), 224.
30 Appadurai, 224–225.
31 Nigel Thrift, *Non-Representational Theory: Space/Politics/Affect*. London: Routledge (2008).
32 Richard Grusin, "Radical mediation", *Critical Inquiry*, vol.42 (2015), 125.
33 Saskia Sassen, "Interactions of the technical and the social: digital formations of the powerful and the powerless", *Information, Communication & Society*, 15.4 (2012), 455.
34 Sassen, 469.
35 Masha Gessen, *The Brothers: The Road to an American Tragedy*. New York: Riverhead Books (2015).
36 Gessen, 234.
37 Gessen, 235.
38 Arun Kundnani, *The Mulims are Coming! Islamophobia, Extremism, and the Domestic War on Terror*, London: Verso (2014), 117.

39 ibid.
40 Lawrence Grossberg, "Theorising context", in David Featherstone and Joe Painter (ed.) *Spatial Politics: Essays for Doreen Massey*, Oxford: Wiley-Blackwell, (2013), 32.
41 Grossberg, 34.
42 Jacques Derrida, in Borradori, 94. Emphasis in the original.
43 Derrida, 108. Emphasis in the original.
44 Derrida, 94. Emphasis in the original.
45 Ben O'Loughlin, Carole Boudeau & Andrew Hoskins, "Distancing the extraordinary: audience understandings of discourses of 'radicalization'", *Continuum*, 25:2 (2011), 153–164.
   Marie Gillespie, "Security, media and multicultural citizenship: a collaborative ethnography", *European Journal of Cultural Studies*, 10(3) (2007), 275–293.
46 Gillespie, 280.
47 Gillespie, 282.
48 Jeffrey Di Leo and Uppinder Mehan, "Theory ground zero: terror, theory and the humanities after 9/11", in Jeffrey di Leo and Uppinder Mehan (ed) *Terror, Theory and the Humanities*. Open Humanities Press (2012), 18. Emphasis in the original.
49 David Altheide, *Terrorism and the Politics of Fear*. Lanham: Rowman & Littlefield (2006), 127.
50 Ghassan Hage, "'Comes a time we are all enthusiasm': understanding Palestinian suicide bombers in times of exighophobia", *Public Culture*, 15(1) (2003), 87–88.
51 R. Harindranath "Malign images, malevolent networks: social media, extremist violence and public anxieties", in Elena Marellozzo and Emma Jane (ed) *Cybercrime and its Victims*. London; Routledge (in press, 2017).

5 Audiencing through Social Media

Darryl Woodford, Katie Prowd and Axel Bruns

Introduction

In most developed and many developing nations, general-purpose social media platforms such as Facebook and Twitter, as well as more application-specific tools such as YouTube, Instagram, and Vine, have by now become a key and central part of the media repertoires of the wider population. They are used for practices ranging from everyday phatic engagement with friends[1] through crisis communication[2] to political debate,[3] but an especially important practice which has emerged over recent years has been their use as ancillary and backchannel media alongside mainstream, mass media channels such as radio and television, as well as during major live events. Many broadcast and live events now advertise 'official' Facebook pages and Twitter accounts and hashtags for viewers to engage with, for example, while in the absence (or even in the presence) of such official offerings social media users are also frequently establishing their own *ad hoc* alternatives.

Such forms of audience participation through social media are now frequently described as 'second-screen' viewing[4] or more narrowly as 'social TV'.[5] They constitute a new form of the active engagement of audiences with the shared texts of mainstream media content which earlier cultural studies work has recognized as a form of 'audiencing',[6] but in using social media for the first time make such practices widely visible beyond the living room or other loci of mass media reception, as well as offering a greater opportunity for further engagement by fellow audience members well beyond the immediate 'personal public'[7] of the individual listener or viewer. This therefore also constitutes a shift away from what, in the tradition of Benedict Anderson,[8] we might be able to describe as an 'imagined' audience or community around the shared media text, and towards a more tangible and indeed more measurable audience (which may or may not also constitute a community, in any meaningful sense of the term).

This is not to say that – other than utilizing new communication platforms – television audiences are necessarily doing anything dramatically different today, compared to previous practices. Research into the uses of television, especially from cultural studies perspectives,[9] has long recognized that 'audiences are far from passive':

> We are not consuming a product but using the imaginative resources of story, song, sight, and sound ... to think about identity, relationship, and community, in real time and space.... We make ourselves up as we watch.[10]

But when we do so *and* use social media to share that process with others as it happens, it becomes amplified – we think aloud, or at least louder than previously, and we think with others beyond the familiar space of the living room. Watching television is already an inherently social process, as John Hartley's reference to the key social concepts of 'identity, relationship, and community' indicates, and television itself is a social medium in this sense; its combination with what we have now come to call 'social media' in a narrower sense simply makes the active audience described by television scholars for the past half-century considerably more visible, and tangible.

This more tangible sense of the active audience emerges most centrally through the tracing, capturing, and quantification of audience activities which state-of-the-art social media analytics make possible.[11] By gathering and evaluating potentially large datasets on the audiencing practices of individual listeners and viewers it becomes possible to identify the patterns of audience responses to media texts, both to examine their engagement with individual broadcasts and events and to compare and benchmark such individual observations against each other. This is valuable in the first place as a significant extension of conventional audience measurements (such as television ratings), providing a substantially more fine-grained and detailed picture of audience responses, but indeed also has substantial value well beyond the assessment of conventional media audiences; such engagement metrics also have applications in areas from brand communication to political campaign management, in fact.

As part of an ongoing effort to establish and standardize rigorous, robust, and reliable methods and metrics for the assessment and evaluation of audience engagement with broadcast content and live events (and to facilitate their extension and application to other fields beyond these core uses), this chapter presents an overview of relevant approaches and outlines the potential for further methodological advancement. We focus here especially on the development of audience engagement metrics that draw on Twitter activity in the Australian television context, but these principles are transferable and extensible to other social media platforms, mainstream media texts, and national contexts as well.

Measuring the Audience

While there is an ever-increasing range of social media platforms, both generally targeting global audiences (*e.g.,* Facebook, Twitter, Instagram, YouTube) and specific to particular countries (*e.g.,* Sina and Tencent Weibo (China), VKontakte (Russia)), the ease with which data on the public activities of their users can be collected and analyzed through their various Application Programming Interfaces (APIs) varies widely. For example, many of the metrics that would be useful for analyzing YouTube, such as the view count over time for a video, are only available to the channel owner. Even those platforms with relatively open access have their quirks.

Facebook, for example, limits the ability of automated software accounts (as opposed to regular human-operated accounts) to access a number public pages which would otherwise have age limits, such as those for R-Rated movies. This is because application accounts do not have an 'age' associated with their profile, and thus the Facebook age-verification algorithm denies the application access to the page data. Instagram provides a far more limited range of data than the other platforms (for instance, it does not provide information such as the account creation date for a given user account), and throttles requests more aggressively.

A comparison between API access limits for Twitter and Instagram illustrates this. Using the Twitter API it is possible to make 180 calls to retrieve user profile data in every 15-minute window, and each of these calls can query up to 100 user accounts; this enables researchers to query up to 18,000 accounts in each quarter-hour, or up to 72,000 accounts per hour. Other types of queries (for example for tweets themselves) are subject to a different limit, and can be made in parallel to retrieving user profile data. Instagram, on the other hand, has instituted a general limit of 5,000 API calls per hour, across all types of data, and each such call can only query one individual user profile, rather than a list of accounts. Compared to Twitter's up to 72,000 user profile queries per hour, Instagram thus allows only 5,000 such queries.

It is not least for this reason that most scholarly and commercial social media research has focused on Twitter: a platform which is public by default and shares a comparatively large volume of information through the public API. However, Twitter, Inc., too, is increasingly limiting access to publicly available information as it continues to revise its API functionality; for example, it is now only possible to retrieve detailed information on the previous 100 retweets by a user. This tightening of API capabilities is having significant chilling effects on scholarly research that draws on the Twitter API.[12]

However, there is still a large volume of data available, and even data which appears not to be immediately publicly available can often be gathered through a combination of other data sources. Here, we outline a range of methods developed for studying public communication on Twitter, Facebook and Instagram, outlining how such data may be useful for studying the social media activities of audiences.

Activity Over Time

Perhaps the most obvious metric for analyzing social media data is time-series data, or the volume of posts over time. This metric allows both comparisons of the long-term performance of specific events and topics, and the identification of key periods (*e.g.,* of intense activity, or no activity at all) that warrant further attention. The data could be drawn from a myriad of use cases, including in the first instance discussion around a particular keyword or hashtag, or posts from or mentioning specific accounts. However, more complex time-series tracking is also possible, to show for example the volume of images or videos posted to Twitter through Instagram, the split between retweets, @mentions, and original posts, or other measures of activity (Figure 5.1).

However, time-series charts can also be based on a further processed version of the data. For example, by running tweets through a sentiment engine,[13] it is possible to generate sentiment scores for each tweet. While the accuracy of sentiment analysis, particularly for social media data where sarcasm and humor can be difficult to detect, is still in question, often such an approach does at least provide a general trend of the sentiment within a conversation. Having performed this classification, it is then possible to graph tweets where sentiment is above or below particular levels, in order to track the shape of the conversation over time (Figure 5.2).

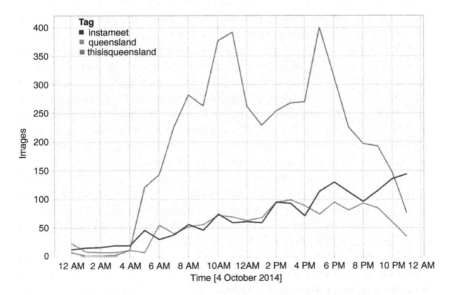

Figure 5.1 Total volume of the #instameet, #queensland, and #thisisqueensland hashtags for Tourism and Events Queensland Instameet Campaign on Instagram (4 October 2014).

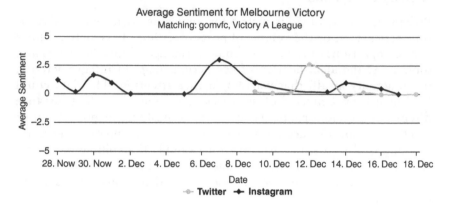

Figure 5.2 Average Twitter and Instagram sentiment over time for posts containing #gomvfc and 'Victory A League', referring to the Melbourne Victory football team in the Australian A-League.

Finally, these data streams can also be used to measure the activity of particular users, for example to find the most active users within a keyword or hashtag community. It is then possible to graph the activity of particular users or groups of users within the community over time, and to apply the same filters as discussed previously (*e.g.,* images, retweets, sentiment) to gain deeper insight, and to drill down into the details of their engagement.

Such time-series analyses thus illustrate audience engagement with television content as viewers encounter the shows live; they trace viewers' interpretive practices as they read media texts, and indeed can highlight the evolution of such practices from minute to minute and episode to episode, as social media users explore and establish their own conventions for interpreting and critiquing a shared text (on Twitter for example in the form of common hashtags and memes surrounding show and cast). In doing so, they can point to both the gradual development of individual audience members' practices, and the establishment of an interpretive community[14] with commonly held readings, as individual viewers connect and share their interpretations through social media.

While time-series data in the forms discussed above is widely covered in existing literature, it is mentioned here because it can also be further refined to provide metrics which give an insight into the underlying nature of the conversation. Two examples of this are the Weighted Tweet Index and Excitement Index,[15] both of which take data over time as core inputs. In the case of the Excitement Index, we measure the volatility of a conversation over time so as to generate a measure of 'excitement' within the conversation, following an approach developed by Brian Burke[16] for excitement around NFL games.

As we apply the Weighted Tweet Index to analyzing social media activity around television broadcasts, we measure the tweet volume not only during the show itself, but also in between shows. In doing so, we not only capture those who are talking about the show as it airs, but crucially also those who are communicating some form of anticipation for the show. We use these data in combination with other factors, such as the network on which a show aired, the time of day, day of week, month of year, position within the season, and country of broadcast, to compare the social media engagement for different shows. By accounting for the impact of each of these contextual factors, it is possible to place each show into a 'neutral' environment and normalize the observed tweeting activity by eliminating the effects of such factors. This allows for more direct comparisons between shows across timeslots, channels, and seasons, and offers an opportunity to develop more sophisticated social media strategies around these broadcasts.

Audience Overlap

Given that we are able to filter time-series data by users, we can thus also determine which users have contributed to which particular conversations. This enables us to map the overlap between audiences, both between specific cases (*e.g.*, *Masterchef* vs. *My Kitchen Rules* or *National Football League* vs. *Major League Baseball*) and on a wider scale, across the Twittersphere. In its most simplistic form, this enables us to visualize overlaps in the social media audience, based on the users taking part in particular hashtag- or keyword-based communities.

Figure 5.3 maps the overlap between three Australian sporting conversations on Twitter; the 2014 Australian Rules (AFL) Grand Final, the Rugby League (NRL) Grand Final, and the opening rounds of the FFA Cup Soccer tournament. Due to the differences in audience size, the image is not proportional, but serves to identify those 1,880 users who could be considered to be 'hardcore' sports fans, those who are dedicated to a specific sport, and perhaps those who watch on only major occasions such as the grand finals.

Similarly, we are able to map the conversations around television shows such as the political talk show *Q&A*, public affairs show *60 Minutes*, and evening news panel *The Project*, drawing on data gathered over several weeks in 2014 for each case (Figure 5.4).

Within a particular broadcast context, this approach also allows a measurement of continued engagement, in the television example, for instance by contrasting the audience for the premiere of a show with that of subsequent episodes. In this way, audience retention can be measured, and those users who have dropped from a conversation can be targeted for further study, for example by identifying whether they constitute a particular segment of the audience. A key tool in such further analysis is the study and mapping of user profiles across the Twittersphere, as we discuss below.

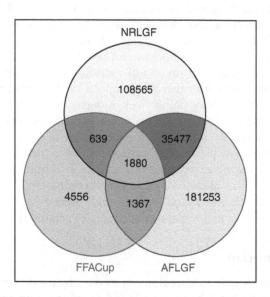

Figure 5.3 Twitter audience overlap between the #NRLGF, #AFLGF, and #FFACup hashtags in 2014.

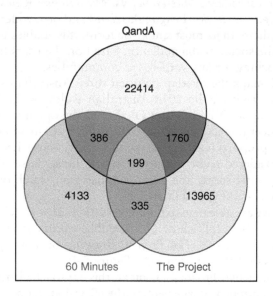

Figure 5.4 Twitter audience overlap between the hashtag use for Q&A (#qanda), 60 Minutes (#60mins, #ExtraMins) and The Project (#theprojecttv) over several weeks in 2014.

Such analyses, then, enable further research into the contextual factors which influence audience activities – from the impact that programming decisions and the broader political economy of the contemporary television industry may have on the formation of interpretive communities around specific TV shows to the strategic and tactical choices made by viewers as they consider which broadcasts to engage with, and how. They place the active audience within the context of the wider mediasphere, including both broadcast and social media and their operators.

Mapping the Twittersphere

What is still missing from the analytical approaches we have outlined so far is any further background information about the users participating in the social media conversations relating to one or more television broadcasts. For example, it would be of considerable value to determine whether users participating around any given topic or event have well-established social media presences with a substantial following in the network, or are relative newcomers with very limited visibility; from a broadcaster's perspective, it is no doubt important to attract at least a sizeable number of well-connected lead users to its shows, as their engagement is likely to attract further participants. Additionally, it would also be desirable to develop a better understanding of the day-to-day interests of participating users in order to determine whether a show managed to attract only the 'usual suspects', or reached a broader audience – a political talkshow addressing a crucial controversial topic would aim to reach a broad audience beyond the 'political junkies',[17] for example, while other programming might be more interested in narrow but deep engagement by its target audience.

Such an assessment of the quality, reach, and depth of a broadcast audience depends crucially on the availability of sufficient background data on the overall make-up and structure of the social media population in the broadcast region, then. The development of such background knowledge is often difficult and time-consuming, but not impossible; as part of our long-term effort of researching the Australian Twittersphere, for example, we have developed a comprehensive database and map of Australian Twitter users, their interests and networks.[18]

We present the outcomes of this work here in the form of an annotated network map of follower/followee relationships in the Australian Twittersphere, which is current to September 2013 (Figure 5.5). The map comprises the 140,000 Australian Twitter accounts which had a total of 1,000 or more follower and/or followee connections by that point, and plots them as a network graph that locates densely connected areas of the network close to each other (as network clusters) while showing less connected areas at greater distance. We further examined the user population in each cluster to infer from the lead users' profile descriptions what the guiding themes of each cluster are. This does not imply that users in each cluster tweet *only* about the cluster's key topics, but that they largely define their Twitter presence by this guiding theme.

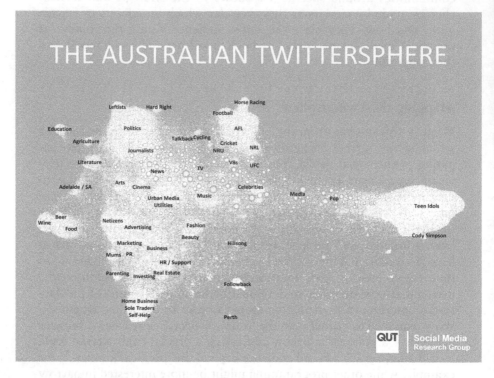

Figure 5.5 Network map of follower/followee relations in the Australian
Twittersphere, as of September 2013. 140,000 accounts with 1,000
or more network connections shown, out of a total of 2.8 million
identified Australian accounts. Cluster topics identified through
manual analysis.

This map is valuable in its own right as it provides detailed information about the structure of the Australian Twittersphere and documents
the key thematic areas and communities of interest represented in or
missing from the overall network. However, it also becomes important
background information to the further analysis of audiencing practices:
given the overall map of follower/followee connections in Figure 5.5,
for example, it now becomes possible to overlay the patterns of actual Twitter activity for any one given broadcast or event, and to compare these patterns across a number of datasets, as the comparison in
Figure 5.6 illustrates. This enables an assessment of the relative breadth
and depth of social media activity around such broadcasts, and an identification of the prominence of specific pre-existing interest clusters in
the follower network as participants in the Twitter conversation.

Figure 5.6, for example, compares the Twitter footprints of the weekly
political talkshow Q&A (#qanda) and the 2014 Australian Football
League Grand Final (#AFLGF). Perhaps unsurprisingly, the core areas in
the overall Twittersphere that engage with these events are, respectively,
the clusters centered around politics and sports, but it is also obvious

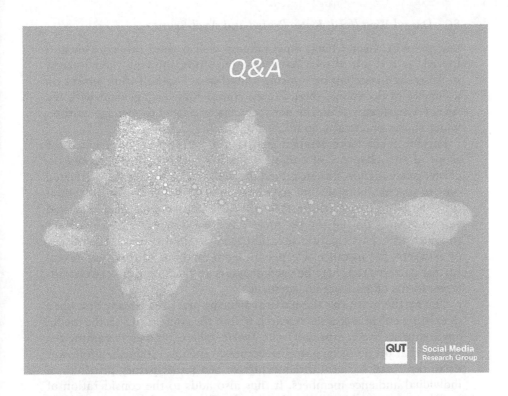

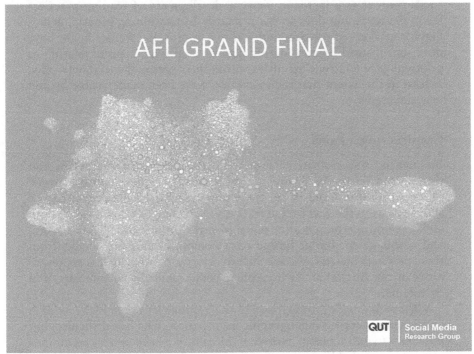

Figure 5.6 a and b Location of #qanda and #AFLGF participants in the overall Australian Twittersphere.

that the AFL Grand Final finds take-up well beyond this core cluster; indeed, as a result of teen band One Direction showing their interest in Australian Football by wearing Hawthorne Football Club jerseys on a number of occasions, there is even considerable engagement with the #AFLGF hashtag within the network cluster related to teenage culture, which shows practically no interest in *Q&A*.

Further, much more detailed analysis is possible here (but beyond the scope of this chapter), of course: we may query whether such out-of-cluster participation was sustained throughout the broadcast, or related only to specific moments; we may examine whether the most influential (*i.e.,* the best-connected) users in the core cluster were also activated as participants during the broadcast; and we may examine the extent to which user participation manifested in original tweets, @mentions, or retweets, for instance. Deeper in-depth analyses of this type reveal further patterns that may be used to assess and distinguish between different forms of audience engagement.

This further positions the active audiencing practices already described in existing cultural studies research within the context of specific media environments (here, especially, the Twittersphere), and can examine the impact that pre-existing social structures – such as established follower networks – can have on the interpretive and participatory practices of individual audience members. It thus also adds to the consideration of social context as a factor in viewers' development of reading practices for media texts, but does so not primarily by examining generic, demographic markers of socioeconomic status as previous studies might have done, but instead by considering post-demographic aspects relating to positioning of audience members within their personal social networks, at least to the extent that such networks have been made visible by and in social media.

Constructing a Panel

Building on the measurement of the overlap between audiences, and their spread across the Twittersphere, is the idea of developing a 'panel' of users that can stand in for the wider user base. This operates on a similar basis to the way that market research companies such as Nielsen seek to build a representative panel of users to measure TV audiences, and is subject to similar limitations. Combining our knowledge from these previous metrics, we are able to select a panel which is representative of the Australian Twittersphere geographically, by interests, and by volume.

What is missing in comparison to the approaches taken by firms such as Nielsen is detailed demographic information, which is difficult – but possible – to extract from Twitter.[19] Already, we have developed an estimate of the probable gender of each account holder, which is calculated using a user's stated real name and also takes into account their likely location (for example, 'Kim' may be predominantly a female name in Australia, but in Scandinavian countries is also used for males). The development and testing of additional methods to estimate the age and socio-economic status of account holders is the next step towards establishing robust demographic estimates for a given user base. Such approaches have clear limitations – not least that users cannot always be relied upon to provide accurate profile details – but are necessary in order to enable further demographically informed social media analytics.

A panel-based approach to social media analytics also addresses and works around important technical limitations for social media research. We have already highlighted the limits of social media APIs; for instance, Twitter limits the tracking of larger groups of users, and a single streaming API connection is able to collect the tweets from a maximum of 5,000 accounts only. For researchers who are unwilling to pay the significant access fees demanded by commercial social media data resellers such as GNIP, and who are therefore limited to Twitter's public, freely available API, tracking 5,000 users at a time is therefore a hard limit. The panel-based approach works well within such limitations, and given that the OzTam service in Australia uses a sample of 3,500 homes to derive its free-to-air national television ratings, for a national population of over 23 million, it is reasonable to suggest that 5,000 accounts out of a total user base of some 2.8 million Australian Twitter accounts would provide a very workable approximation of overall tweeting patterns in the country.

Constructing such a panel allows for the real-time analysis and reporting of Twitter usage patterns by a representative sample of the Australian user base, enabling researchers to identify trends in conversation beyond the hashtag- or keyword-level analyses which have dominated scholarly Twitter research to date. Combining such an approach with methods to dynamically identify conversations and begin tracking new keywords enables the gathering of a much larger percentage of the social media conversation around given topics. The same approach of building panels of users could also be applied to Instagram, where it is possible to gather a limited amount of user-level and relationship data, although ensuring such a panel is representative would be a more significant challenge here. By contrast, comparable user-level information is not readily available through the Facebook API.

Content Analysis

In discussing volume over time, we have already detailed a number of ways in which the time-series data could be processed and analyzed, including sentiment analyses. However, there are other forms of analysis that are possible through natural language processing. Content analysis is possible both on a hashtag- or keyword-based stream, such as the conversations about a television show or around a political debate or crisis, and at the user level, analyzing the archived tweets of a user to determine the subjects that particular users are interested in.

In its simplest form, this may be identifying and counting keywords, bi-grams (combinations of two words) and tri-grams (combinations of three words) within the social media conversation. By doing this, common phrases and keywords can be identified, providing a first indication of the overall shape of a conversation, which can be further filtered to a particular group of users, to a specific period of time, or to a given hashtag or keyword community.

A more advanced extension of this approach is topic modeling, which uses machine learning techniques to automatically categorize segments of text according to a particular theme. This moves current practice beyond the simple word-based analysis to begin to account for the context in which those terms are used, enabling us, for example, to separate conversations around sporting events into sub-communities (*e.g.*, home team, away team, gambling, popular culture, etc.), which can then be further studied using the other techniques discussed in this chapter.

There are also other means of presenting data. One famous example of sentiment is the 'worm', which is often used in televised political debates to assess the immediate response of the audience. We have developed a similar approach using sentiment analysis techniques on popular Australian political hashtags (*e.g.*, #auspol, #qldpol) to measure – in real time – the popularity of Australian politicians, and will use this to track sentiment during the 2015 Queensland and New South Wales election campaigns.

Whether condensed to such simple measures, or forming the basis of a much more detailed study of the key terms, themes, and topics of social media conversation amongst a television audience, such approaches draw on the way that electronic media such as Twitter provide a space for the public expression and exchange of viewers' readings and interpretations of the televisual text. From a textual point of view, the picture of audience practices that emerges from this analysis can be considerably richer and more detailed than that which can be solicited through participant observation during the viewing, or through interviews and surveys with viewers after the fact, as it draws on first-hand evidence of audience responses as contributed by a potentially very large audience itself, without being prompted by a researcher. On the other hand, however, it should also be noted that the actively posting social media community constitutes only a fraction of the total television audience in most cases, and that its observable activities are therefore not simply and directly representative of the full range of interpretive processes taking place amongst the overall audience. A combination of such social media analytics with more conventional research methods in audience studies will be able to generate an even richer and more detailed perspective on audiencing practices.

Follower Accession

Elsewhere, we have detailed a methodology for examining what we describe as 'follower accession': the growth in followers of specific Twitter or Instagram accounts.[20] Importantly, our method enables such an assessment retrospectively, without a need to take regular snapshots of follower numbers; this is facilitated for example by the user-level information provided through the Twitter API, such as the order in which accounts followed a particular user, and the account creation date for the various following accounts. Such an analysis enables both a benchmarking of the popularity of different Twitter accounts, and an identification of specific moments of particularly strong follower growth (which may be traced to particular events surrounding such accounts). Again, beyond the evaluation of audience activities themselves, such analyses may provide useful and important further background data.

Such approaches may also be valuable beyond Twitter, for example to understand which events lead to a growth in Instagram followers. In Figure 5.7, for example, we see a large increase in growth linked to the 'Instameet' event on 4 October 2014,[21] which brought together Instagram users across Queensland to meet up and take photos that were ultimately used by Tourism Queensland for promotional purposes.

As discussed previously, the Instagram API provides more limited user-level data, and most notably for our purposes does not include the date at which a given account was created. However, it is relatively simple to identify the date at which a user first posted an image, which

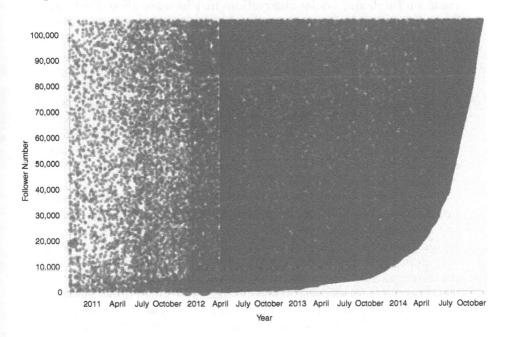

Figure 5.7 Follower accession for the Tourism Queensland account on Instagram.

provides a good proxy for their sign-up date. The precision of this can be further enhanced by collecting the first photo date for a sample of Instagram accounts, and thus building up a pairing of account IDs – which are allocated sequentially – and dates. As discussed in Bruns & Woodford (2014), we are thus able to build a list of dates before which we know the user could not have signed up.

The Instagram API also provides a chronologically ordered list of followers (except for a small number of the account's most recent followers, which are listed alphabetically). As with Twitter, using this ordered list (the accession number) and the first photo date (as a proxy for date on which an account was created), we can generate accession charts for Instagram users. As illustrated by Figure 5.7, such charts provide a useful set of indicators about the growth dynamics of a given account's follower base, and provide a tool to evaluate the success or otherwise of specific promotional campaigns.

Longer-term Engagement with Social Media Content

Beyond the assessment of an audience's immediate activities in relation to broadcast content and live events, it is often also important to examine the longer-term resonance of and engagement with specific topics and issues, potentially on a post-per-post basis. On Twitter, this may manifest for example in the longevity of a specific hashtag, or the period of time over which new retweets of or @replies to relevant posts continue to be made; on Facebook, similar observations may be made about the length of time during which specific posts are liked, shared, or commented on.

Collectively, we define such longitudinal patterns as the lifecycles of posts. By plotting the temporal distribution of activity around a given post we are able to distinguish a range of engagement patterns, ranging from rapid but brief engagement to slower but more sustained responses. Figure 5.8, which shows these temporal data for posts on the Facebook page of the *Captain America* movie, is one example of this. It charts the percentage of comments which have been posted by a specified point in time after the post itself, and shows that approximately 60% of engagement with posts on the *Captain America* page comes within the first 400 minutes (6 hours, 40 minutes) of new content being posted.

Given a sufficient number of observations, these individual patterns may also be compared and benchmarked against an aggregate baseline that describes the 'typical' dynamics of engagement with content on each platform, and can thus highlight especially strongly or poorly performing posts and pages. Further, this approach also enables us to compare typical user engagement patterns across different genres of content. Figure 5.9, for example, compares aggregate longitudinal audience engagement patterns with two movies to engagement with a television show and an online newspaper, and points to notable differences in the dynamics of such audience engagement.

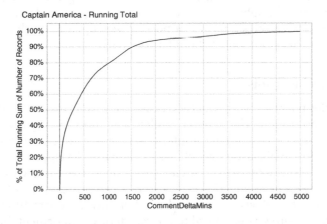

Figure 5.8 Lifecycle of posts on the *Captain America* Facebook page.

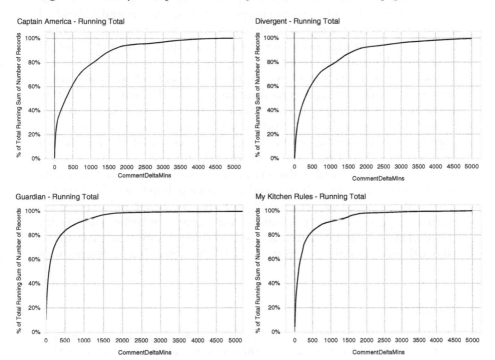

Figure 5.9 Comparison of post lifecycles on the Facebook pages for movies *Captain America* and *Divergent*, for reality TV show *My Kitchen Rules*, and for online newspaper *Guardian Australia*.

As this comparison shows, engagement with *Guardian Australia* content tends to be significantly faster (and shorter-lived) than engagement with movies, for example, reflecting the divergent shelf-life of such content. Such observations also provide valuable information to the content providers and may be used for further developing their social media strategies: most simply, the different speeds of engagement which emerge here suggest that the frequency of posting new updates on these providers' official Facebook pages should also differ.

Public-facing Tools

While the purpose of the methods discussed here may not always be readily apparent to the general public, a number of them can easily be adapted to public-facing applications. One example of this is our 'Hypometer' application, which was originally developed to generate daily indicators showing the social media hype around upcoming television shows. The application now also reports daily and weekly engagement figures for television; this includes both raw numbers and the more complex measures (*e.g.*, Weighted Tweet Index, Excitement Index) we have discussed above. Beyond generic uses related to television, the tool has also been adapted to show engagement with and around individual contestants on reality television shows, sentiment and volume for politicians, and user engagement with global events such as the G20 Summit held in Brisbane in November 2014 (Figure 5.10).

Such applications serve two primary purposes: first, they are a way of communicating engagement metrics to the general public in a meaningful manner; for example, assigning a 'hype' score to television shows immediately makes it clear which shows are receiving significant audience attention beyond the context of their expected performance (based on broadcast network, time of day, day of week, etc.) in a way that neither displaying raw tweet totals, nor the results of the Weighted Tweet Index and Excitement Index would. Second, they could be used as active interventions, for either industry or research purposes. We might examine, for example, whether viewers are more likely to watch a particular show if they know that their social network has been discussing it and is likely to watch and discuss it in real time.

Conclusion

It is possible to ascertain a wide range of post-demographic information through social media. That information can be used to describe, analyze, and target audiences at a range of levels, from the global user base of a platform through geographically bounded audiences, as shown in the case of the Australian Twittersphere, to the audiences of specific TV shows or sporting events. In each case, such information is valuable to researchers, but also to marketers, sales teams, and others who seek more detailed information on the social media users whom they engage with on a day-to-day basis.

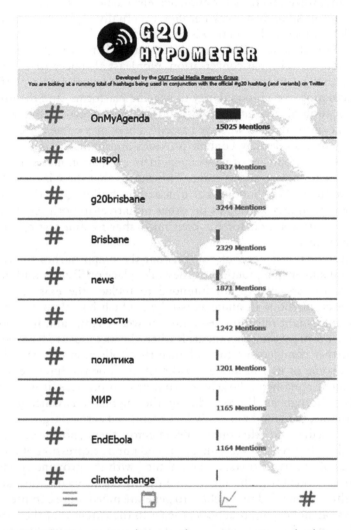

Figure 5.10 G20 Hypometer showing the most prominent hashtags used in association with #G20, 'G20', #g20cultural, #g20brisbane, or colourmebrisbane.

In this chapter we have outlined a collection of interrelated methods and metrics for assessing social media-based audience engagement with broadcast media and live events, focusing for purposes of illustration mainly on Twitter, but also flagging the translatability of such approaches to other key social media platforms, especially including Facebook and Instagram. This is part of an ongoing effort to promote a broader conversation about new approaches to tracking, measuring, and evaluating audience engagement with media texts, and to develop new standardized metrics for audience engagement which may complement (and in some instances perhaps eventually replace) conventional television ratings and similar existing metrics.

The methods and metrics we have presented here are intended to further, not to curtail, that conversation. Not least also because of the continuing changes to the functionality of current social media platforms, the fluctuating overall popularity of specific platforms, and the growing sophistication of content providers in their engagement with social media, some of the metrics we have presented here may come to be obsolete within years, while new content provider and audience practices may enable the development of new engagement evaluation methods that we are unable to foresee at this stage. This means that there is considerable need for further methodological innovation, building on the work we have presented here as well as on other initiatives in both scholarly and industry contexts, and for the continued sharing and testing of these new approaches.

It must be noted here, of course, that these approaches to studying television audiencing practices as they take place on Twitter and in other social media spaces are not intended to replace the existing arsenal of research methods in audience studies, which has already generated significant insight into how television viewers engage and interpret the broadcast content they encounter. Rather, the methods we have outlined here further complement and enhance that collection of methods, and address some of its traditional weaknesses: while the interpretation of TV content remained a largely internal or oral practice, it was best researched through small-group data-gathering methods which generated rich insights, but could not easily be generalized across larger audiences.

Social media (and other online media before them), however, have contributed to the greater externalization and public expression of audience readings of televisual texts, and combined with the growing sophistication in methods for gathering and analyzing social media data at large scale, this has enabled researchers to generate much more comprehensive datasets on audiencing practices at least to the extent that they are taking place in such spaces. Further, data gathering here is unobtrusive and can be done without affecting the contexts in which audience responses are generated; social media analysis is able to observe audiencing *in situ*, rather than in the more artificial setting of an interview or focus group.

But given the comparative ease with which such data may now be gathered from social media, there is also a danger that the most vocal social media users, who will be most visible in the dataset, are going to be seen as representative of all participants in social media environments, or even that social media-supported audiencing practices are going to be regarded as straightforwardly representative of all other, offline as well as online, internal as well as externalized, interpretive practices. Such misrepresentations must be avoided by continuing to employ the entire range of audience studies methods, rather than relying only on now comparatively readily available social media analytics tools, and by comparing the observations made by using these different methods against each other. We also stress, therefore, that our contribution here should not be misread in any way as an argument for an increased emphasis on quantitative over qualitative methods – instead, the analytical approaches we have outlined here will indeed often help to pinpoint the most promising areas for further in-depth qualitative research (for example by highlighting participants to be approached for follow-up interviews, or by identifying a corpus of social media messages that should be studied further through close reading).

What is required next, then, is the rigorous application and evaluation of the methods we have outlined here in production-grade contexts, and the sharing and benchmarking of results in order to develop a more comprehensive picture of, in the first place, social television audiencing practices. We must also pursue the application and extension of these methods to address a broader range of audiencing practices well beyond television, to test whether similar social media user activity patterns exist across areas as diverse as brand communication and political debate. And finally, we must work to more fully integrate these methods with the existing research toolkit employed by audience studies research. It is our hope that the eventual outcome of such research will be not only a range of important domain-specific insights, but also a stable and flexible toolkit of research methods and metrics for the study of social media engagement.

Notes

1 Alice E. Marwick and danah boyd, "I Tweet Honestly, I Tweet Passionately: Twitter Users, Context Collapse, and the Imagined Audience," *New Media & Society* 13, no. 1 (2011): 114–133; Zizi Papacharissi, *A Private Sphere: Democracy in a Digital Age* (Cambridge: Polity, 2010).

2 Amanda L. Hughes and Leysia Palen, "Twitter Adoption and Use in Mass Convergence and Emergency Events," *International Journal of Emergency Management* 6, nos. 3–4 (2009): 248–260; Aleksandra Sarcevic, Leysia Palen, Joanne White, Kate Starbird, Mossaab Bagdouri, and Kenneth Anderson, "'Beacons of Hope' in Decentralized Coordination: Learning from on-the-Ground Medical Twitterers during the 2010 Haiti Earthquake," *Proceedings of the ACM 2012 Conference on Computer Supported Cooperative Work* (New York: ACM, 2012), 47–56; Axel Bruns, Jean Burgess, Kate Crawford, and Frances Shaw, *#qldfloods and @QPSMedia: Crisis Communication on Twitter in the 2011 South East Queensland Floods* (Brisbane: ARC Centre of Excellence for Creative Industries and Innovation, 2012), http://cci.edu.au/floodsreport.pdf.

3 Anders O. Larsson and Hallvard Moe, "Twitter in Politics and Elections: Insights from Scandinavia," in *Twitter and Society*, eds. Katrin Weller, Axel Bruns, Jean Burgess, Cornelius Puschmann, and Merja Mahrt (New York: Peter Lang, 2014), 319–330; Theresa Sauter and Axel Bruns,

"#auspol: The Hashtag as Community, Event, and Material Object for Engaging with Australian Politics," in *Hashtag Publics: The Power and Politics of Discursive Networks*, ed. Nathan Rambukkana (New York: Peter Lang, 2015), 47–60; Axel Bruns and Jean Burgess, "#ausvotes: How Twitter Covered the 2010 Australian Federal Election," *Communication, Politics & Culture* 44, no. 2 (2011): 37–56.

 4 Stephen Harrington, Tim Highfield, and Axel Bruns, "More than a Backchannel: Twitter and Television," in *Audience Interactivity and Participation*, ed. J.M. Noguera (Brussels: COST Action Transforming Audiences, Transforming Societies, 2012), 13–17, http://www.cost-transforming-audiences.eu/system/files/essays-and-interview-essays-18-06-12.pdf; Tim Highfield, Stephen Harrington, and Axel Bruns, "Twitter as a Technology for Audiencing and Fandom: The #Eurovision Phenomenon," *Information, Communication & Society* 16, no. 3 (2013): 315–39, doi: 10.1080/1369118X.2012.756053.

 5 Axel Bruns, Darryl Woodford, Tim Highfield, and Katie Prowd, "Mapping Social TV Audiences: The Footprints of Leading Shows in the Australian Twittersphere," paper presented at the Association of Internet Researchers conference, Daegu, 22–25 Oct. 2014.

 6 John Fiske, "Audiencing: A Cultural Studies Approach to Watching Television," *Poetics* 21, no. 4 (1992): 345–359.

 7 Jan Schmidt, "Twitter and the Rise of Personal Publics," in *Twitter and Society*, eds. Katrin Weller, Axel Bruns, Jean Burgess, Cornelius Puschmann, and Merja Mahrt (New York: Peter Lang, 2014), 3–14.

 8 Benedict Anderson, *Imagined Communities: Reflections on the Origin and Spread of Nationalism* (London: Verso, 1991).

 9 See e.g., Raymond Williams, *Television: Technology and Cultural Form* (London: Fontana, 1974); John Hartley, *Uses of Television* (London: Routledge, 1999); John Hartley, *Television Truths* (Malden, Mass.: Blackwell, 2008).

10 John Hartley, *Television Truths* (Malden, Mass.: Blackwell, 2008): 6.

11 Cf. Stefan Stieglitz, Linh Dang-Xuan, Axel Bruns, and Christoph Neuberger, "Social Media Analytics: An Interdisciplinary Approach and Its Implications for Information Systems," *Business & Information Systems Engineering* 6, no. 2 (2014): 89–96, doi:10.1007/s12599-014-0315-7.

12 Cf. Axel Bruns and Jean Burgess, "Methodological Innovation in Precarious Spaces: The Case of Twitter," *Digital Methods for Social Science: An Interdisciplinary Guide to Research Innovation*, eds. Helene Snee, Christine Hine, Yvette Morey, Steven Roberts, and Hayley Watson (Houndmills: Palgrave Macmillan, 2016), 17–33.

13 Mike Thelwall, "Heart and Soul: Sentiment Strength Detection in the Social Web with Sentistrength," *Proceedings of the Cyberemotions* (2013), 1–14.

14 Stanley Fish, *Is There a Text in This Class? The Authority of Interpretive Communities* (Cambridge: Harvard Unversity Press, 1980).

15 Darryl Woodford, Katie Prowd, Axel Bruns, Ben Goldsmith, Stephen Harrington, and Jean Burgess, "Introducing Telemetrics: The Weighted Tweet Index," Paper presented at the Association of Internet Researchers conference, Daegu, 22–25 Oct. 2014.

16 Brian Burke, "Best Games of The Decade," *Advanced NFL Stats* (22 June 2009), http://www.advancednflstats.com/2009/06/best-games-of-decade.html.

17 Stephen Coleman, "A Tale of Two Houses: The House of Commons, the *Big Brother* House and the People at Home," *Parliamentary Affairs* 56, no. 4 (2003): 733–758.

18 For further details on this process, see: Axel Bruns, Jean Burgess, and Tim Highfield, "A 'Big Data' Approach to Mapping the Australian Twittersphere," in *Advancing the Digital Humanities: Research, Methods, Theories*, eds. Paul Longley Arthur and Katherine Bode (Houndmills: Palgrave Macmillan, 2014), 113–129.

19 Shawndra Hill and Adrian Benton, "Talkographics: Using What Viewers Say Online to Calculate Audience Affinity Networks for Social TV-Based Recommendations," *SSRN* (2012): 2273381, http://papers.ssrn.com/sol3/papers.cfm?abstract_id=2273381; Isaac Hepworth, "Demographic Insights via Nielsen Twitter TV Ratings," *Twitter Blog* (19 May 2014), https://blog.twitter.com/2014/demographic-insights-via-nielsen-twitter-tv-ratings.

20 Cf. Axel Bruns and Darryl Woodford, "Identifying the Events That Connect Social Media Users: Charting Follower Accession on Twitter," *SAGE Research Methods Cases* (London: Sage, 2014), doi: 10.4135/97814462730 5013516710.

21 Cf. Darryl Woodford and Katie Prowd, "Measuring the Success of Tourism and Events Queensland's 'Instameet' Campaign", in *CAUTHE 2015: Rising Tides and Sea Changes: Adaptation and Innovation in Tourism and Hospitality*, eds. Erica Wilson and Mieke Witsel (Gold Coast, Qld.: School of Business and Tourism, Southern Cross University, 2015), 775–780, http://search.informit.com.au/documentSummary;dn=226599693886701;res=IELBUS.

6 The Challenges of Using YouTube as a Data Resource

Craig Hight

The era of Big Data has begun. Computer scientists, physicists, economists, mathematicians, political scientists, bio-informaticists, sociologists, and many others are clamoring for access to the massive quantities of information produced by and about people, things, and their interactions. Diverse groups argue about the potential benefits and costs of analyzing information from Twitter, Google, Verizon, 23andMe, Facebook, Wikipedia, and every space where large groups of people leave digital traces and deposit data. Significant questions emerge. [...] Will it transform how we study human communication and culture, or narrow the palette of research options and alter what 'research' means?[1]

Introduction: Big Data and the Computational Turn

These are challenging and vexing times for audience researchers. The ecosystem of social media platforms, search engines, and other infrastructures still emerging offer demonstrated expertise in Big Data analytics, and form one part of a broader drift toward an acceptance of overwhelmingly quantitative paradigms toward analyzing culture. There are a host of assumptions to this new era, not least that they represent an 'unprecedented opportunity to observe human behavior and social interaction in real time, at a microscopic level yet on a global scale',[2] and in forms that are the 'vernacular datasets of the digital age', helpfully generated by users themselves[3] through practices of self-archivization, self-surveillance and the full spectrum of human performance. Audience researchers need to address this widespread belief in the network and what appear to be networked forms of archive, and more generally the notion that history is being 'archived live'[4] through social media platforms.

And similarly the tools to study such phenomena have proliferated as part of what Berry, in a widely cited essay, refers to as the 'computational turn' in the humanities: 'computational technology has become the very condition of possibility required in order to think about many of the questions raised in the humanities today'.[5] The focus of this chapter is on YouTube as a platform, exploring both the possibilities of the platform as an object of study itself and more particularly the implications of attempting to use

YouTube as a mechanism to explore other areas of social, cultural, and political practice. Among the dilemmas faced by audience researchers engaging with platforms such as these are how to align an expertise in new computational tools with more traditional concerns with complexity, nuance, historical context, analytical subtlety and interpretation.

As Rob Kitchin notes, debates over Big Data have yet to provide a consensus on its definition, although he provides a more than useful summary which includes features such as: huge in volume, high in velocity, diverse in variety, exhaustive in scope, fine-grained in resolution, relational in nature, and flexible.[6] Big Data is offered as a new paradigm in science,[7] one marked by belief in the inherent truth of data free of theory,[8] and an attendant faith in algorithms to uncover patterns through data mining and machine learning, and a preoccupation with fostering an ability to predict rather than explain.[9]

> There is a powerful and attractive set of ideas at work in these arguments that runs counter to the deductive approach that is hegemonic within modern science. First, that big data can capture the whole of a domain and provide full resolution. Second that there is no need for *a priori* theory, models or hypotheses. Third, that through the application of agnostic data analytics the data can speak for themselves free of human bias or framing, and that any patterns and relationships within big data are inherently meaningful and truthful. Fourth, that meaning transcends context or domain-specific knowledge.[10]

Social media offers the promise of an ocean of data, and not just any data. It promises to map onto national size populations, and to collate data intimately related to what people actually do, to how people actually think about things.[11] Critics have provided labels such as 'data fundamentalism',[12] and 'datafication'[13] to term a discursive regime that obscures the monetizing agenda behind social media platforms and promotes quantification as an objective paradigm for humanity. Social data, in this regime, is raw, untainted, waiting to be culled, scraped and made sense of by researchers inside and outside of platforms. In Kitchin's terms this is 'data determinism',[14] where the data simply speak for themselves.

Opposing arguments come from those who represent the beginnings of 'critical data studies',[15] which this chapter falls loosely within. Building from earlier work questioning the nature of Big Data and claims made for its findings,[16] and calls for a critical reflexivity toward Big Data methodologies, critical data studies argues that

> Responsibility for maintaining credibility of the ecosystem as a whole also resides with academics. The unbridled enthusiasm of many researchers for datafication as a neutral paradigm, reflecting a belief in an objective quantified understanding of the social, ought

to be scrutinized more rigorously. Uncritical acceptance of datafication's underpinning ideological and commercial premises may
well undermine the integrity of academic research in the long run.
To keep and maintain trust, Big Data researchers need to identify
the partial perspectives from which data are analyzed; rather than
maintain claims to neutrality, they ought to account for the context
in which data sets are generated and pair off quantitative methodologies with qualitative questions.[17]

As Lisa Gitelman has noted, data is never 'raw'; it is always constructed.[18] As researchers we need to remain suspicious of the variety of
ways in which data is collected, and the tendency to assume that biases
can be avoided through changes in methodology and technique.[19] In this
new terrain, the role of academics should be one of experimentation and
robust forms of reflexivity, particularly toward the forms of construction and interpretation which are central to all social phenomena. Big
Data is embedded within its own agendas, and the favoring of particular
methods which have their own impact on the nature of what is and is
not collected.[20]

These ontological and epistemological issues have been long understood by audience research as we attempt to construct and make sense
of 'audiences'. And these issues are unavoidable in social media research
as there is an 'increasing asymmetry between those who capture, store,
access, and process the tremendous amounts of data produced by the
proliferation of digital, interactive sensors of all kinds'.[21] Lev Manovich
has discussed the notion of data-classes; three categories which people
and organizations fall into within the Big Data era. There are those
who create data (both consciously and leaving digital footprints through
social media and mobile use, for example), those who have the means
to collect it, and those who have the expertise to analyze it.[22] The last
two groups are where audience research aims to position itself, but as
researchers we are in an increasingly tenuous position, with demands
for new kinds of specialized data-gathering and analytical skills, demands that need to be met while audience researchers are on the outside,
looking in.

We are the perpetual third-party to a data-centered ecosystem,[23] in
thrall of its databases and standing in a new set of relationships with
users which consequently moves us into potentially new ethical terrain
(more on this later). Our targets are 'datafied' audiences – collectives of
users which do not exist outside of data, they do not necessarily map
onto a clear population (rather, they are the users who operate most
effectively within the automated environments of social media). In inter-
facing with these datafied users we consequently need skills such as making use of programming interfaces, manipulating unstructured data and
nested data structures, creating web pages and databases to collect and

store surveys or online experiments, manipulating and storing large data sets, machine learning, sentiment analysis, and topic modeling.[24] And more broadly, we need debate over the new agenda for audience research which emerges in the wake of these new possibilities. It is clear that the computational turn 'reconfigures the field itself, enlarging the scope of our potential objects of study' [25] and hence refashions the nature of our inquiries, and not least the relationships which we explicitly and implicitly construct with new forms of audiencing. As much as we need to develop new skills and research techniques, we also urgently need to embed these within ethical debates and a reflexive commentary on the nature of our own research agendas.

This chapter outlines an approach toward the nature of YouTube as a data resource, one informed by the intersection of critical data studies and software studies. While YouTube is somewhat atypical in terms of its ease of use as a data resource for audience research, examining it in this way also provides insight into the broader opportunities and challenges for research practices involving other parts of the digital ecosystem.

A Software Studies Approach to Audience Research

> For us, software needs to be theorized as both a contingent product of the world and a relational producer of the world. Software is written by programmers, individually and in teams, within diverse social, political, and economic contexts. The production of software unfolds – programming is performative and negotiated and code is mutable. Software possesses secondary agency that engenders it with high technicity. As such, software needs to be understood as an actant in the world – it augments, supplements, mediates, and regulates our lives and opens up new possibilities – but not in a deterministic way. Rather, software is afforded power by a network of contingencies that allows it to do work in the world. Software transforms and reconfigures the world in relation to its own systems of thought.[26]

Software Studies is a comparatively new field of enquiry that Manovich and others have championed.[27] Here software is claimed to be, in Manovich's words, 'the [new] engine of contemporary societies'[28] and there is a consequent need for all disciplines to recognize and address the increasing softwarization of contemporary culture, which *'represents a fundamentally new stage in the history of human media, human semiosis and human communication'* (emphasis in original).[29] While this represents a somewhat totalizing statement it nonetheless serves as a useful prompt for reflection on the nature of platforms and infrastructures which offer new hybrids of human-machine assemblages, where human agency itself takes on complicated forms.

Rather than seeing software platforms and applications as neutral tools,[30] software studies insists we need a more critical literacy toward the nature of software as it operates at the level of platforms such as YouTube, in terms of the affordances provided for users, as well as the nature of tools which we use ourselves to conduct data-scraping and data mining (including those fostered by the platforms themselves).

> Significantly, software engenders both forces of empowerment and discipline, opportunities and threats. Software is enabling the realization of many new forms of creative technology and novel kinds of art, play and recreation; it makes social and economic processes more efficient, effective, and productive; it creates new opportunities and markets. At the same time, software has underpinned the development of a broad range of technologies that more efficiently and successfully represent, collate, sort, categorize, match, profile, and regulate people, processes, and places.[31]

These concepts of empowerment and discipline are useful ways of considering the tension in the ways in which software might play out in everyday contexts for users, in combination with a particular notion of performance. All forms of software need to be initiated, to be 'run', in order to function. Programming code only becomes of interest when it is put into action by users (or perhaps by other software which has been initiated by users elsewhere). Drawing in particular from Brenda Laurel's work,[32] Manovich uses the term 'performance' more generally to describe all of the ways in which we interact in professional or more everyday settings with software.[33] In this sense, there is assumed to be a complex interplay between affordance and performance, which plays out in a unique way each and every time a user engages with any application. At a fundamental level, we are *collaborating* with programming code when we engage with, respond to, or create content using an application or platform. But this is also the point where the 'empowering' or disciplining' possibilities of software are actualized. In terms of social media, our performance as users is in response to the affordances of highly sophisticated, automated systems which are drawing upon a range of resources in constructing elements within a frame in real-time.[34]

Users populate platforms with a variety of content, prompted by the platform and the manner in which it presents content from other users. The complex dialectic between human and (software-based) machine defines this new assemblage. Platforms are active mediators, but also shaped by use.[35] User agency is a complex phenomenon within social media; it evolves within the set of affordances, interfaces and algorithms that characterize these as forms of media engagement, experience and interaction. This notion of software performance also applies to some of our own research practices. We also 'perform' the affordances provided by platforms to gather data – either directly through their user interfaces, or attempting to use other software tools such as the Application Programming Interfaces (APIs) provided by platforms (as discussed below).

But as Kitchin argues, 'data do not exist independently of the ideas, instruments, practices, contexts and knowledges used to generate, process and analyze them'.[36] To understand the nature of the data available on YouTube, we need to develop an understanding of the nature of the software as interface, a set of algorithms, and data structures they generate; we need to consider the nature of YouTube as a 'data assemblage',[37] as 'bundles of contingent and relational processes that do work in the world'.[38]

The Nature of YouTube as a Platform

[YouTube] is essentially a hybrid constellation, since users provide semantic input, which the machine then processes algorithmically, producing different clustering with a corresponding organization of video files and metadata. Ultimately, this technological infrastructure can be seen as a specific affordance enabling new forms of media practice. In this way, understanding YouTube means describing it in terms of a 'hybrid' interaction where humans and machines - users and information management systems - are inextricably linked.[39]

YouTube is a core part of the social mediascape, a key platform focused on video distribution, and also an entity deeply embedded within algorithmic culture.[40] Its sheer scale is difficult to appreciate, something which immediately poses problems for anyone considering a comprehensive approach toward its content. From the statistics published by YouTube itself, the platform claims it has over one billion users, a global audience larger than any television network and incorporating multiple languages, and an exponential growth curve increasingly driven by mobile devices.[41] Implicit within these statistics is the sense that this is all 'authentic', 'raw' data, provided on a platform which is itself neutral, simply facilitating and enabling these forms of communication.

As the quote above suggests, YouTube should not be conceptualized nor approached as an 'archive', or at least this term needs to be redefined in order to include this kind of entity. Rather than offering a space for permanent storage, YouTube is an infrastructure for the distribution of video content for end user viewing,[42] 'an infrastructure and a cultural resource [which] constitutes the raw material for a new media practice of perpetual uploading, viewing and deleting of material, as well as streaming it to a variety of other Web services and sites'.[43]

And crucially, this is an *infrastructure which is co-created with its users* through a dynamic and evolving relationship between software-based architecture and huge numbers of individual users. YouTube provides affordances which may be performed by users, although only a small number of these affordances are utilized by most YouTubers. A basic YouTube account allows a user to upload, comment, rate videos, designate favorites, create a personal channel, subscribe, and share links to content. Other accounts are provided for different purposes; comedian, musician, guru, non-profit, and partners (allowing revenue sharing through advertising). The dominant acts on the platform are searching and viewing video content, while commenting on content, favoriting, and generating playlists are comparatively minor activities.[44] Only a small percentage of users engage in uploading video content, and an even smaller proportion of these users provide an accurate and complete user profile, or contribute detailed metadata to their uploads (including title, description and tags). Users, then, generate useful data both directly, through metadata, and indirectly through the 'exhaust' generated by their other actions. These all contribute somewhat unevenly to the operation of the YouTube infrastructure, as they provide data to feed a host of machine-learning algorithms which perform much of the invisible but necessary work of structuring a working hierarchy of data which characterize this 'archive'.

The description above highlights the basic 'weaknesses' of the data available for the infrastructure to work with. It is important to recognize that most user activity is not tracked, or at least is measured only indirectly. Crucially, most YouTubers are anonymous, and their primary activity is 'lurking', in the sense that they are just watching or browsing. Much of user-provided data is incomplete, including user profiles (which are not verifiable even if completed), poorly completed metadata including misspelling of titles, tags, descriptions, and the prominence of folksonomies (user-generated taxonomies) which make comparisons across material difficult. Many users create fake or multiple identities in order to post comments. There is also a wide variety of applications of privacy settings; users apparently have different degrees of understanding of default settings and how to adjust these for content they would like to remain private or for just their personal networks.

There are ironies here of course, in terms of the ethical dimensions of these kinds of data. Scott Golder and Michael Macy refer to a 'privacy paradox', where data begins to become too revealing in terms of privacy protection, yet also not revealing enough in terms of providing the demographic background information needed by social scientists.[45] In a broader context, this also raises the ethical dilemma of whether, as audience researchers, we are implicitly aligning ourselves with dataveillance procedures which are fundamental to the digital economy. Dataveillance procedures, or the automated tracking of traces of user activity, have been integral to the monetizing of data streams operating through social media platforms,[46] and are the increasing focus of privacy debates in a post-Edward Snowden era.[47] The dilemma of aligning to such procedures is generated by a set of competing assumptions about the degree of agency and literacy which users themselves have, in engaging with globalized services such as these which are engineered toward monetizing their online activities. To cull data from social media platforms means assuming that users have implicitly given informed consent by accepting a platform's terms and conditions,[48] even if it is not clear whether all users understand the implications of participating online.[49] There is the possibility, for example, that much audience research in this field is exploiting less savvy online users, and constructing 'audiences' from the datafied performances of a skewed population.[50] In other words, a crucial (but to a large extent unanswerable) question is: What kinds of software literacies[51] do users themselves have in engaging with the platform?

As noted above, the nature of commentary, community, or network which develops within YouTube is quite distinct from other social media platforms.[52] Most users do not provide a detailed account of how they may be interpreting video content, or if they do post a response it is couched within the particular forms of public posturing fostered by YouTube. There is a different quality to the discourses on offer here, certainly in comparison to a platform such as Facebook, for example, where users' primary activities might involve engagement with others' content, commenting, uploading their own material, and particularly operating within an assumed network of 'friends'.

Video content itself does not remain indefinitely on the platform. It has a life span, it erodes; if this is an archive it is 'is simultaneously stable and unstable'.[53] Many videos are taken down by users, either voluntarily or as a result of YouTube being notified of copyright infringements.[54] By the same token content might appear or reappear through different users, or on different platforms, or might proliferate in multiple versions (let alone those which incorporate layers of extra material intended to serve as commentary, or be bookended by user commentary). Video content, then, is flickering, difficult to pin down in its origins, appearing in multiple guises and subject to erasure at any time. When you conduct research on YouTube, therefore, you are seeking a snapshot rather than an infinitely detailed historical record of video distribution and reception.

And most importantly of all, video content is effectively invisible to the infrastructure itself. YouTube's algorithms are currently not indexing video content based on what happens within the frame; its algorithms do not see what we see as users. Relying on folksonomies and the volunteered or generated data of users, YouTube offers us content which it can not categorize outside of the descriptors and responses of users themselves. YouTube's interface provides a number of video discovery mechanisms, such as keyword-based search engine, related video recommendations, and video highlight on the YouTube homepage.[55] These mechanisms feed off the volunteered and inadvertent data of users, and attempt to mitigate for the weaknesses of these data streams. Again, there is a fundamental tension at the heart of this infrastructure which reflects broader dynamics at play within the 'algorithmization' of the social web.

> YouTube's interface design and its underlying algorithms select and filter content, guiding users in finding and watching certain videos out of the millions of uploads, for instance through buttons for 'most popular' videos. The site controls video traffic not by means of programming schedules but by means of an information management system that steers users' navigation and selects content to promote. Even though users feel they have control over which content to watch, their choices are heavily directed by referral systems, search functions, and ranking mechanisms (*e.g.*, PageRank). In other words, ranking and popularity principles rule YouTube's platform architecture.[56]

This is the cutting edge of algorithmic culture, but they are also forms of automation which effectively serve as black boxes for third-party researchers. They are machine-learning operations designed to function at scales and forms of complexity that are impossible to examine directly, and to some extent operate in concert in ways that may not be fully understood even by the engineers who helped to design them.[57] For researchers external to YouTube / Google, their operations and effects can only be examined indirectly. Both 'search' and 'highlight' functions appear to create a rich-get-richer effect, while 'related videos' recommendations equalizes the overall video distribution and helps users find niche videos.[58] So different mechanisms work against each other, in complementary and recursive ways, feeding off different combinations of data values. Some of their essential metrics are necessarily incomplete or misleading or skewed toward some kinds of interaction over others.[59] The YouTube recommendation engine is weighted toward recommending videos with similar titles and descriptions, so popular videos drag other similar videos with them,[60] but there are also other factors such as audience retention (the extent to which users watch an entire video). In comparison, the YouTube search engine's ranking algorithm appears to draw upon factors such as ratings, playlist additions, flagging, embeds, shares, comments, age of video, channel views, subscribers, and inbound links (from external domains).[61]

To look at these patterns in another way, it is important not to confuse activity on YouTube with spontaneous, or 'raw' evidence of audience activity. Instead of every social media platform having a naturally occurring distribution pattern which looks like Anderson's 'long tail',[62] the nature of 'popularity' here needs to be recognized as something which emerges through the interaction between a collection of machine-learning algorithms working together and the selective, partial forms of (software) performances by users. Datafied 'audiences' are not an accurate reflection of publics 'out there' but are constructed in particular and partial ways.[63] Given the instability of some of this (video and metadata) material, as discussed above, researchers are inevitably constructing snapshots of particular kinds of data structures, which are evolving as algorithms and users' performances change over time.

APIs and Automated Research Workflows

Another means of gathering material from YouTube is to use APIs provided by the platform (a research option outlined particularly in Chapter 5 of this book). Most social media platforms now make data publicly available on their platform through APIs, which operate as an extension of the management style of social media platforms, and are an increasingly core part of the digital ecosystem. They are at the center of efforts by internet giants like Amazon and Google to foster third party applications which build upon and add value to their own infrastructures.

> Open APIs enable interfaces, services, and applications to connect seamlessly with one another, making digital content accessible within and outside of existing websites via: social games, mashups, widgets, social plugins, share buttons, and data syndication (*e.g.,* Real Simple Syndication). A wide range of social applications enable users to talk back, play, comment, recommend, and share in an increasing number of ways and spaces within social media sites and outside them. These applications add value to social networks and make them central to a users' online experience, even when they have left the SNS.[64]

These parts of algorithmic culture are designed to foster programming applications for creating, consuming, interacting with and sharing multiple types of content. Allowing networked software components to communicate with each other using standards based technologies, APIs represent the next generation of the internet. They are helping to generate software development which builds upon the dominance of existing platforms, and allows the internet to be extended seamlessly with mobile devices and beyond. Google Maps is a good example of the possibilities of using a platform as a base to foster extensions to its functionality, building layers of extra content and allowing a cottage industry of mashups to emerge which helps to transform the capacities of the platform itself without interrupting revenue streams. YouTube's APIs, available from 2006, allowed for the embedding of the platform's video content across the internet. They helped to transform YouTube from a website which you visit to an infrastructure with content which could be surfaced anywhere online.

The growth of APIs dates from the early 2000s, when companies such as eBay (2000), Amazon (2002) and Google (2002) first began to respond to aggressive raiders of their databases by establishing rules of engagement, formalizing and controlling access. The growth and success of third-party developers in scraping and financially exploiting the material available on the databases of platforms and Flickr and Facebook prompted these platforms, particularly during 2003–2006, to increasingly consider the design of APIs as part of their core business model. In the case of Amazon S3, APIs have helped to foster the emergence of cloud computing, allowing the company to serve as an infrastructure offering fast, reliable, inexpensive computational and storage capacities that allow other companies to rapidly scale up their operations.

It is tempting to consider APIs, a less visible part of the automated work of online infrastructures, as simply tools available for automating research workflows. In contrast to trying to web crawl material through a platform's interface, APIs allow researchers to engage with the platform's databases and nonintrusively harvest large amounts of metadata, offering the possibility to scale up data-gathering depending on the nature of the tools used, or endlessly repeat data-scraping exercises as part of longitudinal research designs.[65]

However as Taina Bucher notes, APIs are far from neutral.[66] They are an essential means through which social media platforms seek to govern their environment. The design of APIs are a key part of competition between social media platforms and competing services. In Robert Bodle's words, 'we see how interoperability is used strategically to align with allies and discriminate against rivals in order to establish market dominance'.[67] For example;

> Facebook's development and integration of Open APIs demonstrate a strategy of controlled openness, innovation, and dominance. Facebook utilizes Open APIs to provide valuable user data to developers and online partners in order to encourage the proliferation of social applications that ultimately harness inbound links from external sites and devices by redirecting traffic to Facebook's servers. By colonizing online spaces of the Web with 'Like' buttons, Facebook successfully solicits user participation making it a conduit for online interaction and a center of gravity for the social space of flows.[68]

To engage with and make meaningful use of APIs, audience researchers must either have either computational skills or collaborate with programmers, and perhaps more crucially, acquire a basic knowledge of software and its advantages and disadvantages.[69] Researchers are here co-creating knowledge in collaboration with automated software tools, and it is important to recognize that the nature of the software fundamentally shapes the types of questions which can be asked.[70]

APIs are themselves evolving black boxes – so we are still dependent upon the actions of the platform itself. To some extent APIs *compound* the limitations of data assemblages such as YouTube; you get a tightly prescribed set of data values to choose from and can access only a thin slice of predigested data (and, again, there is no escaping the weaknesses of the data itself).[71] There are obviously different kinds of limitations within the API regimes. For YouTube, some limitations are set by users themselves (through privacy controls) but most are prescribed through API code. Overall, however, there is a lack of transparency on the supply side – we have little to no insight into the possible sampling and selection mechanisms of the data which are made available through the API.[72]

A brief overview of a case study is useful to this discussion to illustrate some of the limitations and constraints of engaging with YouTube as a data resource. As part of a broader study investigating online documentary culture within New Zealand, a small nation where YouTube is a dominant video distribution platform, this case study looked to explore the role of the platform in lowering the threshold for new kinds of practitioners in fostering user-generated documentary practices (and where 'documentary' might be defined quite broadly). Key goals were to attempt to map the nature and scale of 'documentary' related video content distributed through YouTube by New Zealand-based users, in the process identifying content generated by users themselves, and ultimately use this information to identify users who might be approached for more qualitative research encounters. The types of data this case study sought, then, were geographically bound, and associated with content that was not necessarily easily definable prior to data-gathering but needed to be discovered through an iterative process.

There were a number of technical constraints which hampered this research, such as the YouTube API's limit on 500 results per search, daily limits on data access, and tools which were faster than available bandwidth connections with YouTube's databases. Changes to both the YouTube interface and the YouTube APIs over the course of the project were other, more frustrating factors, undermining efforts to have research design emerge through experimentation with automated workflows, and to develop a longitudinal research approach. The instability of YouTube's material was another complication, with generated data sets needing to be cleared of 'ghost' links to content already taken down (and in some cases, with some content disappearing even between the short period when it was identified by videoID and the video itself was downloaded using another mechanism). Another, more theoretically driven, complication was the effort to keep the search for types of content relatively broad, as 'documentary' tends to be both an elastic category and something understood and applied rather loosely by users.

This lack of a clearly defined set of content characteristics necessitated first developing a flexible, iterative workflow designed to identify and map out a folksonomy which could then be used as parameters to feed into other automated data scraping techniques. These are all issues known before initiating this case study, and inherent to the 'fuzziness' and 'noise' endemic to user generated content and metadata on social media platforms – to be useful in a research sense, such data needs to be 'cleaned', in the process becoming one step further removed from an accurate mapping of actual audiences.

A more fundamental obstacle for this case study, and ultimately one which was not resolvable with the then current API, was the difficulty of identifying content uploaded specifically by New Zealand-based users (a key imperative for approaching YouTube as a resource in the first place). Outside of that content uploaded by users explicitly (and hopefully accurately) labeling themselves as based in the country, the API would not provide material based on geographic location. This was a limitation presumably designed to satisfy privacy concerns, but there were no satisfactory workarounds which might, for example, generate an aggregated listing of material through triangulating different data sets. In effect, then, New Zealand as a locality was invisible within the global content streams on YouTube (outside of those explicitly identified in some way by users themselves). Collectively, such constraints meant that the case study's original objectives and aims had to be refined and adapted to suit the types of data which were available. This is an outcome which, scaled up to apply to the wider body of research on and through YouTube, has profound implications for the nature and scope of research in the field.

Some of the concerns outlined above are not limited to the study of YouTube. Jean Burgess and Axel Bruns have outlined a useful genealogy of the Twitter API, drawing upon their own considerable experience in using the APIs over number of years, engaging with a platform which is more amenable to automated data generation.[73] Twitter has occupied a special place in Big Data audience research for both audience and industry-based researchers as it provides arguably the most open access to its data.[74] Burgess and Bruns, however, note a variety of frustrations with using Twitter APIs, derived from the fact that they are not under their control, not primarily designed for use by audience researchers, and continually updated for commercial reasons. They note one implication is the resulting abundance of 'hashtag studies', fostered by the relatively easier access to these kinds of metadata through the Twitter APIs. They essentially outline a cycle of dependency centered on the APIs; changes to these APIs can undermine established workflows, requiring programming expertise to maintain the usefulness of software-based research tools, and preventing the kinds of replication of research techniques which can foster longitudinal research. The more technically difficult to reach forms of data (which they term 'hard data', compared to easier to cull 'soft data'), and the cost of generating larger data sets (those which more properly could be defined as Big Data) mean that these types of analysis remain out of reach of most academic researchers. More fundamentally, these constraints inevitably shape and constrain the overall nature of possible research into and through Twitter as a platform.

> If very little intellectually hard research on Twitter is able to draw on large data sets, and most of the technically hard, 'big data' Twitter research is conducted by commercial and market researchers, our understanding of Twitter as a media platform and of Twitter-based communication as a sociocultural phenomenon must necessarily suffer.[75]

If we translate these concerns onto research practices related to YouTube, this tends to mean that there is something of a divide between research which simply considers YouTube as *an object of study*, and that research which aims to use YouTube *as a mechanism* for approaching broader social, political, economic and cultural questions. The 'easy data' of YouTube research involves studying the nature of popularity on the platform, accepting the data associated with rankings generated by its machine learning algorithms and the (limited) access to these provided by the platform's APIs. In contrast, 'hard data' approaches might include those looking to custom design API-centered workflows, be driven by more theoretical concerns, or necessitate triangulating metadata from a number of different locations (spatial, temporal, categorical or otherwise) into more meaningful collectives. The latter set of approaches obviously requires more patience, persistence, resources and, not least, critical literacy toward the nature of software tools that are involved and the consequent nature of data which are generated through such research designs.

In an era of Big Data, then, audience research needs to be recognized as a new set of research practices fundamentally shaped by rapidly evolving aspects of software culture. As researchers, we need to remain cautious of the broader paradigms underlying Big Data itself, and the manner in which the discursive regimes they foster tend to obscure the full complexity of data assemblages that characterize entities such as social media platforms. Platforms such as YouTube are fundamentally shaped by the nature of programming code which operates at a variety of levels in new hybrid infrastructures of human and machine. Everything from the affordances designed for users, the hierarchy of affordances embodied through interface design, the scale and complexity of algorithmic processes controlling recursive loops of data to and from users, to data management tools such as APIs, become factors to be negotiated in designing research instruments which can generate substantial, meaningful and ultimately useful audience data. Audience research in this context remains a third-party enterprise, operating outside of social media infrastructures and encompassing forms of inquiry and analysis requiring not only a critical understanding of the forces shaping data assemblages more generally, but a set of literacies associated with software operating simultaneously as phenomena to be studied, the context in which data is generated, and tools integral to our methodologies. These are epistemological and ontological implications which need to be acknowledged, understood and debated by researchers operating in this field.

Acknowledgments

The author wishes to acknowledge Marsden funding administered by the Royal Society of New Zealand (project UOW1008 'Playing with reality? Online documentary culture and its users').

Notes

1 danah boyd and Kate Crawford, "Six provocations for big data", paper presented at *A Decade in Internet Time: Symposium on the Dynamics of the Internet and Society,* Oxford Internet Institute (21 September, 2011), available at http://papers.ssrn.com/sol3/papers.cfm?abstract_id=1926431, 1.
2 Scott A. Golder and William W. Macy, "Digital footprints: opportunities and challenges for online social research", *Sociology*, 40, no. 1 (2014), 146.
3 Tara McPherson, "Some theses on the future of humanities publishing", in *Future Publishing: Visual Culture in the Age of Possibility* (with K Behar et al.). London: International Association for Visual Culture, March, (2013), 7. Available at: http://iavc.org.uk/2013/future-publishing-visual-culture-in-the- age-of-possibility.
4 Marquard Smith, "Theses on the Philosophy of History: The Work of Research in the Age of Digital Searchability and Distributability", *Journal of Visual Culture*, 12, no. 3 (2013), 381.
5 David M. Berry, "The computational turn: Thinking about the digital humanities." *Culture Machine* 12.0 (2011), 2.
6 Rob Kitchin, *The data revolution: Big data, open data, data infrastructures and their consequences.* (Sage, 2014), 68.
7 Kitchin, *The data revolution*, 129.
8 Chris Anderson, "The end of theory: The data deluge makes the scientific method obsolete," *Wired Magazine*, 16–07. (2008).
9 Kitchin, *The data revolution*, 132.
10 Kitchin, *The data revolution*, 132.
11 Kari Steen-Johnsen and Bernard Enjolras, "Social research and Big Data - The tension between opportunities and realities", in Hallvard Fossheim and Helene Ingierd (eds.) *Internet research ethics*, Institute for Social Research (2015), 125.
12 Kate Crawford, "The hidden biases in big data." *HBR Blog Network* 1 (2013).
13 José Van Dijck, "Datafication, dataism and dataveillance: Big Data between scientific paradigm and ideology." *Surveillance & Society* 12.2 (2014): 197–208.

14 Kitchin, *The data revolution*, 135.
15 Craig Dalton and Jim Thatcher. "What does a critical data studies look like, and why do we care? Seven points for a critical approach to 'big data'." *Society and Space open site* (2014), and Rob Kitchin and Tracey P. Lauriault. "Towards critical data studies: Charting and unpacking data assemblages and their work." (2014).
16 boyd and Crawford, "Six provocations for big data", 12.
17 Van Dijck, "Datafication, dataism and dataveillance", 206.
18 Lisa Gitelman, *Raw data is an oxymoron*, (MIT Press, 2013).
19 Nate Silver, *The signal and the noise: the art and science of prediction*. Penguin UK, 2012.
20 Kitchin, *The data revolution*, 136.
21 Mark Andrejevic, *Infoglut: How too much information is changing the way we think and know.* (Routledge, 2013), 17.
22 Lev Manovich, "Trending: The promises and the challenges of big social data," in M. K. Gold (ed.) *Debates in the Digital Humanities*, (The University of Minnesota Press, Minneapolis, 2011), 460–475.
23 See boyd and Kate Crawford, "Six provocations for big data", and Steen-Johnsen and Enjolras, "Social research and Big Data", 131–2.
24 Scott A. Golder and Michael W. Macy, "Digital footprints: Opportunities and challenges for online social research." *Sociology* 40.1 (2014), 145–6.
25 Jean Burgess and Axel Bruns, "Easy data, hard data: The politics and pragmatics of Twitter research after the computational turn," *Compromised data: From social media to big data* (2015), 95.
26 Rob Kitchin and Martin Dodge. *Code/space: Software and everyday life* (MIT Press, 2011), 43–44.
27 See Steven Johnson, *Interface culture: How new technology transforms the way we create and communicate* (New York: Basic Books, 1997), Matthew Fuller, *Behind the blip: Essays on the culture of software*, (New York: Autonomedia, 2003), Matthew Fuller, *Software studies: A lexicon*, (MIT Press, 2008), Byron Hawk, David M. Rieder, and Ollie O. Oviedo, eds. *Small tech: The culture of digital tools.* Vol. 22. (University of Minnesota Press, 2008), Kitchin and Dodge, *Code/space*, and Lev Manovich, *Software takes command.* Vol. 5. (A&C Black, 2013).
28 Manovich, *Software takes command.*
29 Manovich, *Software takes command*, 46–7.
30 Fuller, *Behind the blip*, 16.
31 Kitchin and Dodge, *Code/space*, 10–11.
32 Brenda Laurel, *Computers as theatre.* Addison-Wesley, 2013.
33 Manovich, *Software takes command*, 17.
34 Manovich, *Software takes command*, 17.
35 Burgess and Bruns, "Easy data, hard data", 96.
36 Kitchin, *The data revolution*, 2.
37 Kitchin and Lauriault, "Towards critical data studies".
38 Kitchin, *The data revolution*, 21.
39 Frank Kessler and Mirko Tobias Schäfer. "Navigating YouTube: Constituting a hybrid information management system." *The YouTube Reader* (2009), 279.
40 Ted Striphas. "Algorithmic culture." *European Journal of Cultural Studies* 18.4-5 (2015): 395–412.
41 YouTube Statistics: http://www.youtube.com/yt/press/statistics.html, accessed May 17 2015.
42 Kessler and Schäfer, "Navigating YouTube", 276.

43 Kessler and Schäfer, "Navigating YouTube", 287.
44 Meeyoung Cha, et al. "I tube, you tube, everybody tubes: analyzing the world's largest user generated content video system." *Proceedings of the 7th ACM SIGCOMM conference on Internet measurement*, ACM, 2007.
45 Golder and Macy, "Digital footprints", 141.
46 José Van Dijck, *The culture of connectivity: A critical history of social media*, (Oxford University Press, 2013).
47 See Van Dijck, "Datafication, dataism and dataveillance", David Lyon "Surveillance, Snowden, and big data: Capacities, consequences, critique." *Big Data & Society* 1.2 (2014): 2053951714541861, Sylvia E. Peacock"How web tracking changes user agency in the age of Big Data: The used user." *Big Data & Society* 1.2 (2014): 2053951714564228, 1–11, Sara Degli Esposti, "When big data meets dataveillance: the hidden side of analytics." *Surveillance & Society* 12.2 (2014): 209–225, and Helen Kennedy and Giles Moss, "Known or knowing publics? Social media data mining and the question of public agency," *Big Data & Society* 2.2 (2015): 2053951715611145, 1–11.
48 Stine Lomborg and Anja Bechmann, "Using APIs for data collection on social media." *The Information Society* 30.4 (2014), 262.
49 Merja Mahrt and Michael Scharkow, "The value of big data in digital media research." *Journal of Broadcasting & Electronic Media* 57.1 (2013), 26.
50 Cédric Courtois and Peter Mechant, "An evaluation of the potential of Web 2.0 API's for social research," *COST Action ISO906: New challenges and methodological innovations in European Media Audience Research*, 2011, 222.
51 Craig Hight, "Software Studies and the New Audiencehood of the Digital Ecology." *Revitalising Audience Research: Innovations in European Audience Research* 5 (2014), 62–79.
52 Fabio Giglietto, Luca Rossi, and Davide Bennato. "The open laboratory: Limits and possibilities of using Facebook, Twitter, and YouTube as a research data source." *Journal of Technology in Human Services* 30.3-4 (2012), 148.
53 Kessler and Schäfer, "Navigating YouTube", 286.
54 See https://www.youtube.com/yt/copyright/.
55 Renjie Zhou, et al. "How YouTube videos are discovered and its impact on video views," *Multimedia Tools and Applications* (2016), 2.
56 Van Dijck, *The culture of connectivity*, 113.
57 Burgess and Bruns, "Easy data, hard data", 98.
58 Zhou et al., "How YouTube videos are discovered and its impact on video views.".
59 Giglietto et al., "The open laboratory", 148.
60 Renjie Zhou, et al. "Boosting video popularity through recommendation systems." *Databases and Social Networks*. ACM, 2011, 18.
61 Gloria Chatzopoulou, Cheng Sheng, and Michalis Faloutsos. "A first step towards understanding popularity in youtube." *INFOCOM IEEE Conference on Computer Communications Workshops, 2010*. IEEE, 2010, 4.
62 See Chris Anderson, *The long tail: how endless choice is creating unlimited demand*, (Random House, 2007). Anderson argues that all forms of online distribution, if optimised with effective recommendation engines, takes on a distinctive pattern of a large 'head' of popular content, and a 'long tail' of products which appeal to niche consumers.
63 Kennedy and Moss, "Known or knowing publics? Social media data mining and the question of public agency," 4.
64 Robert Bodle, "Regimes of sharing: Open APIs, interoperability, and Facebook." *Information, Communication & Society* 14.3 (2011), 325–6.

65 Courtois and Merchant, "An evaluation of the potential of Web 2.0 API's for social research," 215.
66 Taina Bucher, "Objects of intense feeling: The case of the Twitter APIs." *Computational Culture* 3 (2013).
67 Bodle, "Regimes of sharing", 328.
68 Bodle, "Regimes of sharing", 333.
69 Lomberg and Bechmann, "Using APIs for data collection on social media," 258.
70 Lomberg and Bechmann, "Using APIs for data collection on social media," 258–9.
71 See Lomberg and Bechmann, "Using APIs for data collection on social media," 259, and Courtois and Merchant, "An evaluation of the potential of Web 2.0 API's for social research," 216.
72 Courtois and Merchant, "An evaluation of the potential of Web 2.0 API's for social research," 221.
73 Burgess and Bruns, "Easy data, hard data", 103.
74 Robert N. Procter, Alex Voss, and Ilia Lvov, "Audience research and social media data: Opportunities and challenges." *Participations: journal of audience and reception studies* 12.1 (2015), 478.
75 Burgess and Bruns, "Easy data, hard data", 106.

7 U Tried!

Failure in a University Social Network Site

Erika Pearson and Adon C. M. Moskal

Online Social Networks and 'Failure'

The success or failure of social networks is complex, with both offline and online factors to be accounted for. These include pre-existing network structures, the needs and expectations of actors on the network, time constraints, and both existing and potential social tie structures. This chapter examines the complex interplay between actors, ties, networks, and need, and explores how these factors can influence the potentiality of an online social network to *fail*. This chapter draws on a case study of a non-successful social networking initiative set within an existing Higher Education staff network to discuss how failure, and indeed success, is not the linear outcome of a specific initiative—such as the introduction of a social networking tool—but rather the product of various shifting and often hidden interacting factors.

Social network sites, or SNS, are heavily-studied phenomena, with the high profile, open, international sites dominating the discussion. We use the nomenclature first put forth by danah boyd and Nicole Ellison who describe SNS as 'web-based services that allow individuals to (1) construct a public or semi-public profile within a bounded system, (2) articulate a list of other users with whom they share a connection, and (3) view and traverse their list of connections and those made by others within the system'.[1] SNS are a fascinating form of media in that the user is the product; to remain viable the site is dependent on users to visit, use, and interact.

Successful social network sites have been subject to everything from metric-based studies[2] to more qualitative evaluations of trust, ties, or other functions of virtual networks.[3] Even though 'success' is subjective and contextual, we feel we 'know' what a successful network looks like—large, active, and typically high profile. They exhibit shared markers that are taken to proclaim their success, such as total number of users on the site, rate of user joins, or total number and frequency of message postings. Failure in social networks, when studied at all, is typically understood in terms of once-successful networks that have fallen from grace. The cause of failure in these cases can mostly be inferred as the introduction of technical restrictions that disenchant users, or the emergence of a competitor that better meets a need and thus incites a mass migration of the social network to the new platform (both factors influenced the decline of SNS Friendster, as discussed by boyd[4]).

However, such studies are limited in two key ways. First, they isolate failure as a singular, terminal state, rather than considering the entirety of the SNS lifecycle. Online social networks are dynamic and evolving as users join and depart, and wider social and technological contexts shift and change. Thus, 'snapshot' measures (such as total users signed up at any given moment) can only ever provide one piece of an inherently elaborate puzzle. Second, often the identified 'causes' are, in themselves, merely symptoms of deeper issues arising from the complexity of the social processes at work. As such, failure evaluation should go beyond the most obvious failing factors and examine the underlying constraints on user activity.[5] Deeper interrogation is necessary when, as in the case study presented in this chapter, no causes for site failure are immediately discernible. It is important to see failure as more than just a decline.

The case study presented here is of a university social network that was defined by its own users as not only having failed, but also as never having succeeded. We use this case study as a starting point to discuss the question of failure more deeply, drawing attention to some of the dynamic factors that can shape success and failure on online social networks. Social networks are highly dependent on the context in which they are used; as such, case studies are useful for exposing context-specific use practices.[6] Though we cannot account for every variable here, it is still worth exploring some in detail to emphasize the complexity of factors that influence network development.

Our inquiry was informed by a mixed-methods approach, designed to interrogate the concept of 'failure' more deeply than a metrics-based network analysis on its own (*e.g.,* measuring rates of new user joins, frequency of posts, or connectedness of nodes in the network). An overview of this process is outlined below, with each step detailed later in the chapter.

As a starting point, we analyzed network metrics and graphed the network structure to give insight into the current 'state' of the campus SNS, and suggest how the network had evolved since its genesis. We conducted a genre analysis of communicative events on the platform (messages sent by users) to identify common behaviors and perceived motivations of network participants. From this we formed initial hypotheses around the (non)use of the network. We then tested these hypotheses in interviews with key users who had relatively frequent posting behavior, or proportionally large follower/following stats. Users discussed their perceptions of the network status and activity, their motivations for participating, and how the campus network compared with other social networks they belonged to.

The platform that forms the basis of this evaluation is Yammer, a free-to-use, closed-access enterprise social network tool. Organizations create a private site for their employees, and users access the site by logging in with their corporate email address. Yammer[7] defines itself as being able to facilitate better communication and collaboration, and has been shown to be a useful networking tool in some corporate settings.[8]

The Case Study: Yammer on Campus

Yammer arrived at the studied university campus in 2008, though its exact origins and who introduced the site to the campus are unclear. Word of mouth was generally how new users in the early phase of uptake heard of the site, and most signed up to explore. As an experimental and external service, no restrictions from the institution were explicitly placed on staff use. The only functional restrictions were instituted by Yammer, who required users to have an institutional email address to gain access to the site. Once registered with the site, staff were free to 'follow' their colleagues, post messages, create groups, and invite others to join the site within the boundaries of the provided infrastructure.

Preliminary analysis of the campus Yammer showed slow but steady uptake by staff. Increasingly, there were 'clusters' of joins, probably as members of functional teams made collective decisions to sign up at once. Around July 2013 there was a noticeable spike in new users joining the site (Figure 7.1).

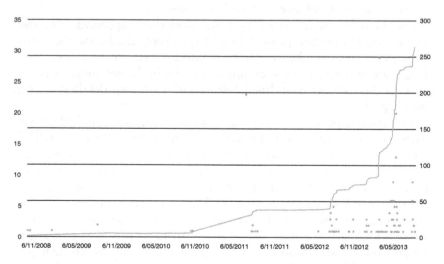

Figure 7.1 User joins on the university Yammer network, 2008–2014. Dots indicate daily numbers of joins; the line depicts a cumulative total of join activity.

Initially, we thought that the observed spike in users signing up to the site might signal a tipping point to widespread adoption. Rogers[9] discusses how innovations tend to be adopted by a general population, offering five criteria that can influence adoption behavior:

1 The innovation must demonstrate a relative advantage over established practices;
2 The innovation must be compatible with existing processes;
3 The innovation must be relatively simple to use;
4 Users must be able to observe the innovation in use; and
5 Users must be able to trial the innovation to assess its effectiveness.

Over the initial uptake period of 2008–2011 (the *early adopter* period), the campus Yammer platform appeared to embody many of the characteristics that would foster widespread user adoption. Throughout 2008–2011, Facebook and Twitter were becoming well-established and familiar online social environments, and the principles of online text-based social networking were recognizable to Yammer's target user groups. As such, Yammer was compatible with users' existing norms and expectations (criterion 2, as above). In terms of complexity, the platform presented itself as a relatively simple interface—described by one user as 'Facebook in a fancy dress', its core functionality was familiar and easy to navigate (criterion 3). Finally, the campus Yammer was openly trial-able by staff; once signed up, users were *encouraged* to invite others to trial (criterion 5). The inference of all these traits is that if the platform proved useful to the early adopter group (criterion 1), and the benefits were observable to the wider population (criterion 4), the innovation should diffuse itself throughout the social network, eventually reaching a critical mass of users.

The genesis of a network represents a key influential point in the SNS lifecycle. It is here that the foundations for widespread adoption (and, by inference, success) are first established. If users do not arrive at the site with a preformed 'need' to be satisfied (for example, by a lack of existing social networking behaviors, or being directed to use the site by a superior), they will expect the benefits of the site to reveal themselves. This can be through their own experiences (weighing up the return on investment (ROI) for their efforts in participating in the online community), or by observing the behaviors of other 'opinion leaders'[10] on the site. One interviewee summed it up as:

I think that's the main thing, it's getting back to the need. What need do people have to use it, if they don't see a need, they're not going to use it, if they're not going to benefit. – USER A

Many open networks collectively work to produce emergent behaviors that are adopted and refined into expected practice—in other words, organically and informally, a culture and practice of use emerges, including language and tone, appropriate content for the platform and network, and a loose understanding, usually uncodified, of 'acceptable' behavior.

The genesis of this particular closed campus Yammer network was unclear to many users. Some believed it was originally set up by a senior manager as part of an institutional initiative; others understood it to be an ad-hoc innovation started by a junior peer. Ultimately, these competing mythologies would prove to be influential factors in how some users approached the site. That Yammer was perceived by some to be a formal, official space (created and managed top-down rather than bottom-up) led to a sort of 'self-censorship' among some users interviewed. Users were reluctant to post casual or informal messages to the site, which are used in building and reinforcing social connections and developing new social capital within the emerging network.[11] For those who understood it to be a bottom-up initiative, the 'so what?' question remained unanswered.

The generation and circulation of social capital is a key predictor of the strength of bonds between users on a network. In particular, the ideas of bonding and bridging social capital can be used to explore how homogenous and heterogeneous networks, respectively, maintain cohesion and reinforce tie relations.[12] Francis Fukuyama defines social capital as the 'shared norms or values that promote social cooperation, instantiated in actual social relationships'.[13] These relationships can be virtual or face-to-face, institutionally structured (such as within silos of a campus network) or more organic and emergent. There is already a significant body of work dealing with the development and exchange of social capital in virtual networks which will be discussed further later in this chapter, but what is key to emphasize here is that the exchange and creation of social capital not only strengthens existing ties, but also builds trust and expectations of reciprocity.[14] This sense of trust, and of accumulated social capital in active circulation, are critical to understanding the role of the early adopter group in this Yammer network.

In this case study, the early adopter group held a number of characteristics that were not replicated in the wider network. The early adopters were identified as core 'innovators', beyond their participation in the fledgling Yammer group. Indeed, closer analysis in the interview phase of the research revealed that these on-campus members were mostly known to each other prior to joining Yammer. This group *did* exhibit some signs of a successful social network, namely in terms of close interconnectivity, organic network structures and relatively high levels of trust relations. Indeed, trust developed between these users in other spaces was likely an enticing factor in encouraging them to form this unique core early adopter network.

But, even from the beginning (especially when compared to other, open social network sites) the campus Yammer group was never particularly active, either in terms of new users joining or message posting activity. Even among the innovators, the majority of messages sent on the site were automatically generated *system* messages. When the strongest, or perhaps more accurately, the *loudest* actor on the network is a non-human agent, it could be argued that the ties within and between network groups are not being strongly expressed within the network space.

We analyzed communicative events (message postings) in this phase more closely to better understand how users were participating in the online community. We concluded that there was an absence of exemplar online behavior, which left many new joining members wondering what the purpose of the site was and how it could best be used for maximum return on the investment of time and social effort. For example, users noted:

I sort of thought, hang on a minute, what is the purpose of this here? ... I think there's only a point in doing it if there's a point in doing it... I didn't find a real purpose for it, in my role. And, if we were supposed to be using it for work, that wasn't articulated. – USER A

You expect something to happen, and since you don't know what could happen yourself, you're not the one doing the first step. And, if everybody is in that situation, then nothing is going to happen. – USER B

[talking about encouraging others to use Yammer] I don't think [previously] I explained enough about it... this time, I actually spent more time explaining what Yammer was and actually how to access it...even still, they're not quite sure what it's about. – USER C

Some later adopters expected the site to function as a news stream, which they would 'dip in and out of' in the hopes of finding relevant content. However, a distinct lack of meaningful messages left this need ultimately unsatisfied. Other users attempted to force production habits and generate content by 'shouting into the void' and frequently posting general public announcements. Again, this behavior was seen either as not coming from people worth responding to, or from users whom others felt they could not interact with (perhaps due to perceived hierarchy, or a lack of accumulated social capital). Alternatively, such posts were read by other users as not inviting a response or conversation, and thus were mostly disregarded as 'spam', or low value messages.

In interviews, key participants from the early adopter group suggested a number of reasons for the observed low level of activity. Respondents reflected that their networking needs were already facilitated through existing connections, in both face-to-face and technologically-mediated situations. There was no new ROI offered by the site, and thus little personal motivation to invest time and effort in a new platform, learning its features and codes (both technical and social). The closed and institutionally-centric nature of the Yammer site meant that actors on the network could only draw connections from a limited user base, with there being a high likelihood of users already knowing each other, and what they had to contribute.

> [talking about internal-only Yammer communication]...[T]hat would be a disadvantage to me, by my own way of thinking... you learn a lot by talking to people from outside this place. – USER D

> People collaborate here through old-school 'I know him who knows her'... So, the social network is people's relationships, talking and meeting and going to lunch and going across campus. That's the social network. – USER E

In interviews, these users often referred to other, more open tools that could more efficiently satisfy wider networking needs, such as forming new ties with associates outside the campus network.

Within the campus environment itself, the mixed perceptions as to the origins of the site further dampened any emergence of 'best practice' or shared social norms on the site. As one user noted when reflecting on the success and failure of social media on campus:

> [T]here's two components about [success]. The first one, from the top-down, there's an acceptance that this is valid work, so if I'm looking at Yammer, that it's actually something that's going to impact positively on my work performance. So there needs to be that level of acceptance...but I think that the use of it actually comes from the bottom-up. – USER C

Outside Influences on Closed Network Development

Closed networks also emphasize the importance that structural factors can play in influencing the growth (or failure thereof) of SNS, such as this campus Yammer group. On the surface, the campus Yammer appeared, if not overly 'successful', at least stable. Its presence as an institutional tool was accepted by most users, though they represented only a small fraction of the campus staff who potentially could have accessed the network. Despite little activity, a cursory examination would have suggested a burgeoning 'popularity' as more and more users came onboard. A more nuanced analysis, however, revealed not only perceived failure by users, but also that the site was failing at its core stated purpose—to facilitate better communication and collaboration across the disparate functional units and departments of the organization.[15]

To illustrate the influence of the institutional structure, Figure 7.2 shows the network plotted as a graph. By employing certain rules for where nodes should be placed within the graph (*i.e.*, highly-connected nodes are pulled together while less-connected nodes are repelled from each other), distinct communities are revealed, interconnected to each other by only a few key nodes. These communities were subsequently identified to closely follow the divisional/departmental boundaries of the offline university structure.

At this point, it is worth considering these recurring questions of social ties and social capital, and how they influence the structure of mediated social networks like this Yammer case study. The shape and structure of networks has been thoroughly discussed elsewhere[16] referring to both on and offline networks. Different approaches highlight how factors such as structure, agents, and ties all influence network development, and,

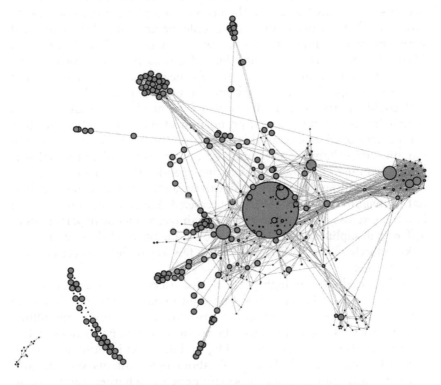

Figure 7.2 Graph of the university Yammer network. Size of nodes represents relative amount of posting activity (i.e., larger nodes are users that posted more messages). Pulling together highly-connected nodes (and repelling less-connected nodes) reveals community clusters within the network structure.

conversely, how networks can shape user behavior, both as network participants and as individual actors.

Most of this work, however, isolates single networks for study, with the *interplay* between networks only now coming under scrutiny.[17] Open networks pose a difficult research problem for trying to analyze the relations between online and offline networks. As social network use and access becomes increasingly portable, overlapped and invisible, it becomes difficult to tease out the specific influence of various network and social ties on the development and success of any SNS.

When considering how social ties move and form within and across social networking spaces (such as a university campus and a third-party social networking site), different types of ties have the potential to affect network formation, stability, and 'success' in different ways. In exploring this case study, the presence of various tie types (or lack thereof) stands out as an important consideration for understanding this network.

Ties play different roles within a network structure. We rely on strong ties (the relationships between close intimates) as a key part of our social network apparatus because of the deep trust and reciprocity we feel to those ties.[18] Weak ties (those with people we are not tightly associated with, the distant associates we know *of* but not *well)* and latent ties (those ties that exist *in potentia* but which, as yet, have not been activated by social contact) are critical for new ideas, opportunities and fresh social capital to be injected into the social network.[19]

It could be argued that the very nature of closed social networks strictly limits the number and proportion of weak and latent ties that can be developed or leveraged by actors on the network. In the case of our university Yammer network, the online and mediated social network (Yammer) mirrored the existing, geo-local social network (the campus), meaning the number of weak or latent ties that had the potential to invigorate the network were reduced. Here, weak and latent tie bonds lay across disparate units—for example, academic departments in different disciplines. As Figure 7.2 shows, members of these units were linked mostly to each other, with only a few key nodes connecting units to each other.

In theory, there was high potential for users to exploit these cross-divisional weak and latent ties to find value in participating in the online network. However, in practice, the structure and culture of the offline campus network constrained user behavior in realizing this potential.

The organizational structure of Higher Education institutions is complex. J.L. Bess and J.R. Dee[20] talk about determinants such as size, environment, culture and tasks influencing whether institutional organization tends to be more *organic* or *mechanistic*. Organic structures decentralize authority and responsibility and typically have more cross-over between functional groups; mechanistic structures, on the other hand, revolve around a clear hierarchy of command and clear boundaries between functional groups. Many institutions (particularly larger institutions) are organized as mixed structures; for example, the overall organization of a university can be mechanistic with individual departments functioning more organically.[21]

It has been noted in the literature that the complex manner in which Higher Education institutions are structured does not inherently encourage collaboration. The concept of disciplinary or departmental silos is well-documented,[22] and is further supported by observations and reflections from interviewees on this university's culture:

> [I]t's the culture of the place... our siloed way of dealing with things means that we just don't have that inbuilt way of thinking about how we do things... Trying to do [something centralized], there's so much devolution of control in the university, it makes it really, really difficult to kind of come up with a single system that people should use. – USER D

Or, as another user put it more pithily:

> [T]hat's just the culture of the university, its historic independence of each mini ivory tower... you're never going to break that. – USER E

That these silos were replicated online does not, in itself, predicate failure of the online social network. As R.S. Burt[23] and others have argued, even siloed or closed social networks of strong or close ties can still connect and leverage other weaker or latent ties by brokering relations using key nodes. No social network structure exists without 'holes' or gaps, whether these are driven by structural, institutional or personal factors. Burt argues that nodes who possess a tie that connects across these gaps in the social network—like the key nodes identified in this campus Yammer group—can act as 'brokers', and may, by taking on this role, gain both individual prestige and social capital as well as benefit from a more heterogeneous social network. However, brokerage requires extra effort and expenditure (of time, of social resources, of capital, etc.), and may be seen as irrelevant by the potential brokerage nodes for a variety of reasons. This may be further reinforced if the silo or network unit is not outward-looking in its networking practices (regardless of the technology or medium of networking). As one interviewee noted:

> It's not the technology, it's buy-in, with your stakeholders, then process, what's the right, you know, process. Then the technology's the last thing. – USER E

The closed nature of the site (relying on institutional email as a condition of entry) further closed off brokering relations with actors and networks beyond the silos of the campus network. Many of the interviewees made reference to the stability of their internal networks—they had built ties with all actors in that network they wished to expend the effort to form a tie with. As one interviewee noted:

> I mean, for what, really, what could you say there that you couldn't say in the corridor, what could you say there that you couldn't say by meeting somebody? – USER B

This raises a point for further discussion: across the field of Higher Education and academic research, much is made about the need for cross-silo collaboration.[24] However, much of the rhetoric about technologically-mediated collaboration presupposes a commonality of identity, or shared purpose. When comparing the emergence of the campus Yammer network with the case studies of successful Yammer deployment,[25] we identified key differences in the cultures of the respective organizations, and this gives clues as to why our instance of the platform failed to reach a critical mass of users.

First, university users operate under a far less consistent organizational identity than their private corporation counterparts. One interview respondent touched upon this issue of identity:

> The university is actually quite a unique environment. One of the things that always fascinates me [...] is the sense of differentiation, you know, 'I don't work for the university, I work at the School of Business'. Each of these units are actually quite discrete units, there's a lot of diversification within the university in terms of segmentation of roles and actually where people see themselves. – USER C

This lack of a shared institutional identity could be one of the reasons why staff replicated their organizational boundaries online, despite having the potential to redefine these existing structures. In comparison, examples of successful social networking within the business sector show that corporations have an overarching brand identity consistent across all countries and service divisions, which likely helps foster cross-departmental communication despite the different roles individuals may play (often across national borders).[26]

Second, corporations tend to be under pressure from external competition with other companies, which helps to reinforce their sense of collective identity—employees in different areas and roles all work towards a shared goal. Academic institutions, however, are subject to internal competition, as different departments/units (and academics within the same department/unit) compete for resources (whether they be money, students, time, or prestige). As a result, while the institution may drive collective, high-level goals (*e.g.,* 'excellence in teaching', 'excellence in research'), individual departments/units are left to implement their own strategies to attain these goals, and as a result cross-departmental collaboration is perhaps not as automatic a reflex.

Interestingly, several interviewees commented that, in theory, cross-department collaboration was desirable, and noted the potential of SNS tools to bridge organizational divides:

> I'm just generally enthusiastic about trying to establish links between different parts of the university because one, it's one thing that frustrates me it's people doing things like this and this [draws separate circles on the table]. So they never even know the other person even exists, or that they're doing something very similar. – USER D

> Talking about cross-campus collaboration, well that's what should be in it... because you might be researching a similar thing from Physics to Education. – USER E

In practice, though, as the following exchange on Yammer illustrates, the idea of crossing departmental boundaries confused some users:

> [with regards to a departmental group] This might be a silly question, but it appears that of the 16 members, only 7 are actually associated with [Department X]. – USER F

> Hi [User F], You may want to consider the administrator changing the settings for group access. – USER E

> Hi [User F], Just to wade in: I joined because working at [Department Y] we're sort of a 'friend' of [Department X], so I wanted to participate in the community. I wasn't sure if it was set up as a private operational group only for [Department X] people. – USER G

> I think the question being asked is 'Why aren't there more [Department X] people in the group?' :) – USER H

> Actually both 'Why aren't there more [Department X]?' and 'Why are there quite a few non-[Department X] people, including names I don't recognize?' – USER F

Dynamic Proportions

A further limitation of the literature highlighted by this research is that much of the work done on the function of social networks deals with stable and successful networks (or networks that recently had such characteristics). For example, one model of user production/consumption habits in established (successful) networks describes users as typically falling into a pattern of:

- 90% of users generate little or no content themselves, existing on the site merely to consume others' content ('lurking' behavior);
- 9% of users serve mostly to relay others' generated content (for example, through reposting links, 'retweeting', or liking/commenting on content to draw attention to it);
- 1% of users actively generate original content for others to consume.[27]

Another model suggests a ratio of 50–30–20, where a stable site has 50% of 'sporadic' or passive content consumers, 30% 'intermittent contributors' and 20% 'heavy contributors'.[28] Putting aside the critiques of these ratios, we hypothesize that, while successful social networks might *settle* into the above patterns of content generation, the proportions needed in the genesis phase are likely to be quite different. New, casual users coming to the site with no predetermined need are perhaps more likely to lurk as they come to terms with the site, essentially testing the waters before deciding whether to produce their own content. As such, a seed contingent of content producers, usually the early adopter group, is required at the genesis of the network to model exemplar behavior and the social normative parameters that the new users are seeking. This early adopter contingent has huge influence in shaping the future social direction of the site. If they don't engage actively with the site or network, it may put the future of that site and network in jeopardy. Therefore, it is arguable that a 90% lurker ratio might not reflect the activity required for an early adopter group to 'seed' a site with activity that encourages subsequent growth.

This hypothesis was strengthened by analyzing activity in our case study over time, and wondering how different snapshots of activity reflect or contrast the reported overall experience of users. While it is possible that this case study is an outlier (and more work needs to be done in the area), our preliminary findings suggest that different proportions of users and activity can mark success change over time. For example, a snapshot approach taken in early 2012 (as the early adopter group peaked in numbers, network connections, and activity) would have suggested that this Yammer group was either successful or well on the way to success. However, interviews with those early adopters revealed, both subjectively and in terms of Yammer's goals for the site, that the campus Yammer was in fact failing.

This ties back to both the idea of looking at success as a snapshot measure, and how complex and subtle socio-personal factors have strong influences over developing networks. We argue that we should perhaps be wary about looking at social network success in a way that isolates the network from both structural and interpersonal influences. The campus

Yammer network, which is closed and bounded yet also deeply embedded within pre-existing interpersonal and structural networks, makes that explicitly clear. Even without looking at any other factors or criteria, Yammer would define this case as a failure of its tool to achieve its goal—it did not establish a thorough cross-institution networking and communication space, it did not break down barriers or bring its users together.

Conclusion

Social network successes and failures are complex and multifaceted phenomena. Failure and success as concepts are difficult to define and operationalize, and even working with a subjective, user-centric notion of success or failure, there is still a lot of grey area to navigate when studying a social network in growth or decline. For instance, focusing on generalized 'snapshot' measures of success or failure offers a limited view of the entirety of the social network lifecycle—what appears as 'success' or 'failure' at any given point in time may not accurately reflect the actual state of the network in question. And, it is important to remember that such social networks exist not in quarantined isolation, but are tied to and interlink with other online networks as well as physically situated social groupings. As such, both on- and off-line factors can affect SNS development. As with any media, the audience is at the core of success or failure; as such, to develop deeper understandings of mediated social networks it is important to acknowledge and incorporate the complexity of network actors.

In studying the campus Yammer network, this chapter has highlighted the particular complexity of social networks in the earliest stages of their development, underlining the importance of social and bridging capital in the genesis phase of social networks, especially in relation to *overlapping* social network spaces. In order to stake out cognitive space, new networks need to prove value and worth in their development stages, and they cannot duplicate an existing need or service (be it social, enterprise-related, or other) without adding to the capital already in circulation. Essentially, to survive, new networks must extend. To do this, however, there needs to be the development of new capital among the early adopters, and this capital needs to be observable to entice other adopters.

This capital, needed to sustain emerging online social networks to maturity, emerges from the small social bonds that form in networked spaces – through simple phatic rituals ('Hi, how are you?'), bridging existing groups across key nodes ('Have you met X?'), or freely offering intangible value now under the implicit understanding of return later ('let me do you this favor...' which is collectively remembered and repaid later on in the overall balance of networked exchange). As was seen in this failure case study, none of these activities could be said to be systematically occurring — phatic rituals were self-suppressed out of fear of top-down censure; internodal exchanges were limited due to the existing wider network structure of the geo-social campus; and a culture of exchange did not take root in among the 'shouting', the machine messages, and the general sense among the early adopters that they could make such exchanges much more easily through other network spaces.

As M.L. Small writes of the generation of social capital in organizational contexts:

> understanding people's connections... requires understanding the organizations in which those connections are embedded. It requires conceiving of people as organizationally embedded actors, as actors whose social *and* organizational ties... respond to institutional constraints, imperatives, and opportunities.[29]

The influence of these actor constraints at the genesis of our campus Yammer, and the subsequent lack of social / bridging capital development, doomed the network to 'failure', despite the outward appearance of successful hallmarks (*e.g.*, a steadily increasing user base), and the perception of network users that an enterprise social network would be valuable to connect staff cross-institution.

In our university case study, even though Yammer's original target audiences were small to medium commercial enterprises, on paper at least, the needs of a university network should have fit within Yammer's own frameworks of collaboration, cooperation and communication. Corporations, though, have a coherent identity that is readily accommodated by the structures implicit within Yammer as a communication and collaboration network. The fractured, siloed, and multi-layered identity of the university (including division, unit, discipline, location) is less translatable. Although universities talk of (research) collaboration, the pre-existing institutional behaviors and structures are often resistant to taking advantage of more open communicative and collaborative spaces like Yammer. On top of this, existing networks of trust and social capital exchange (both mediated and face to face) further diminish the use value of such a closed, restricted, and ill-defined networking space.

This, we argue, is why we see the replication of silos on the Yammer map – cross-silo communication barriers are still too much for the actors on the edges of the network to broker connections for, and there is insufficient impetus to go over them when it is easier to go around (use another channel) or not even try (stay within silo). Put another way, mediated networks cannot be (re)formed in a vacuum, but must also account for the socio-personal and structural influences users bring to the new networking space. Enclosure of the network throws into stark relief the impact of wider social factors such as existing trust relationships, bridging actors, and institutional structures, especially when dealing with a campus network, where these pre-existing issues around network boundaries and silos further put pressure on the growth — and the potential for success or failure — of a network.

Notes

1 danah boyd and Nicole Ellison, "Social Network Sites: Definition, History, and Scholarship," *Journal of Computer-Mediated Communication.* 13, no. 1 (2007): 210–230, p. 211.

2 K-Y.Lin, & H-P. Lu, "Why people use social networking sites: An empirical study integrating network externalities and motivation theory." *Computers in Human Behavior,* 27, no. 3, (2011): 1152–1161; O. B. Brandtzæg,, & J. Heim, "Why People Use Social Networking Sites" in *Online Communities and Social Computing: Third International Conference, OCSC 2009, Held as part of HCI International 2009, San Diego, CA, USA, July 19–24, 2009 Proceedings,* eds, Ozok, A.A., & Zaphiris, P. (Springer Berlin Heidelberg, 2009): *143–152.*

3 danah boyd, "Friendster and Publicly Articulated Social Networks." Conference on Human Factors and Computing Systems (CHI 2004). Vienna: ACM; E. Pearson, (2009). "The World Wide Web's A Stage: The performance of identity in online social networks." *First Monday.* 14, no. 3 (2009): http://firstmonday.org/article/view/2162/2127.

4 boyd, "Friendster and Publicly Articulated Social Networks."

5 Pearson & Moskal, "The Failure of Defining Failure in Social Networking Sites."

6 A. Richter, and K. Riemer, "The Contextual Nature of Enterprise Social Networking: A multi case study comparison." *Proceedings of the European Conference on Information Systems (ECIS 2013).*

7 Yammer Corporation (2014). "About Yammer." Retrieved from: https://about.yammer.com/.

8 K. Riemer, P. Overfeld, P. Scifleet, and A. Richter, "Oh, SNEP! The Dynamics of Social Network Emergence-the case of Capgemini Yammer." (2012): Retrieved from http://prijipati.library.usyd.edu.au/bitstream/2123/8049/3/BIS%20WP2012%20-%2001%20-%20RIEMER.pdf; K. Riemer, P. Scifleet, and R. Reddig, "Powercrowd: Enterprise social networking in professional service work: A case study of Yammer at Deloitte Australia." (2012): Retrieved from http://prijipati.library.usyd.edu.au/bitstream/2123/8352/6/BIS%20WP2012%20-%2002%20-%20RIEMER.pdf.

9 E. M. Rogers, *Diffusion of innovations.* (New York: Simon and Schuster, 2010).

10 Rogers, *Diffusion of innovations.*

11 D. Halpern, *Social Capital.* (Cambridge, UK: Polity Press, 2005).

12 R. D. Putnam, *Bowling Alone: The collapse and revival of American community.* (New York: Simon and Schuster, 2000); Francis Fukuyama, "Social Capital and Development: The coming agenda," *SAIS Review.* 22, no. 1. (2002): 23–37.

13 Fukuyama, "Social Capital and Development: The coming agenda," p. 27; Francis Fukuyama, "Social Capital, Civil Society, and Development," *Third World Quarterly.* 22, no. 1, (2001): 7–20.

14 Pearson, "The World Wide Web's A Stage: The performance of identity in online social networks."

15 Yammer Corporation "About Yammer."
16 V. Buskens, *Social Networks and Trust.* (Norwell, MA: Kluwer Academic Publishers, 2002).
17 R. Agarwal, A.K. Gupta, and R. Kraut. "Editorial Overview—The Interplay Between Digital and Social Networks," *Information Systems Research* 19, no. 3, (2008): 243–252.
18 Barry Wellman, A. Quan-Haase, J. Witte, and K. Hampton "Does The Internet Increase, Decrease, or Supplement Social Capital? Social networks, participation, and community commitment," *American Behavorial Scientist.* 45, no. 3, (2001): 436–455; H. H. Hiller, and T.M. Franz. "New Ties, Old Ties and Lost Ties: The use of the internet in diaspora," *New Media and Society,* 6, no. 6, (2004): 731–752; A. Quan-Haase, and Barry Wellman. "How Does The Internet Affect Social Capital?" in. *Social Capital and Information Technology,* eds. Huysman, M & V. Wulf, (MIT Press: USA 2004): 113–132; Nicole B. Ellison, C. Steinfield, and C. Lampe. "Connection Strategies: Social capital implications of Facebook-enabled communication practices," *New Media and Society.* 13, no. 6, (2011): 873–892.
19 M.S. Granovetter, "The Strength of Weak Ties," *American Journal of Sociology.* 78, no. 6, (1973): 1360–80.
20 J.L. Bess, & J.R. Dee, *Understanding College and University Organization: Dynamics of the system (Vol. 2).* Stylus Publishing, LLC (2008).
21 Bess, & Dee, *Understanding College and University Organization: Dynamics of the system (Vol. 2).*
22 See for example: R.M. Kanter, "Collaborative advantage: the art of alliances." *Harvard Business Review,* 4 (1994): 96–108; A. Kezar, "Redesigning for collaboration within higher education institutions: An exploration into the developmental process." *Research in Higher Education,* 46, no. 7, (2005): 831–860; P. Senge, *The Fifth Discipline* (Doubleday, New York, 1990).
23 R.S. Burt, *Brokerage and Closure: An introduction to social capital.* (Oxford: Oxford University Press 2005).
24 See for example: J. Finch, *Accessibility, Sustainability, Excellence: How to expand access to research publications.* Report of the Working Group on Expanding Access to Published Research Findings. London, UK. (2012): Retrieved from http://www.researchinfonet.org/wp-content/uploads/2012/06/Finch-Group-report-FINAL-VERSION.pdf.
25 D. Richter, K. Riemer, J. von Brocke, and S. Große Böckmann, "Internet Social Networking - Distinguishing the Phenomenon from its Manifestations," Proceedings of 17th European Conference on Information Systems, Verona (2009); Riemer, Overfeld, Scifleet, & Richter, "Oh, SNEP! The Dynamics of Social Network Emergence-the case of Capgemini Yammer."; Riemer, Scifleet, & Reddig, "Powercrowd: Enterprise social networking in professional service work: A case study of Yammer at Deloitte Australia."
26 K. Riemer, S. Diederich, A. Richter, and P. Scifleet. "Tweet Talking: Exploring the nature of microblogging at Capgemini Yammer." *Business Information Systems Working Paper Series.* (University of Sydney, Australia, 2011).
27 J. Nielsen, *The 90–9-1 Rule for Participation Inequality in Social Media and Online Communities.* (2006): Retrieved from http://www.nngroup.com/articles/participation-inequality/.
28 P.B. Brandtzæg, & J. Heim, "A typology of social networking sites users." *International Journal of Web Based Communities,* 7, no. 1, (2011): 28–51.
29 M.L. Small, *Unanticipated gains: Origins of network inequality in everyday life.* (Oxford University Press, 2009): p5, emphasis original.

8   Beyond 'the profile'

Multiple Qualitative Methods for Researching Facebook Drinking Cultures

Ian Goodwin, Christine Griffin, Antonia Lyons and Tim McCreanor

In this chapter we reflect on the insights made available through the multiple methods deployed in a large scale, team-based qualitative research project conducted in Aotearoa New Zealand on Facebook use. In this specific study, our aim was to investigate the convergence of young people's drinking cultures and their practices of online social networking and self-display. Young people's drinking cultures, often associated with particularly heavy, hedonistic and 'risky' alcohol consumption, have always attracted a heightened degree of societal interest and concern, both from the media and policy makers as well as from academic researchers.[1] As drinking cultures have incorporated the online environments made available through social networking sites (SNS), they have produced new forms of heightened visibility for youth drinking practices. Much of the growing research in this area has primarily focused on examining the drinking-related content young people generate on their SNS profiles. Such content, for example digital photography depicting drinking and drunken behavior, seems so self-evidently relevant to what is at stake in new forms of online drinking displays that the rationale for focusing analysis on 'the profile' is rarely explicated in contemporary literature. Moreover, profile content is not only readily accessible to the user's peers but can become much more publicly viewable, and hence seems to carry even greater analytical weight in terms of influencing emerging youth cultural practices around SNS and alcohol consumption.

Examining Facebook drinking displays through user profiles has produced valuable insights, particularly in terms of public health research seeking to minimize the negative health outcomes associated with alcohol consumption. However, in this chapter, we argue that the deployment of multiple, complementary qualitative methods reveals the limitations of focusing solely, or too heavily, on the content of users' profiles. We also contend that using multiple qualitative methods, derived from more 'traditional' audience research projects and adapted for online contexts, allows for productive (if equally partial) insights into the nature of Facebook as a technological platform and into user engagement with its affordances. Indeed, following Christine Hine's earlier work on qualitative online research, we use this chapter to illustrate that understanding the distinctive features of Facebook as a technological platform, and relatedly 'bounding' an appropriate approach for their study, is far from a clear cut exercise.[2] While 'the profile' seems to be a logical, common sense place to begin any study, in fact complex problems always emerge about what to focus *upon* and where to *begin*, and these complexities are always bound up with the types of questions we are seeking to ask and answer. Rather than producing a simple contrast between our approach and dominant approaches for studying Facebook drinking displays, we hope our discussion demonstrates that productive understandings of Facebook as a technology, and associated understandings of its users, can usefully emerge through reflexively managed critical enquiry, as end points of an adaptive research process.[3] This critical reflexivity suggests user profiles, while clearly being pivotal to the design and use of Facebook (and SNS generally) may not always be the appropriate place to start analysis, and cannot necessarily be straightforwardly 'read' more or less 'textually' without missing key elements of the novel dynamics they introduce to social life.

We first broadly describe the established literature on SNS and youth drinking, focusing on its key insights and limitations, and the relationship of both these factors to the types of methods deployed which tend to privilege analyzing user-generated content posted on profiles. We then provide a methodological overview of our research design that focuses on how it was planned and implemented as we collected different strands of data. We will outline the three major stages of data collection, the ethical issues raised, and the participants involved. We then explore how these methods provide specific insights, often occluded in dominant approaches, into how online youth drinking cultures are related to processes of meaning-making, online display of user-generated content, participation, and interaction on Facebook. As a brief illustrative example, we then reassess the drinking photo as a form of user-generated content. Finally, we point to how our approach allows for different forms of theorizing that enable a broader critique of Facebook and the power relations framing Facebook use.

Youth Drinking and Social Networking: Emphases, Findings and Methods of Enquiry

Over the past few years a burgeoning literature has developed, overwhelmingly focused specifically on the activities of young people, examining alcohol use and social media. This research has, in the first instance, usefully established detailed evidence of the sheer prevalence of alcohol-related content on young people's profiles. Here content analysis of SNS profiles is common. For example Kathleen Beullens and Adriaan

Schepers found that 95.62% of the 160 Belgian college student Facebook profiles they analyzed contained references to alcohol in either profile pictures or status updates.[4] They found 2,575 pictures and 92 status updates referring to alcohol use, which 'represented about 6.50% of the pictures in the sample and 2.90% of the status updates'.[5] Similarly, content analysis of 225 male college student Facebook profiles in the USA found 85.3% contained alcohol references. Here the researchers extended their analysis of profile content beyond pictures and status updates, to include group names, the personal information section and the use of an application for downloading and posting tailored icons (Bumper Sticker).[6] These studies are indicative of broad patterns. For example further analysis of profile postings on Bebo in New Zealand[7] and MySpace in the USA[8] revealed young people's profiles to be replete with alcohol references, suggesting strong relationships have rapidly developed between young people's use of SNS, their drinking, and their associated online self-displays and socializing.

This phenomenon could be conceptualized and studied in a variety of ways. Previous research has identified youth drinking cultures as increasingly important sites of leisure, where the social practices involved become linked to broad processes around the formation of (class, gender, ethnic) identities as well as the development of friendships and wider social networks.[9] Ties between drinking cultures and broader contextual factors like alcohol deregulation and links to night time economies, increasingly central to wealth generation in cities and in turn linked to the corporate promotion of alcohol, have also been highlighted.[10] Some critical attention has been paid to aspects of these issues in SNS research examining drinking cultures.[11] Yet the predominant reaction to the documenting of large amounts of alcohol content within young people's SNS profiles has been to raise concerns about the 'effects' such content may have on the health and wellbeing of young people. This is perhaps understandable as a first response given the well documented negative health impacts of alcohol consumption, which affect young people disproportionately.[12] Several researchers have created and manipulated fictitious Facebook profiles in studies designed to interrogate how drinking content on profiles influences SNS users' attitudes to alcohol. For example Angela Fournier and colleagues used a 'between-subjects experimental design... in which participants viewed a fictitious Facebook profile with or without alcohol-related content and then reported their perceptions of college student drinking norms'.[13] Results suggested those exposed to drinking content viewed this content as indicative of actual alcohol use, and estimated higher college drinking norms than those who did not.[14] A similar experimental design used by Dana Litt and Michelle Stock led to similar conclusions for a younger user cohort; *i.e.,* that 'descriptive norms for alcohol, as portrayed by Facebook profiles' positively affects 13 to 15 year old students' willingness to use alcohol and attitudes towards alcohol.[15]

The major concern here is that alcohol-related profile content may encourage greater alcohol consumption, and tracing the 'impact' of user generated alcohol content on actual drinking behavior has therefore become the central thread that much subsequent research has followed. A US study of 5,679,008 tweets, examining keywords that are synonyms for 'drunk' (wasted, shit-faced, buzzed etc.), suggested tweets relating to intoxication on Twitter peaked between 10 pm and 2 pm on Friday and Saturday nights, correlating to time periods of highest consumption.[16] Numerous survey-based studies, often combined with analyses of profile content and employing multivariate statistical analyses, have established strong correlations between posting alcohol content, alcohol consumption, and higher AUDIT (Alcohol Use Disorders Identification Test) scores.[17] For example Brad Ridout and colleagues had 158 US university students 'complete a range of alcohol measures [including survey-based AUDIT scores] before providing access for researchers to view their Facebook profiles'.[18] Profiles were analyzed to assess the extent to which they portrayed alcohol content in profile photography and wall postings. They found content-driven 'alcohol identities' on profiles to be commonplace, and to be correlated with 'alcohol consumption and problematic alcohol–related behaviours'.[19]

One of the key issues likely to strike a reader of this volume, focused on studying digital media audiences, is that despite the novel context this research examining alcohol-related content on social media has moved firmly into territory previously covered by established debates over 'media effects'. However media and communications/audience research scholars are not the ones driving this research forward. As Sonia Livingstone recently noted, many diverse disciplines are justifiably interested in social media and they understandably bring with them their own particular perspectives on 'the social' and 'society'.[20] In this instance health promotion, behavioral medicine, public health and health psychology researchers are driving the agenda. The ultimate concern is that young people's peer-generated alcohol content on SNS profiles may be producing potent, new 'intoxigenic digital spaces'[21] – online alcohol promoting environments – that are potentially damaging to public health. In terms of building broader theoretical understandings from this body of research, the over-riding concern with establishing relationships between drinking content, drinking practices, and negative health outcomes has led to an interest in models like Social Learning Theory, the Media Practice Model, and even the tentative development of a conceptual approach entitled the Facebook Influence Model.[22] Here young people's alcohol-related content on their profiles is presumed to have a potentially 'predictive capacity, especially in relation to health behaviour'.[23]

There are two issues we wish to highlight here. First, like *all* studies of SNS, this research agenda does not straightforwardly reflect the 'reality' of the issues at stake. Rather, it effectively brings into focus particular, partial versions of both the 'user' and the technology(ies) they are engaged with. While authoritative creators of their own content, young people as active 'users' remain open to the powerful effects of co-created online environments that encourage drinking, which is conceived of primarily as a health risk. In this way they remain ambiguously caught between being a traditional 'audience' and being more active 'users' (in the contemporary sense where, notwithstanding the nuances of active audience research, the two terms are often juxtaposed). While both drinking and SNS use are social practices, users are considered in a de-contextualized fashion and primarily *as individuals*, and their reactions/uses are measured in an individuated fashion. These constructions dovetail with dominant media and health policy frameworks, prone to segregating 'youth' as a problematic 'other', which frequently construct young people's drinking practices and associated uses of SNS as individual, risky behaviors.[24] The technology itself is also considered in an individuated and de-contextualized fashion. The focus remains firmly on individual profiles, which does allow for a consideration of certain key affordances of social network sites that relate to content creation and networking capacities. Yet, aside from considering user-generated content on profiles and young people's associated friendship ties, the technology/media itself is largely black boxed.[25] The way the user may negotiate, appropriate or resist the affordances of specific, variegated SNS user interfaces is underexplored, as is the broader nature of the platform(s), and the meaning of content is 'read' off SNS profiles as a form of new 'self-textual' representation without exploring the complex social context in which profiles are produced.

Our second major concern is that the limited and partial nature of the insights any research agenda produces points to a need for a broad range of methods and methodologies to be applied in understanding social media, sociality and alcohol. We need to illuminate as much as possible about the complex processes of change underway without prematurely foreclosing productive avenues of enquiry. Here we argue, alongside others,[26] that – especially given the nature of the issues and limitations described above – methodologies associated with the rich history of 'audience studies' can be usefully adapted for the purpose of studying 'new'/social media. This certainly does not mean that user profiles become irrelevant, but it does mean that studies focusing on drinking cultures and SNS could usefully recreate the sort of rich, contextualized accounts of media and media audiences associated with this tradition of scholarship. This in turn suggests we need to consider using differentiated points of beginning – beyond the profile – and broader emphasizes, and to look for new ways of exploring the significance and 'effects' of user generated content.

Rethinking Facebook Drinking Displays Using Multiple Qualitative Methods: SNS, Meaning Making and Drinking Cultures

With this critical context in mind, our study aimed to explore the role of SNS in young people's alcohol consumption and leisure practices from an epistemological perspective which emphasized capturing rich, contextual and interpretative data. We argue both SNS use and drinking alcohol are situated, complex, meaning-laden social and cultural practices. In essence our major goal was to identify these meanings, from young people's own perspectives in their everyday lives, and their subsequent implications. While not wishing to minimize health concerns, we aimed to explore in detail why young people choose to post alcohol content, and the social and cultural practices it enables. Rather than 'reading' the meaning of profiles from their content alone, we were interested in using a 'socio-culturally grounded study of people's activities in context'[27] as part of developing a more nuanced approach to the role of SNS in online drinking cultures. That is, one that would enable us to interrogate how the specific affordances of SNS technology, that is the 'functional and relational aspects which frame, while not determining, the possibilities for agentic action',[28] were taken up, resisted, or appropriated by young people as part of their social lives and alcohol-based leisure practices.

The first set of choices we had to make revolved around how to choose research participants. Aotearoa New Zealand has a deregulated alcohol regime, a well-established alcohol-based night time economy, and a pervasive culture of intoxication similar to that of the United Kingdom.[29] Our society is made up of multiple ethnic strands, and has patterns of power relations heavily influenced by the colonial history of the country. To provide insight into New Zealand's drinking cultures and SNS practices, it was important to specifically explore these issues within three major ethnic groups, Māori (indigenous people), Pasifika (Pacific descent), and Pākehā (European descent). More Pākehā drink and do so more frequently at lower volumes, while Māori and Pasifika people drink less often, and are more likely to drink to intoxication when they do.[30] Engaging with ethnic diversity therefore fundamentally matters to the framing of our study. We then developed three inter-related stages of data collection and obtained approval from the university's human ethics committee.

Stage one, being the period where we 'entered' the field, was a particularly important phase. Here we decided to focus attention first on young people's alcohol consumption as a highly *social* activity, which research suggests is firmly based in *group*-related practices of having fun with friends.[31] We wanted to obtain situated meanings of drinking practices within the context of friendship groups, to examine how groups of friends developed shared, co-constructed understandings of correlated uses of SNS, and how they *collaboratively* made sense of their leisure-based nights out drinking and subsequent self-displays online. Between 2011 and 2012 participants for friendship group discussions were recruited using a mixture of convenience sampling and snowball techniques. Like drinking practices, the form and meaning of friendship can vary significantly across cultural groups,[32] so therefore we recruited friendship groups with naturally occurring networks of friends within each ethnic strand we were studying. Any interested participants subsequently asked 3–6 of their friends to take part in group discussions, so that friendship groups were determined by participants themselves. As groups formed, participants were provided with information sheets outlining the research objectives. In total, 34 friendship group discussions were conducted with 141 participants aged 18–25 years. Twelve were made up of predominantly Pākehā participants, while 12 were predominantly Māori, and 10 predominantly Pasifika. They included 57 male participants, 80 female participants, and 4 Fa'afafine, a third gender category specific to Pasifika cultures for people born male but whose spirit is female. We also sought to build diversity into our sample by recruiting across different geographical locations (including both urban and rural settings), varied workplaces and community centers (capturing differing occupations and unemployed young people), and educational institutions. Discussions were held wherever participants felt most comfortable, including workplaces, homes or university halls of residence. Upon arrival, participants were provided information sheets, assured of anonymity, offered the chance to ask questions, and signed consent forms. Discussions were semi-structured with questions about friendships, socializing, drinking behavior, use of media and SNS, and the online self-display of drinking. They lasted 1–2 hours and were video and audio taped, and were facilitated by individual female PhD researchers whose ethnicity was matched to the predominant ethnicity of the groups.

Starting with friendship groups enabled us to explore collaborative meaning making, social processes and interactions in an atmosphere where a wide range of responses can occur. This was important to capturing the *social* and *group* dynamics of online drinking cultures often overlooked in the established literature. However friendship groups can equally make it difficult for individuals to voice views which sit outside friendship group norms. In stage two, the three female researchers undertook individual interviews, again with participants of their own ethnicity, to provide a space where countervailing views might be expressed, and also to provide an opportunity for more nuanced insights into uses of SNS in drinking cultures. Participants from stage one were invited to take part in stage two. A key feature of these interviews involved the use of an internet-enabled laptop. Participants were invited to navigate to favored sites, texts, images and videos. We were interested in participants' varied uses of their own SNS profiles, in all the aspects they considered important, but were specifically interested in asking about their posting of alcohol-related content. Digital navigation capture software stored all online activity, while synchronous video recorded researcher questions and participants' responses (including nonverbal communications). This, we argue, provides a rich multimodal data stream that helps document essential aspects of how participants' make sense of their online social worlds in relation to drinking cultures. Those interested were given information sheets, had questions answered, and were assured of confidentiality and anonymity in any written research reports. All participants were Facebook users, and it was made clear to them that any information from their profiles shared during the interview would be anonymized for research purposes, whereas any information from other people's profiles would not be used in any form of dissemination as the owners of these pages had not consented to use of this material. Interviews lasted approximately one hour, and were open and flexible and driven as much as possible by participants themselves. In total 23 young people aged 18–25 years took part, including 15 females, 7 males, and one Fa'afafine. Seven were Pākehā, 8 were Māori, and 8 were Pasifika.

In order to help interpret the data collected throughout stages one and two, we needed to document and contextualize the online worlds participants were engaged in. In the last stage of the research we collated the web-based content and material, including but not limited to pages on social networking sites, which captured and engaged our participants' time and attention. We began by systematically documenting the sites referred to by our participants in stages one and two, including alcohol brand and bar Facebook pages and websites. To add breadth and depth to this database of content, we then supplemented it through weekly Google searches by research assistants across a 12-month period aimed at collating material concerning alcohol consumption, intoxication, Facebook, social networking and youth culture. Overall, 487 sites/social networking pages, including web addresses and screen captures, were collected. The majority were derived from friendship groups (275) and individual interviews (131). Systematic searching provided a total of 81 additional sites. This database was not analyzed separately. Rather, we used this material to help in the analysis of participants' accounts of their SNS use and drinking as provided by them in stages one and two. Reflecting on this content enabled greater insights into participants' drinking-related leisure activities and associated forms of meaning making, and helped produce a broader context for our interpretations of young people's online social worlds.

In sum, stages one to three deployed a range of methodological techniques aimed at generating rich, detailed, contextually complex data including transcripts, video recordings, online screen captures of browsing sessions, and a database of broader/contextually significant forms of online content linked to audio, visual and textual material not produced by participants themselves but highly relevant to them (for example Facebook pages of bars they frequented). This enabled us to gain insight into how uses of SNS were embedded into young people's social lives, and into how social life online related to young peoples' social relationships generally and drinking cultures specifically. Discussions and interviews were transcribed verbatim. For individual interviews, Transana software was used to bring together and time-synchronize the three strands of data collected, namely the video recording, transcript and screen capture recording. This allowed us to engage with the multimodality[33] evident in participants' accounts of their SNS use, that is, with the dynamic interactions between factors like text, speech, video and photography at play.

Illustrating the Value of the Research Design: Insights into Facebook Drinking Photos

Given the nature and scale of the project, we cannot provide an extensive summary of all our findings. The general point we wish to make is that our interpretative emphasis on capturing young people's processes of meaning making in context has allowed for insights occluded or under-explored in mainstream research into online drinking cultures, while opening up a space for rethinking the nature of Facebook 'users'/ use and for different understandings of the technology itself. For example, our published research has explored how young people appropriate Facebook affordances to not only represent their drinking online, but to engage in pleasurable real-time drinking practices with geographically dispersed friends which involve negotiating tensions around the fun of posting while drunk.[34] We have also explored how young people's sense making of friendship is bound up with their appropriation and negotiation of specific Facebook affordances and associated forms of novel online friendship work,[35] how their Facebook drinking displays present 'airbrushed' versions of a carefully managed and yet 'authentic' self,[36] and how self-display and friendship in online drinking cultures relate to structural constraints and power relations around class, gender, and ethnicity.[37] However, for the purposes of illustration, we will briefly re-examine here several key dimensions of the role of Facebook drinking photos in youth drinking cultures.[38] As we have previously noted, Facebook drinking photos have been singled out for concerted attention in mainstream literature due their documented popularity online, and because of the links made to their 'effects' on young people's health behaviors.

Notwithstanding its centrality to current debates, the first point we would like to emphasize is that our project's central focus on the photography that occurs on Facebook as a platform was derived adaptively from the research process itself. It emerged from young people's own accounts of drinking cultures in focus groups and interviews, rather than from any pre-existing assumptions as to Facebook's technological features or its role and significance for young people. All of our participants reported using Facebook, to a greater or lesser degree, often after having migrated to it from Bebo and/or MySpace, and most often to the exclusion of any other social networking platform (including other fairly popular sites at the time like Twitter). This is important to acknowledge, because if we asked how young people negotiate online drinking cultures today this situation may not hold. Numerous other social networking sites have become prominent since we collected our data across 2011–2012. We may have caught Facebook at the zenith of its exclusivity as a uniquely popular site with unparalleled penetration into daily routines. It may be that a variety of different sites, with different sets of affordances, are now used simultaneously by young people for sharing drinking photos, and if so, then investigating each of them, as well as the *interconnections* between them and their associated social practices, would become central to the analysis. For instance, the growth in popularity of the mobile app Snapchat, with its built in self-destruction of video and picture content, has made new technological affordances readily available for managing drinking, sociality, and self-display online that may well have been taken up by young people. Indeed, Facebook itself continues to change in response to the changing media environment it operates within, recently becoming easier to use in relation to privacy settings and more mobile friendly. Situating the analysis of online drinking cultures historically and temporally in terms of social and technological change therefore matters,[39] and yet is often overlooked in dominant approaches to studying SNS and drinking cultures. In contrast, our interpretative approach to asking young people themselves to circumscribe and describe the technologies that matter to them and how they use them provides one valid means for capturing some of this situated complexity.

Our interpretative approach was also designed to remain open to exploring diverse activities undertaken by participants on the social media platforms they chose to use. However, our thematic analyses of focus group data made it apparent that young people's social lives while on Facebook predominantly revolved around a broad, user-generated visual culture. That is, in describing its role in their everyday lives, participants consistently constructed Facebook as a *visual* medium. For them its utility is linked to its affordances for photo uploading and photo sharing across manifold day-to-day contexts and events, from the ordinary and mundane like having lunch, to the more exceptional like holidays or weekends away. In this sense, Facebook use is tied to a correlated culture of ubiquitous smartphone use, so that photo taking and routine uploading is a thoroughly normalized activity for young people. Facebook photos were valued here in a dual sense. First, as is well established in the dominant literature on drinking cultures, for their referential function. That is, as important forms of profile 'content' that act as 'markers' for self-display, and for recording and presenting (primarily with an 'audience' of peers in mind) life events, places visited, and people you know. However, equally importantly, Facebook photos were also seen as vital *discursive resources* subsequently drawn upon in online conversations. That is, they were means for re-living shared experiences, becoming catalysts for ongoing, recursive social exchanges that helped to make one's social life continually visible to one's peers, while simultaneously helping to cement friendship bonds even while friends are 'physically' absent. The temporal and spatial dimensions of Facebook photo sharing were highly valued because photos enable reflexive sociality. Uploading, sharing, tagging, 'liking', and commenting on photos sustains forms of everyday social connections for young people across time and space. This was not only evident in thematic analyses of focus groups' discussions, but equally in individual interviews as – for instance – participants commonly used photos and profile albums to navigate to other (friends') profiles and highlighted the ways photos generate on-going comments. Indeed screen captures, as well as participants' discussions in focus groups and interviews, suggested a heightened value is accorded to those photos that attract the most attention ('likes') and comments from one's peers.

It is *within* this wider culture of online socializing, tied to technologically mediated visibility, that drinking photos take on specific meanings and functions. Young people's accounts of the pleasures of heavy social drinking have always invoked identity, storytelling, friendships and socializing as key elements. Drinking stories are often told and re-told amongst peer networks, playing a crucial part in identity construction and maintaining friendships.[40] As with Facebook photography generally, our participants' accounts emphasized that Facebook drinking photos 'capture' the moment, and enable reflexive forms of enhanced socializing to ensue online. Moreover, as we have pointed out in detail elsewhere,[41] both the representative and interactive dimensions of drinking photos were constructed as being beneficial in specific, and powerful, ways. First, for young people drinking occurs in the company of one's peers and is often tied to social events, and drinking photos were therefore constructed by participants as providing particularly potent, and yet authentic, connotations of being sociable and popular. That is, they connote a 'successful' social life while carrying less risk of producing inferences that one is overtly seeking attention or 'falsely' claiming popularity. Second, our participants' accounts emphasized that drinking photos were particularly effective at facilitating recursive feedback, enticing multiple comments and attracting numerous 'likes' from one's peers, both in real time and – through leaving searchable and persistent traces of social interaction[42] – asynchronously across time as drinking narratives are stored, modified, and retrieved at will. It was this dual, heightened ability of drinking photos to represent an authentically popular social life, while also being particularly effective at *actively developing* online attention and Facebook facilitated social connections, that was highly valued. This is especially so within a culture of regular and routine photographic documentation, where the sheer weight of images produced daily raises questions as to the traditional truth claims of photography, and where many images were largely ignored.

As Gillian Rose argues, these ways of *using* specific images 'much more as communicational tools than as representational texts' is a key feature of contemporary visual culture which deserves closer scrutiny when developing our forms of methodological enquiry.[43] That is, too often visual research methodologies focus solely on the creation of images as mechanisms for making aspects of the social visible. This focus on *visibility* obscures the *visuality* of contemporary cultural practices where images become meaningful objects central to symbolic and communicative activity, at the same time underplaying the competency of research participants as skilled negotiators of visual culture.[44] In our data, a complex interplay is revealed between the representative and 'social/interactional' functions of Facebook drinking photos, which is important for young people's social lives, but is left under-explored in investigations that focus too closely on the representative aspects of photos as they are displayed on individuated profiles. While drinking photos, as a form of profile 'content', are clearly a key part of individuated self—displays, the 'user' here equally emerges as situated in a broader, more complex and collective cultural context which they constantly negotiate, and which is not reducible to individuated levels of analysis.

There is much more to be said about these processes. In particular, realizing the benefits of drinking displays demanded an enormous amount of online self-management work from young people, in terms of strategically choosing images to upload and on-going processes of monitoring, tagging and un-tagging oneself from images uploaded by others. Participants articulated an acute awareness of the imperative placed upon them to remain in command of the body and its online display while drinking, especially in the knowledge that employers and others (such as parents) may form broader 'invisible audiences'[45] watching peer-orientated drinking displays. The authentic popularity achieved through drinking displays is highly valued, but is always *precarious*. Indeed the continued willingness to transparently reveal/perform drinking practices online to one's peers despite this broader risk of 'outside' moral judgment by others, contributed to the peer-sanctioned, relatively unique form of authenticity drinking photos produce 'within' the peer group. This enhanced their effectiveness as facilitators of young people's online sociality. Moreover, and perhaps most importantly, all these practices are riven with power relations related to gender, sexuality, class and ethnicity. Young people's willingness and ability to engage in online drinking cultures as a site of self-realization and authentic popularity/ sociality, and the associated amount of work drinking photos require in terms of managing self-displays, is always contingent on structural forms of domination that must be actively navigated, and contested, while online.[46] The risks and benefits of drinking displays are unevenly distributed across the social formation.

We don't have the space to explicate these important concerns here. Rather we would end this section by briefly pointing out that the form of detailed, contextual analysis multiple qualitative methods provide enables a different form of theory building from dominant approaches focused on the 'effects' of Facebook content. For example we have argued that the complex, multivalent accounts young people provide through qualitative methodologies can form the basis for a conjunctural analysis.[47] This form of theorizing, following the impetus of the youth (sub) cultures approach developed in Birmingham's Centre For Contemporary Cultural Studies, does not simply ask *why* young people produce drinking photos, but focuses on why *now*? That is, why has 'online youth drinking' become so prevalent in young people's social lives, and why is this attracting such concerted attention from the media, academia, and policy makers? Why is this happening at this moment, and how does this relate to the 'political, economic, and sociocultural changes'[48] of the current time? In our published work in this area we have highlighted connections between the processes young people engage in as we describe them above and broader forces of social, technological and historical change. We examine how, for instance, the affordances and algorithmic structure of Facebook that actively encourage the online display of drinking cultures reflect and reinforce the broader formation a new 'attention economy', where neoliberal forms of popularity have become a dominant means for generating wealth, and where young people are exhorted to recreate themselves as 'brands'.[49] In this way, the contextual, situated richness of qualitative methodologies enables a wider, more 'generalizable' form of critique pertinent to understanding contemporary media technological forms and their users/audiences.

Conclusions: Adapting, Applying and Re-valuing Qualitative Audience Methodologies in Studies of Social Media

In this chapter we have described the design of a team-based, qualitative research project into the nature of new online drinking cultures, and have outlined some of the alternative insights that qualitative designs generate which are occluded in the development of more mainstream research into SNS and drinking. In doing so we have argued that qualitative methodologies like focus groups, interviews and broader archival research approaches, traditionally associated with 'audience studies' of 'mass media', can be productively adapted to study contemporary online contexts like SNS. This is an important point to re-make in the current moment. As Martin Hand argues, qualitative social research has shifted markedly over time in response to changes in online phenomena, but 'arguably finds itself in 'crisis' when faced with algorithms and ubiquitous digital data'.[50] In current data-intensive online environments like Facebook, so much of the 'social' seems to be automatically 'captured' through the analysis of user-generated data on profiles that the rationale and advantages for generating qualitative research designs – beyond the profile and the data it readily contains – needs to be argued for anew. We have sought to demonstrate how the ability of our qualitative methods to contextualize, situate and critique 'audience'/user practices enables productive new insights into both users and the technologies they engage with.

Acknowledgments

The authors wish to acknowledge Marsden funding administered by the Royal Society of New Zealand (contract MAU0911).The authors would also like to acknowledge the contributions of our fellow researchers on this project: Helen Moewaka Barnes, Fiona Hutton, Kerry-Ellen Vroman, Patricia Niland, Lina Samu, and Dee O'Carroll.

Notes

1 For an overview of these issues in the New Zealand context see Antonia Lyons, Timothy McCreanor, Ian Goodwin, Christine Griffin, Fiona Hutton, Helen Moewaka Barnes, Dee O'Carroll, Lina Samu, Patricia Niland, and Kerryellen Vroman, "Young Adult Drinking Cultures in Aotearoa New Zealand," *Sites: A Journal of Social Anthropology and Cultural Studies* 11 (2004), 78–102.
2 Christine Hine, *The Internet* (Oxford: Oxford University Press, 2013).
3 See Hine, *The Internet*, 29.
4 Kathleen Beullens and Adriaan Schepers, "Display of Alcohol Use on Facebook: A Content Analysis," *Cyberpschology, Behaviour and Social Networking* 16(7) (2013), 497–503.
5 Beullens and Schepers, "Display of Alcohol use on Facebook", 497.
6 Katie Egan and Megan Moreno, "Alcohol References on Undergraduate Males' Facebook Profiles," *American Journal of Men's Health* 5 (2011), 413–420.
7 Richard Griffiths and Sally Caswsell, "Intoxigenic Digital Spaces? Youth, Social Networking Sites and Alcohol Marketing," *Drug and Alcohol Review* 29, 525–530.
8 Megan Moren, Leslie Briner, Amanda Williams, Libby Brockman, Leslie Walker, and Dimitri Christakis, "A Content Analysis of Displayed Alcohol References on a Social Networking Site," *Journal of Adolescent Health* 47, 168–175.

9 See Christine Griffin, Andrew Bengry-Howell, Chris Hackley, Willm Mistral and Isabelle Szmigin, "The Allure of Belonging: Young People's Drinking Practices and Collective Identification," in *Identity in the 21st Century: New Trends in Changing Times*, ed. Margaret Wetherell (London, UK: Palgrave, 2009), 213–230; Antonia Lyons and Sarah Willot "Alcohol Consumption, Gender Identities and Women's Changing Social Positions," *Sex Roles* 59 (2008), 694–712.

10 See Sally Caswell, "Current Status of Alcohol Marketing Policy – An Urgent Challenge for Global Governance," *Addiction* 107, 478–485; Timothy McCreanor,Helen Moewaka Barnes, Hector Kaiwai, Suaree Borell and Amanda Gregory, "Creating intoxigenic environments: Marketing alcohol to young people in Aotearoa New Zealand," *Social Science and Medicine* 67(6) (2008), 938–946.

11 See Rebecca Brown and Melissa Gregg, "The Pedagogy of Regret: Facebook, Binge Drinking and Young Women," *Continuum* 26(3) (2012), 357–369; Nicholas Carah and Michelle Shaul, "Brands on Instagram: Point, Tap, Swipe, Glance," *Mobile Media and Communication* 4(1) (2016), 69–84; James Nicholls, "Everyday, Everywhere: Alcohol Marketing and Social Media—Current Trends," *Alcohol and Alcoholism* 47(4) (2012), 486–493.

12 Jürgen Rehm, Colin Mathers, Svetlana Popova, Montarat Thavorncharoensap, Yot Teerawattananon, Jayadeep Patra, "Global burden of disease and injury and economic cost attributable to alcohol use and alcohol-use disorders," *Lancet* 373 (2009), 2223–33.

13 Angela Fournier, Erin Hall, Patricia Ricke and Brittany Storey, "Alcohol and the Social Network: Online Social Networking Sites and College Students' Perceived Drinking Norms," *Psychology and Popular Media Culture* 2(2) (2013), 86.

14 Fournier et al., "Alcohol and the Social Network".

15 Dana Litt and Michelle Stock, "Adolescent Alcohol-Related Risk Cognitions: The Roles of Social Norms and Social Networking Sites," *Psychology of Addictive Behaviours* 25(4) (2011), 708.

16 Joshua Heber West, Parley Cougar Hall, Kyle Prier, Carl Lee Hanson, Christophe Giraud-Carrier, E. Shannon Neeley, and Michael Dean Barnes, "Temporal Variability of Problem Drinking on Twitter," *Open Journal of Preventive Medicine* 2(1) (2012), 43–48.

17 See, for example, Johnathan D'Angelo, Bradley Kerr, and Megan Moreno, "Facebook Drinking Displays as Predictors of Binge Drinking: From the Virtual to the Visceral," *Bull Sci Technol Soc.* 34 (2014), 159–169; Sarah Stoddard, Jose Bauermeister, Deborah Gordon-Messser, Michelle Johns and Marc Zimmerman, "Permissive Norms and Young Adults' Alcohol and Marijuana Use: The Role of Online Communities," *Journal of Studies on Alcohol and Drugs* 73 (2012), 968–975.

18 Brad Ridout, Andrew Campbell and Lousie Ellis, "'Off Your Face(book)': Alcohol in Online Social Identity Construction and its Relation to problem Drinking in University Students," *Drug and Alcohol Review* 31 (2012), 20.

19 Ridout, Campbell and Ellis, "Off your Face(book)", 20.

20 Sonia Livingstone, "From Mass to Social Media? Advancing Accounts of Social Change," *Social Media + Society* April to June (2015), 1–3. DOI: 10.1177/2056305115578875.

21 Griffiths and Caswsell, "Intoxigenic Digital Spaces?," 525.

22 Megan Moreno and Jennfier Whitehill, "Influence of Social Media on Alcohol Use in Adolescents and Young Adults", *Alcohol Research Current Reviews* 36 (2014), 91–100.

23 D'Angelo, Kerr, and Moreno, "Facebook Drinking Displays as Predictors of Binge Drinking," 159.

24 Brown and Gregg, "The Pedagogy of Regret".

25 See Livingstone "From Mass to Social Media?" for a discussion of this tendency in the broad range of disciplines (outside of media studies) that study social media.

26 See Andy Ruddock, "Media Studies 2.0? Binge Drinking and Why Audiences Still Matter," *Sociology Compass* 2(1) (2008), 1–15 DOI 10.1111/j.1751-9020.2007.00040.x; Sonia Livingston and Ranjana Das, "The End of Audiences? Theoretical Echoes of Reception Amid the Uncertainties of Use," in *A Companion to New Media Dynamics*, eds. John Hartley, Jean Burgess and Axel Bruns (London: Blackwell, 2013), 104–121.

27 Sonia Livingstone, "From Mass to Social Media?," 2.

28 Ian Hutchby, "Technologies, Texts and Affordances," *Sociology* 35(2) (2001), 441–456.

29 Brett McEwan, Maxine Campbell, & David Swain "New Zealand culture of intoxication: Local and global influences," *New Zealand Sociology*, 25 (2) (2010), 15–37.

30 New Zealand Ministry of Health, Alcohol Use 2012/13: New Zealand Health Survey (Wellington, NZ: Ministry of Health, 2015).

31 Griffin et al., "The Allure of Belonging"; Lyons and Willot "Alcohol Consumption, Gender Identities and Women's Changing Social Positions".

32 Liz Spencer and Ray Pahl, *Rethinking Friendship: Hidden Solidarities Today* (Princeton, NJ: Pirnceton University Press, 2006).

33 See Gunter Kress, *Multimodality: A Social Semiotic Approach to Contemporary Communication* (London: Routledge, 2010).

34 Helen Moewaka Barnes, Timothy McCreanor, Ian Goodwin, Antonia Lyons, Christine Griffin, and Fiona Hutton, "Alcohol and Social Media: Drinking and Drunkenness While Online," *Critical Public Health* 26(1) (2016), 62–76.

35 Patricia Niland, Antonia Lyons, Ian Goodwin and Fiona Hutton, "Friendship Work on Facebook: Young Adults' Understandings and Practices of Friendship," *Journal of Community and Applied Social Psychology*," 25 (2015), 123–137.

36 Patricia Niland, Antonia Lyons, Ian Goodwin and Fiona Hutton, "'See it doesn't look pretty does it?': Young Adults' Airbrushed Drinking Practices on Facebook," *Psychology and Health* 29(8) (2014), 877–895.

37 See, for example, Fiona Hutton, Christine Griffin, Antonia Lyons, Patricia Niland, and Timothy McCreanor, "'Tragic Girls' and 'Crack Whores': Alcohol, Femininity and Facebook," *Feminism and Psychology* 26(1) (2016), 73–93.

38 These are primarily adapted from Ian Goodwin, Christine Griffin, Antonia Lyons, Timothy McCreanor, and Helen Moewaka Barnes, "Precarious Popularity: Facebook Drinking Photos, the Attention Economy, and the Regime of the Branded Self," *Social Media + Society* 2(1) (2016), 1–13.

39 It is necessary, in this sense, to set out some of the key technological features of the Facebook profile and the platform's affordances during our specific period of study, and in particular to highlight those features our research participants engaged with most often. Upon logging in users would regularly check their "notifications" and "personal messages" via icons located handily to the right of the Facebook logo (and if indicated via a third icon, also check any friend requests), often responding to new content or messages as they did so. Many female participants reported using notifications, which

could be monitored via mobile phone, to immediately check what photos they were "tagged in" in order to vet them (quickly un-tagging any content deemed inappropriate so it disappeared from their wall). The "friends list" formed a prominent component of the profile occupying the left of the screen. The newsfeed and wall were regularly checked and Facebook chat functionality was highly valued for enabling real time engagement with friends. Friends were automatically highlighted by Facebook as being online at the same time (although it was possible to log in and disengage from chat so that friends could not see you were online – an option utilized for example when users were at work). Facebook's video sharing and photo sharing functionalities, including the ability to upload content, tag content, comment upon and "like" content, were also regularly utilized. "Status updates" were also key, and "events" and "notes" features were available, with the former engaged with much more often and regularly than the latter. The "people you may know" section and "sponsored" links/content were prominently displayed on profiles to the right of the page. The profile went through several minor format changes, and the site's privacy policy and associated settings were regularly changed. Perhaps the most prominent shift that occurred during the study period was the introduction of "timeline" (at the end of 2011/beginning of 2012, after much of our data had been collected). For a detailed discussion of Facebook's specific development from 2004 to 2013 see Niels Brügger, "A Brief History of Facebook as a Media Text: The Development of an Empty Structure," *First Monday* 20(5) (2015).

40 Griffin et al., "The Allure of Belonging"; Lyons and Willot "Alcohol Consumption, Gender Identities and Women's Changing Social Positions".
41 Goodwin et al., "Precarious Popularity".
42 danah boyd "Social Network Sites as Networked Publics: Affordances, Dynamics and Implications," in *Networked Self: Identity, Community and Culture on Social Networking Sites*, ed. Zizi Papacharissi (New York, NY: Routledge, 2010), 39–58.
43 Gillian Rose, "On the Relationship Between 'Visual Research' and Contemporary Visual Culture," *The Sociological Review* 62 (2014), 24–46.
44 Rose " 'Visual Research' and Contemporary Visual Culture".
45 see boyd "Social Network Sites as Networked Publics".
46 Hutton et al., "'Tragic Girls' and Crack 'Whores'"; Goodwin et al., "Precarious Popularity".
47 Ian Goodwin, Antonia Lyons, Christine Griffin, Timothy McCreanor, "Ending Up Online: Interrogating Mediated Youth Drinking Cultures," *Mediated Youth Cultures: The Internet, Belonging, and New Cultural Configurations*, eds. Brady Robards and Andy Bennett (London, Palgrave, 2014), 59–74; Goodwin et al., "Precarious Popularity".
48 Stuart Hall and Tony Jefferson, "Once More Around 'Resistance Through Rituals'," in *Resistance Through Rituals: Youth Subcultures and Post-War Britain*, eds. Stuart Hall and Tony Jefferson (London, UK: Routledge, 2006), vii–xxxv.
49 Goodwin et al., "Precarious Popularity".
50 Martin Hand, "From Cyberspace to the Dataverse: Trajectories in Digital Social Research," *Big Data? Qualitative Approaches to Digital Research* 13 (2014), 1–27.

9 Ambient Liveness

Searchable Audiences and Second Screens

Michele Zappavigna

Introduction: Second-screen Viewing

Posting commentary to social media while watching television has become a pervasive practice. For example, using Twitter to post an observation about a show in real-time is known as 'live-tweeting'.[1] It typically involves the use of a mobile device, such as a smart phone or tablet, that acts as an interactive 'second screen'.[2] Access to social media services on these devices means that viewers are increasingly networked in terms of both the 'synchronicity' of media supporting their communication, and the 'simultaneity' of other audience members present in the ambient social network.[3] Second screens allow these viewers to produce their own texts, and to interact with each other, both directly, and via mass communicative practices such as hashtagging. This chapter employs corpus-based discourse analysis to explore the communicative practices viewers engage in when live-tweeting a particular program broadcast in Australia, *My Kitchen Rules*.[4] In particular the chapter focuses on the kind of opinion and sentiment construed by these viewers as they forge different kinds of attitudinal alignment. This type of communication is at once an emergent practice and embedded in a broader history of people commenting on media via multiple communicative channels. In exploring this meaning-making I will introduce the concept of 'ambient liveness', that is, how the temporal affordances of social media inflect communicative practices, in particular, the expression of attitude regarding televisual media.

The real-time discourse produced by these viewers is available to audience researchers in ways that have not previously been seen. This discourse has also been seen as a 'backchannel' form of communication,[5] in other words, as supplementary to more primary forms of experience, or more principal forms of media consumption. Nick Anstead and Ben O'Loughlin term the emergence of audience backchannels as the rise of the viewertariat, 'viewers who use online publishing platforms and social tools to interpret, publicly comment on, and debate a television broadcast while they are watching it'.[6] Studies of second-screen viewing have focused on a range of genres such as televised election debates[7] and political debates,[8] current affairs shows,[9] and talk shows, as well as differences across genres of TV shows.[10] Other contexts in which back-channeling has been documented include collaborative learning environments,[11] education,[12] conferences,[13] question-and-answer sessions,[14] and other kinds of large events, such as fashion trade shows.[15] Backchannelling has also played a role in elections and debates,[16] and public events and crises.[17] Some studies adopt a cognitive focus, for example, aiming to determine how second-screen viewing affects factual recall,[18] influences users' opinions,[19] and affects the neural indicators of engagement with the primary media being consumed.[20] There has also been interest in how second screens act as a technology of fandom allowing fans to commune around a shared media text.[21] Two-screen viewing not only facilitates real-time audience interaction during TV shows,[22] but also enable fans to engage in creative practices such as roleplaying[23] or simulating characters.[24]

The social connections produced via backchannel communication may form a kind of 'intangible, clandestine community'[25] or 'conversational shadow',[26] operating in parallel to media or real-world events. This loose notion of social-media supported 'conversation' is in keeping with accounts of microblogging as a conversational technology. For example, microblogging has been variously described as a kind of 'conversational exchange',[27] as 'lightweight chat',[28] as 'prompting opportunistic conversations',[29] as 'a specific social dialect, in which individual users are clearly singled out and engaged in a conversation'[30] and as constituted by 'dialogue acts'.[31] However, linguistic study, of the kind undertaken in this chapter, is required to understand the particular conversation-like practices that characterize live-tweeting via second screens, and the particular communicative functions they enact.

Ambient Liveness and 'Real-time'

Microblogging, and social media more generally as a communicative platform, foregrounds time as an important social variable. For example, Twitter describes itself as 'a real-time information network'[32] where instant engagement with the social stream[33] is critical. It is now common for feeds of 'live-tweets' to appear in news broadcasts, or during programs involving audience commentary, such as chat shows and panels. 'Real-time' as a concept ascribes value to an apparent increase in the pace at which we engage with internet-mediated resources, and with members of our social networks. The term is often used uncritically as synonymous to 'clock-time' or 'synchronous time', where social media users are posting about events almost 'as they happen' via mobile media. The classifier 'real', however, also has a legitimating function: web-based time is positioned as being the equal to the 'offline' time of face-to-face social interaction. At the same time it is 'hyper-real', potentially affording superior access to what is happening in our social networks in any given moment. In addition, the discourse of real-time appears to be 'a central ideological feature of global capitalism', involved not only in cyberculture, but in finance culture and the experience of living in city environments.[34]

Agnate to the concept of real-time is the notion of 'liveness',[35] historically associated with broadcast media, and used to classify media as being broadcast at the time that it recorded. With the advent of social media we see new forms of liveness emerging. Practices such as 'citizen journalism', whereby users post about newsworthy events that happen to occur near them, depend on the value ascribed to liveness as a form of eyewitness.[36] Interestingly, the notion also appears to inform more mundane practices, such as the chronicle of daily routine (*e.g.,* posting about your morning coffee at the time that you drink it[37]). Nick Couldry[38] suggests that liveness invokes a potential connection with central social realities shared at the time they are occurring, and that the range of media to which this concept can be applied is expanding. He proposes two new 'rival forms of liveness: 'online liveness', as a form of social co-presence mediated by internet technologies, and 'group liveness', facilitating continuous mediation via mobile technologies.

Social media use has collapsed the distinction between these two forms of liveness, establishing what I refer to as 'ambient liveness'. This kind of liveness presupposes that there are always others, co-present in the social stream, ready to engage with the content posted via a social media service. As such, liveness may be thought of as the ever-present possibility of the attention of multiple participants in a social network. This chapter explores the communicative patterns that are associated with such ambient liveness, in particular, how live-tweeting practices afford the opportunity for forging different attitudinal alignments and forms of 'ambient affiliation'.[39]

The chapter begins by introducing the *My Kitchen Rules* (MKR) corpus used as a case-study, and the reference corpus, HERMES2013, used as a baseline of more generalized tweeting practices. It then details the model of evaluative language used for discourse analysis, and applies this model to the discursive patterns observed in the corpus, with a view to understanding the communicative practices characterizing live-tweeting.

MKR Corpus

The MKR corpus explored as a case study in this paper consisted of 6508 tweets (83,793 words) posted from the morning of March 18, 2015 until the afternoon of March 20, 2015. The posts were about the television show *My Kitchen Rules* and the selection criteria used to construct the corpus was to include all tweets during this period containing the hashtag, #MKR. A limitation of such hashtag-based research is that it does not necessarily capture all the communication surrounding the primary media, since there will be posts that do not use the hashtag, and in particular, posts that are replies may omit the tag. However, hashtags do, at the very least, make obtaining a snapshot of particular discourse at a particular time, achievable. A truly exhaustive corpus would be very difficult to create since it is possible to comment on a TV show without mentioning its name or using an established hashtag, and thus both hashtags and keyword searches will result in patchiness in terms of exhaustivity. In addition, since 2010, due to its increasing commercial development, Twitter has not made the 'firehose' of all tweets available at an affordable price for most research projects,[40] and instead many researchers rely on the 'garden hose' feed which is a randomized (via an algorithm that Twitter do not disclose) selection of the more comprehensive feed.

The posts in the MKR corpus were scraped from the Twitter Application Programming Interface (API) using the DMI Twitter Capturing and Analysis Toolset (DMI-TCAT).[41] The corpus collection period aimed to approximate a 48-hour cycle and spanned two episodes of MKR that screened in Australia. As Table 9.1 suggests, the number of posts across these two days was also reasonably consistent, in terms of overall tweeting, and in terms of the amount of tweets with links, hashtags and mentions, as well as the level of retweets and replies. This suggests that the live-tweeting occurring has some level of communicative consistency across different episodes of the show. Of particular note is the relative infrequency of posts with replies. If backchannel commentary is to be thought of as conversational, analysis that moves beyond turn-taking as a conversational strategy is needed.

Tweets were collected on March 20, 2015 until 4 pm, deliberately stopping collection three hours prior to the screening of the show to demonstrate that minimal posting occurred outside the time in which the TV show aired (*i.e.,* around 7 pm). The frequency of tweeting is presented visually in Figure 9.1 which shows the frequency of tweets along the *y* axis, and time along the *x* axis. This figure also gives some indication of the number of users compared with tweets, suggesting that there are users who post multiple times during the broadcasts.

Table 9.1 General composition of the MKR corpus

Date	Number of tweets	Tweets with links	Tweets with hashtags	Tweets with mentions	Retweets	Replies
18/03/15	2963	245	2956	907	520	157
19/03/15	3243	258	3239	1018	603	188
20/03/15	161	84	159	82	49	7

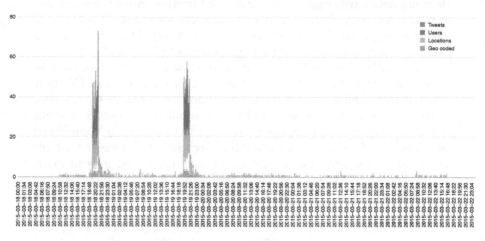

Figure 9.1 Tweets in the MKR corpus over time.

The concordance software, AntConc,[42] was employed to explore the communicative patterns in the corpus, with concordance lines used for investigating particular instances. Concordance lines are samples of particular lexical or grammatical patterns presented together with a pre-defined amount of co-text (*e.g.*, five words to the left and five words to the right of the search word). For example, concordance lines for the temporal adverb '*right now*' are shown in Table 9.2. These differ from traditional concordance lines, which offer only limited windows of co-text compared to the length of the entire text, in that the entire post can be displayed because Twitter posts are such short texts.

Evaluative Language and Live-tweeting

Given that live-tweeting involves responding to some form of primary media and affords the opportunity for expressing opinion and making observations, it is unsurprising that evaluative language plays an important role in this form of discourse. However, in order to understand the functions of this communication, it is necessary to employ a framework,

Table 9.2 Concordance lines for 'right now' from the MKR corpus

The stress levels are so high	**right now!**	#MKR
The stress levels are so high	**right now!**	#MKR
I'm on edge	**right now.**	#MKR
Devastated	**right now**	:(I can't hold it together #MKR
Heartbroken	**right now.**	:(Tears are flowing. #MKR #friendsforever
Freaking out	**right now!**	Want them both to win! #MKR

grounded in linguistic theory, for exploring evaluative language. The model adopted in this paper is known as the Appraisal Framework,[43] developed within Systemic Functional Linguistics. This framework details three regions of meaning in which evaluation is construed in language: AFFECT (expressing emotion), JUDGMENT (assessing behavior) and APPRECIATION (estimating value).

The choices between these different meanings are represented in Figure 9.2 as a system network,[44] that is, a network of interrelated options that are organized paradigmatically, in terms of 'what could go instead of what', rather than syntagmatically in terms of structure.[45] The examples shown in the boxes are taken from HERMES2013. Each example illustrates a type of ATTITUDE and the network may be further specified to greater levels of delicacy depending on the kind of analysis for which it is being used. ATTITUDE that is INSCRIBED is realized via explicit evaluative choices, while ATTITUDE which is INVOKED is suggested via linguistic choices that imply evaluation but do not employ evaluative lexis.

For example, consider the types of ATTITUDE realized in the following posts about the contestant Drasko:

Drasko kinda **annoys** me.....#mkr
Drasko is a **walking fiasco** #MKR
Drasko and Bianca are my **fav** couple #mkr

In the first post Drasko is the trigger of negative emotion, with '*annoys*' realizing negative AFFECT. In the second post he is the target of negative moral opinion, with '*walking fiasco*' realizing negative JUDGMENT in terms of capacity. In the final post, together with his partner, Drasko is assessed in terms of aesthetic opinion, with '*fav*' realizing positive APPRECIATION.

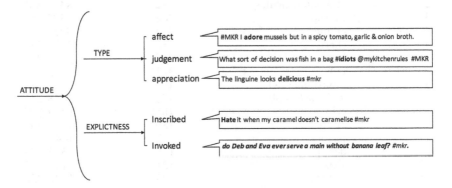

Figure 9.2 The system of attitude.

Comparing the MKR Corpus to a Reference Corpus

In order to understand the communicative practices observable in the MKR corpus, and make claims about how this live-tweeting might differ from general tweeting, it is necessary to use a larger, randomized Twitter corpus as a baseline. This is what is known in Corpus Linguistics as a 'reference corpus'. The reference corpus used in this study was HERMES2013, a 100 million word corpus of approximately 10 million randomized tweets collected in 2013. The MKR corpus contained fewer @mentions (3% of the total words) compared with the reference corpus (6.5%). This is perhaps due to the preference, which we explore later in the chapter, of referring to contestants in the show using vocatives rather than @mentions. Assessing the difference in hashtagging levels is problematic, since a hashtag was used in the selection criteria for the MKR corpus. Approximately 19% of posts in the MKR corpus were retweets, a similar level to the reference corpus (25%). These kinds of structural differences are not particularly illuminating. What is more interesting is to compare the different kinds of meanings that are made in the corpora.

Unsurprisingly, the discourse in the MKR corpus conformed to a more restricted field (semantic domain) than the reference corpus. A keyword analysis was performed to determine which words in the MKR corpus were key when compared with HERMES2013, that is, which words occurred at a significantly different frequency to the reference corpus (Table 9.3).

Table 9.3 Keywords in the MKR corpus using HERMES2013 as a reference corpus

N	Word	Freq.	Keyness
1	#mkr[1]	6759	96386.374
2	@mykitchenrules	582	8331.808
3	drasko	308	4395.811
4	emilie	312	3921.515
5	sheri	285	3623.213
6	kat	355	3170.227
7	pub	322	2683.606
8	#mkrpubcrawl	186	2662.743
9	#friendsfaceoff	178	2548.216
10	celine	185	1944.095
11	andre	189	1669.646
12	teams	237	1644.847
13	debra	133	1585.843
14	shaz	121	1442.721
15	sudden	175	1328.036

[1]Since #MKR was part of the selection criteria it can be ignored.

It is also unsurprising that tweets to the official @mykitchenrules account are key. More interesting is the general types of words that were key:

- MKR-specific hashtags, *e.g., #MKRpubcrawl*
- Contestant names, *e.g., Drasko*
- Competition-related lexis, *e.g., teams*
- Cooking-related lexis, *e.g., cooking*
- Evaluative language about the above, *e.g., 'fantastic food'*

The sections which follow later in the chapter explore the types of meaning associated with each of these and how they afford forms of ambient affiliation. As Table 9.3 suggests, discourse about the show's contestants was the most prevalent area of semantic difference between the corpora. The discourse was typically highly evaluative in nature, spanning the three types of attitudinal meaning introduced in the previous section. The most frequent key attitudinal lexis in the corpus (Table 9.4) was predominately APPRECIATION, typically invoking JUDGMENT targeted at the capacity of the contestants.

For example, consider the concordance lines for 'raw' in Table 9.5. What without context might appear to be a purely ideational reference to an uncooked state, is in fact charged with negative value, invoked through co-occurring exclamation of incredulity (*e.g.,* 2, 3, 4) and mock-delight (*e.g.,* 1, 6). While this evaluation is realized in the texts as

Table 9.4 Key evaluative lexis in the MKR corpus

N	Evaluation	Freq.	Keyness	Example
69	raw	78	419.371	Don't serve the judges **raw** seafood. #MKR
71	moist	48	406.934	New drinking game: Whenever some says '**MOIST**', drink! #mkr
106	refined	25	252.961	Apparently **refined** palates only like rare steak #MKR
139	rare	46	178.725	**Rare** steak is such an acquired taste! GREAT FOR FOOD CRITICS-RISKY FOR GENERAL PUBLIC!!! #MKR
158	mmmm	31	157.136	**Mmmm** banana dessert #banana #dessert #yum #saltedcaramel #LicksLips #MKR
166	sad	103	151.483	It's so **sad** that one of these teams will leave us tonight. #MKR @mykitchenrules
192	yum	34	128.595	#MKR. I suddenly feel like a curry. That looks **yum**

Table 9.5 Concordance lines for 'raw'

1	Mmmmmm a slab of refrigerated	raw	meat rolled in grass! Yes, please!! #MKR
2	Damn, i don't know how people can eat	raw	beef #MKR
3	#MKR how can anyone	raw	eat meat?
4	Is that	raw	or still alive, I can't tell#MKR
5	#MKR thats not carpaccio, thats	raw	steak
6	Mmm	raw	seafood again! #MKR
7	Aww that prawn is	raw!	:(#MKR
8	Damn, you don't want to hear the words "It's	raw"	when someones eating your dish #MKR

APPRECIATION, it invokes JUDGMENT of the abilities of the contestants who have made the dishes being assessed. Rallying around such shared negative assessment is a form of communing affiliation in which the live-tweeters create ambient solidarity through shared critique. We will return to this form of affiliation later in this chapter.

Communing: The function of Hashtags in Live-tweeting

Social tagging, for example inserting a hashtag such as #MKR into a social media post, plays an important role in live-tweeting. Hashtags are a form of linguistic innovation[46] that have spread from microblogging to different forms of social media and have been integrated into other mediated contexts such as television and advertising. Hashtags are prefixed by the # symbol which at a typographic level, acts as a particular kind of linguistic marker, indicating the beginning of a tag, and its special status as metadiscourse. The # symbol has an interesting semiotic history, originating with the pound symbol as an abbreviation derived from the Latin *libra pondo* (pound in weight) and subsequently taking on a range of uses depending on context, for instance as an 'octothorpe' on Touch-Tone phones developed by Bell Labs in the 1960s.[47] Hashtag use may have arisen 'from a history among computer programmers of prefacing specialized words with punctuation marks, such as $ and * for variables and pointers, or the # sign itself for identifying HTML anchor points'.[48] Special characters of this kind are typographic conventions used in markup languages to indicate when something is part of the 'markup' rather than the 'content' being annotated.

Michele Zappavigna,[49] drawing on M.A.K. Halliday's[50] notion of linguistic metafunctions, identifies three important discursive functions that hashtags can play in live-tweeting:

- An *interpersonal* function of enacting ambient relationships and construing ambient community.

- A *textual* function of organizing the post (acting as a form of punctuation) and affording aggregation (intertextually associating the tweet with other tweets containing the same tag).
- An *experiential* function of classifying the post a being about a particular topic.

Table 9.6 presents the 10 most frequent hashtags in the corpus. The most obvious function of hashtags in the MKR corpus is an experiential function of indicating the topic of the tweet. Indeed, this function was leveraged in creating the corpus, the assumption being that tweets tagged with #MKR were about the show. An example of this topic-marking function is the following, where without the hashtag providing context, the particular target of the positive AFFECT construed in the tweet is unclear:

I need a lot of tissues tonight. Omg! I love both of the teams **#MKR**

The tag indicates that the teams appraised are part of the TV show. However, hashtags can have functions beyond such topic-marking, in particular interpersonal functions involved in how attitudinal alignments are negotiated in the discourse. For example:

@mykitchenrules cook-off! Good luck girls! #mkr #mkr2015 **#soexcited**

In this post the hashtag, '*#soexcited*', is an evaluative metacomment with the interpersonal function of construing AFFECT regarding the dimension of the TV show referenced in the body of the post. The broader social function of this type of tag is to invoke solidarity with a potential network of co-emoters who share the sentiment presented in the tweet.

While the most frequent tags have a predominately experiential function, at the other end of the spectrum there was a set of 419 hashtags

Table 9.6 Most frequent hashtags in the MKR corpus

	Hashtag	Freq.	Example
1	#mkr	5935	This is not looking good for Emilie. :(**#MKR**
2	#mkr2015	292	Both teams are so cute and focused, not sure who will win #MKR **#mkr2015**
3	#mkrpubcrawl	176	Someone better make a Parma **#MKRPubCrawl** #MKR
4	#friendsfaceoff	140	This is gonna be massive!! **#friendsfaceoff** #MKR
5	#suddendeath	46	Come on Robert and Lynzey!!! Kill it in **#SuddenDeath** on Monday. #MKR #MKRPubCrawl

(with a frequency of one) that construe highly interpersonal meanings (Table 9.7). These tags clearly do not have marking a particular topic as their primary function, and it is unlikely for anyone to conduct a search using such idiosyncratic tags. Instead the main function appears to be to enact evaluative metacommentary with a humorous edge, for example:

> "It's a lot of pressure in a commercial kitchen!" No shit, Sherlock. #MKR #CaptainObvious

The hashtag in this post construes negative JUDGMENT as a metacomment targeted at the quoted speaker.

The hashtags in the corpus were able to make a large variety of interpersonal meanings about the TV show, the contestants, the judges, and other viewers. For instance, interpersonal hashtags spanned three of the four different types of speech function defined by Halliday and C.M.I.M Matthiessen;[51] *statements, questions, offers,* and *commands*. For example, the following is an instance of a hashtag realizing a *statement* that invokes negative AFFECT:

> Is it wrong that I just bought Pete Evans saying 'The Score Is A Ten' as a ringtone? **#WeNeverGotATen** #MKR

Questions realized in hashtags were often rhetorical and used to produce additional attitudinal metacommentary:

> So Devo! Neither team deserves to be eliminated! #MKR **#Whygod-why** @mykitchenrules

Table 9.7 Examples of hashtags with a frequency of 1

Hashtag	Example
#iwanttobebestfriendswith allofyou	Seriously, #MyKitchenRules? My two favourite teams against each other?! This is madness! **#iwanttobebestfriendswithallofyou** #seriously #MKR
#katandandjefailbigtime	Have #KatAndAndje EVER made a successful fish dish? like... you know... their speciality? #mkr here's hoping **#KatAndAndjeFailBigTime**
#lovelygirls	unlucky Sheri n Emilie #chinup #lovelygirls #mkr
#snobberyatitsbest	Wrong ... a large amount of pub goers won't want to eat "raw" steak.. #stubbornwomen #MKR **#snobberyatitsbest**
#wankers	I've been to a few pubs in life but never had Ling en Pappiote **#wankers** #mkr
#keepingitclassy	Bearded clams as finger food **#keepingitclassy** #mkr

Commands often realized some form of JUDGMENT, for instance the following example targeted at other viewers in the social network:

> OMG! Stop with the fat hate at Celine. Pathetic and horrible people - improve yourself instead of criticising others #mkr **#StopBullying**

The only function not performed was *offers* of goods or services, a semantic function more typical of promotional discourses.

Hashtags could evaluate a particular target in the tweet (*e.g.,* a contestant), the entire body of the tweet (often a situation presented in the show) or the entire post, including other tags. The evaluative hashtags in the corpus were observed to realize all the systems of ATTITUDE[52] introduced earlier. For instance, there were tags construing AFFECT (expressing emotion), often the viewer's reaction to an event in the show:

> Time sure does fly in that kitchen! The stress is really starting to kick in now **#keepcalm** #mkr2015 #mkr @mykitchenrules

The live-tweeters also reacted to the show with hashtags by realizing JUDGMENT (assessing behavior), often as a humorous display, for example:

> If none of these teams doesn't do a chicken parma, they should all go into elimination. **#unaustralian** #pubfood #mkr

This form of evaluation was also targeted at the discourse of other viewers:

> Note to self: stop reading #MKR tweets if I don't want to despair the state of humanity. **#sexismeverywhere #bodyshamers**

In addition, APPRECIATION (estimating value) was deployed in hashtags such as the following, which, interestingly, were accompanied by viewer's images of their own food:

> #MKR Love both Mussels and Beef Carpaccio **#delicious** @mykitchenrules http://t.co/wI7xcO9Qxo
> Special dinner with friends **#yummy** #MKR http://t.co/l9F8Pd29gj

Integrating this type of hashtagged metadiscourse into social life may be the first semiotic movement toward what I term 'searchable talk': computer-mediated communication where we actively leverage the affordances of metadata to make our discourse more 'bondable', in the sense of enabling ambient, ad hoc connections with both putative and real mass audiences. As we have seen, while topic-marking tags might invite alignment with an ambient community of co-searchers actively attempting to find out what people are saying *about* something or *within* some specific semantic domain, interpersonal tags instead invite alignment with putative co-evaluators or co-emoters. The latter, while unlikely to search for the specific interpersonal tag, are ambiently co-present in the social network, potentially sharing the same feelings and values. It may be the case that as our social relations shift in tandem with changes in the social connections made possible with emerging social media technologies, that individuals may engage in purely interpersonal search, actively seeking texts construing similar emotions or values #whoknows!

Enacting Solidarity: Addressing and Evaluating Contestants in Real-time

Evaluation of the contestants in the show is one of the most common communicative patterns in the corpus. The most frequent evaluative lexis in the MKR corpus is shown in Table 9.8 together with the most frequent 3-word pattern in which this appraisal occurred. This provides a synoptic perspective on some of the most frequent domains of evaluation. The instances of evaluation were determined using the word frequency list and then discarding non-evaluative usage (*e.g.,* uses of '*like*' as a softener).

As this table suggests, the most frequent appraisal in the corpus is positive in polarity. For instance the most frequent evaluation was '*love*' (positive AFFECT) most often used in the 3-gram, '*love both teams*'. This phrase co-occurred with additional patterns of AFFECT (shown underlined in Table 9.9) construing the strong emotional reaction the viewers present themselves as having to the fate of the contestants. This outpouring of sentiment also has the function of forging alignments with other viewers who share the same positive feeling.

Negative assessment of characters was also frequent, for instance the pattern 'contestant + is so' (Table 9.10, ATTITUDE shown in bold).

Another prominent communicative practice was addressing comments to participants in the TV show. This was most often the contestants, but could also be the judges, or the MKR twitter account. With the exception of this account, the forms of address were not typically @mentions, presumably because the twitter accounts of the contestants may have

Table 9.8 Most frequent evaluative lexis in the MKR corpus

	Word	*Freq.*	*Most freq. 3-gram*
1	love	298	love both teams
2	good	197	good luck to
3	like	148	like to see
4	well	130	well done girls
5	sudden	175	sudden death cook

Table 9.9 Concordance lines for 'love both teams'

> #MKR sudden death, I can't watch. I **love both teams!** ?¼?
> I <u>wish</u> there was some sort of plot twist and they were both staying, **love both teams** #MKR
> #mkr @mykitchenrules - I would just eat and eat and not <u>complain</u>! What's with a little beard?? **Love both teams.**
> I **love both teams** ! This is <u>stressful</u> to watch ! #MKR @mykitchenrules
> Omg no matter wins Im going to <u>cry</u>! I **love both teams** </3 #mkr @ mykitchenrules
> I **love both teams** i do but if Eva and Debra go home it will be a <u>tragedy</u>. Mind you i <u>don't want</u> Sheri and Emilie to leave either #torn #MKR
> I'd <u>hate</u> to see Sheri and Emilie go but my money's on Eva and Debra. I **love both teams** (Emilie especially) but go WA! #MKR
> @mykitchenrules Nooo I **love both teams!** #MKR
> @mykitchenrules so intense watching this!!! **Love both teams** #MKR

Table 9.10 Concordance lines for 'contestant + is so'

> Josh's mum is so **annoying.** #mkr
> Rose's voice is so **grating** #mkr
> Bianca's voice is so **annoying!!!** #MKR #MKRPubCrawl
> ugh Kat is so **egocentric** I want to burn her face on the pan or something #mkr

not been widely known or promoted. The live-tweeters often addressed the participants in the show as if they were potential conversational interlocutors. This occurred by using the character's name as a vocative (term of address):

> Hey, **Drasko**, you really passionate about becoming a chef? Start peeling potatoes, bitch! #MKR

As this example suggests, the discourse directed at the contestants was predominantly interpersonally charged. For instance, this is apparent in concordance lines for 'you' (Table 9.11, vocatives shown underlined; ATTITUDE shown bold underlined).

Commentary of this kind could spawn conversational exchanges with other viewers. An example is the exchange in Table 9.12, beginning with User 1 addressing a contestant with the vocative, '*Colin*'. This conversation centers on shared negative APPRECIATION (shown bold underlined) of this contestant's hair, with each accumulating instance of evaluation keeping the conversation flowing and solidifying the attitudinal alignment enacted. This kind of discourse has a communing func tion, whereby the coupling of Colin's hair with negative APPRECIATION becomes a value that is shared by Users 1 and 2, realizing a shared social bond within the ambient network.

Table 9.11 Concordance lines for 'you + vocative'

Oh <u>Drasko</u>.	**You**	are such a **douche.** #MKR
Those little things let	**you**	**down** <u>boys</u> #MKR
Seriously? You've never had a pub dish	**you**	<u>Pete</u>? #mkr
in your **strange, pitiful** life, have		
Lol good going <u>Colin</u>. Now if only	**you**	somewhat better #MKR
you could wash your **filthy horrid**		
hair I might like		
<u>Ash and Camilla.</u> Note. Not everyone	**you.**	#MKR #mkrpubcrawl
is as **"refined"** as		
Kat & Andre, go away	**you**	are totally **irrelivant..** #MKR

Table 9.12 An exchange negotiating aesthetic appreciation

User1: Lol good going Colin. Now if only you could wash your <u>**filthy horrid**</u> hair I might like you somewhat better #MKR

User2: @User1 how **bad** is it lol

User1: @User2 tweet him you'll wash it for free lol. I will pay for it! He REALLY needs to wash it though. My head itches looking at it

User2: @User1 hahaha worlds greatest shave was last week, shame lol somehow I think the **greasy** hair works better 4 him than a **bald** head!

User1: @User2 oh god! Hahahah I think his **mop** def <u>**suits him better**</u> than a **bald** head would

Another pattern involving viewers directly addressing contestants is 'hey + vocative' which is also highly evaluatively charged (Table 9.13, ATTITUDE underlined). The instances of negative JUDGMENT inscribed in these posts might be thought of as reminiscent of futilely shouting abuse at the TV. The affordances of social media mean, however, that there is the chance that the contestants might view the unfolding feed of comments and react to the commentary. In addition, the abuse is performed to the ambiently co-present audience communicating via the MKR hashtag. Thus this discourse becomes a kind of rallying affiliation, aligning viewers around shared negative evaluation, and perhaps forging a sense of shared superiority amongst the viewers.

Other patterns of this kind included 'dear + vocative':

Dear Kat, every time you cook it's a complete disaster. Please go home. #mkr

and 'command + vocative':

Use a peeler **Josh!** #MKR #MKRPubCrawl

Table 9.13 Concordance lines for 'hey + vocative'

Hey Carol & Adam It's called En Papillote. You are more <u>bogan</u> than Jac & Shaz #MKR2015 #MKR
Hey, Drasko, you really <u>passionate</u> about becoming a chef? Start peeling potatoes, <u>bitch</u>! #MKR
#mkr **hey Pete.** How about a <u>nice</u> big can of <u>SHUT THE HELL UP</u>! Let's try that.
Em! Em! Em! **hey Em** are you <u>deaf</u>!! oh..right.. oops ... #MKR
#mkr **hey guys** lets go twins do it go go go <u>hope</u> yous <u>win</u>
Hey Josh, just in case you missed it your mums 'so proud of you' #MKR
Banana muffins only available at uni, **hey Kat?**! #mkr #<u>stupid</u>

Again the main function enacted in these examples appears to be both expressing personal assessments about the contestants, at the same time as aligning with the ambient audience. In many instances they are accompanied by underspecified outbursts of ATTITUDE in the form of exclamations such as '*oh my god*' or '*WTF*' (Table 9.14).

All of the patterns of positive and negative evaluation considered in this section are examples of 'ambient affiliation',[53] whereby viewers are aligning around couplings of ideational meaning (*e.g.,* contestants) and shared ATTITUDE. This affiliation is ambient in the sense that the viewers do not necessarily have to engage in direct conversational exchanges with each other to enact this sense of shared values, instead they merely need to occupy the same semantic space within the social network, coordinated, for example, by hashtags and other kinds of metadata (*e.g.,* location).

Metadiscourse About Live-tweeting

While most posts were about the show, there was a set of self-reflexive posts about the practice of live-tweeting itself, typically realizing an

Table 9.14 Examples of exclamations in the corpus

Undercooked prawns is unforgivable **WTF** a 7 is too high #MKR
OMG!! this is gonna be close! #MKR
Oh my God. No Drasko please don't do this for the rest of your career. Or ever #MKR
The hell? "I got married so I don't go to the pub any more?" Man, pub lunches are something the wife and I love doing. #mkr
Sheri and Emillie are in the bottom two? **what the fuck?** what happened? MY BABIES #mkr

attitudinal stance. This discourse included posts that refer to the activity of live-tweeting and to tweets as communicative events. Four main semantic functions were identified (Table 9.15, ATTITUDE shown in bold). For example these included posts expressing desire, via AFFECT, about having one's tweet broadcast on the screen during the show, in other words, a desire for visibility. Parallel to this was pleasure at being recognized in this way, again involving inscribed positive AFFECT and invoked AFFECT via exclamations. In addition there were posts assigning positive social esteem via JUDGEMENT to the viewer whose tweets was shown on screen. At the same time there was negative JUDGEMENT of the propriety of other viewers' tweeting, often featuring hashtags commanding them to change their behavior (*e.g., '#benice'*), as well as APPRECIATION regarding humorous tweets, and positive assessment of Twitter as a backchannel in general. This metadiscourse, aside from having the function of enacting the kind of solidarity already discussed in relation to attitudinally charged posts, foregrounds live-tweeting as a communicative space in which different kinds of relationships with other viewers can be enacted.

Such ATTITUDE typically occurred in tweets without replies, but there were instances where the evaluation was negotiated in conversation-like exchanges, often involving humor. For example, the exchange shown in Table 9.16 involves negotiation of ATTITUDE regarding the visibility afforded by a tweet appearing on the TV screen (ATTITUDE in bold). The appreciation realized in the exchange is targeted at the verbiage of the tweets (*e.g., 'PG rated', 'tamest, lamest', 'sardonic'*) coupled with

Table 9.15 Functions of metadiscourse about tweeting

Function	Example
Desire for visibility	#MKR I just **want** to see my tweet on tv
Pleasure at recognition/ complaint about lack of recognition	Omg! I just saw my tweet on tv!!! I've always **wanted** to see that!!!
	@User1 @mykitchenrules How come my tweets don't make it to the telly???
Positively evaluating visibility	#mkr @User Your tweet was just on screen. **You da man!**
Assessment of other viewers	Just read some of the #MKR tweets and some people are so **mean**!! These are **real** people too! #keyboardwarrior #benice #mkr
	The #MKR tweets are **on fire** tonight. Literally **laughing out loud**. So **hilarious!**
Assessment of Twitter	**If it wasn't for** Twitter I wouldn't bother watching #mkr
	Someone just tweeted 'i **don't know what I'd do without** #mkr'. I **dont know what I'd do without** twitter whilst watching mkr!

Table 9.16 A conversational exchange involving metadiscourse about live-tweeting

User 1: @mykitchenrules Thanks for airing my tweet(s), that's very PUBlic :) #mkr
User2: @User1 @mykitchenrules I think none of mine are **PG rated** to be aired lol
User1: @User2 @mykitchenrules Well, you might have a point there ☻
User3: @User1 @mykitchenrules How come my tweets don't make it to the telly???
User 4: @User1 @mykitchenrules Three years I've been waiting. ...even the **tamest, lamest** ones **don't work. Sigh.** ....
User 5: @User1 @mykitchenrules You're a **star!**
User 1: @User5 @mykitchenrules thanks very munch ☻ ☻ ☻
User 1: @User4 @mykitchenrules Oh my, and you have such a **nice** profile pic as well, very **classy**
User 4: @User1 @mykitchenrules allegedly. **Sardonic sarcasm** might be my **downfall.** ☻
User 1: @User4 @mykitchenrules perhaps, not that there's anything **wrong** with that

self-deprecating humor, construed via hyperbole (*e.g., 'downfall'*). The tenor of these posts is playful, and the ATTITUDE fuels the unfolding of the exchange in a similar manner to the kinds of saturated evaluation seen in casual conversation. Even posts without replies, such as the observations shown in Table 9.15, retain a sense of potential conversationality in relation to the ever present ambient audience who might reply, favorite, or retweet the post.

Conclusion

Social media discourse offers an important resource for audience researchers, seeking to understand new forms of hybrid media use. This chapter has explored the communicative practices involved in live-tweeting television via a second screen, applying a corpus-based discourse analysis method. This method drew upon the Appraisal framework, a linguistic model of evaluative language. The value to audience research of using an analytical approach, grounded in linguistics, is that it offers a systematic way of understanding audience practices that is based on textual evidence about patterns in communication. This type of evidence, as we have seen, can be both quantitative, telling us something about the communicative tendencies of audiences, and qualitative, providing details about the particular stances adopted by audience members through inspection of concordance lines.

An important dimension of the discourse analyzed in this chapter was the use of hashtags to coordinate ideational content and forge attitudinal alignments. Several communicative practices were evident: communing around shared values via interpersonal hashtags, enacting solidarity with other viewers through addressing and evaluating contestants, and construing metadiscourse about live-tweeting as a communal activity. The MKR audience studied actively leveraged the affordances of hashtags to make their discourse more 'bondable' within the social stream. Social tagging, and social media discourse more generally, will undoubtedly become an increasingly important data source for audience studies. The challenge will be to apply systematic and theoretically sound models of language in order to understand the meanings audiences are making with these new semiotic resources

Notes

1 Schirra, Steven, Huan Sun, and Frank Bentley, "Together Alone: Motivations for Live-Tweeting a Television Series," Paper presented at the Proceedings of the 32nd annual ACM conference on Human factors in computing systems, Toronto, Ontario, Canada, 2014.
2 Lochrie, Mark, and Paul Coulton, "Mobile Phones as Second Screen for Tv, Enabling Inter-Audience Interaction," In *Proceedings of the 8th International Conference on Advances in Computer Entertainment Technology*, 1–2. Lisbon, Portugal: ACM, 2011.
3 Laursen, Ditte, and Kjetil Sandvik, "Talking with Tv Shows: Simultaneous Conversations between Users and Producers in the Second-Screen Television Production Voice," *Northern Lights: Film & Media Studies Yearbook* 12, no. 1 (2014): 141–60.
4 *My Kitchen Rules* is an Australian cooking TV game show in which contestants' cooking skills are judged by a panel of celebrity chefs and hosts. The initial format of the show was two teams competing against each other to cook a three-course meal, with variations on this format in later seasons. The show has been running since 2010.
5 Atkinson, Cliff, *The Backchannel : How Audiences Are Using Twitter and Social Media and Changing Presentations Forever* (Berkeley, California: New Riders, 2010), Sarita, Yardi. "The Role of the Backchannel in Collaborative Learning Environments," Paper presented at the Proceedings of the 7th international conference on Learning sciences, Bloomington, Indiana, 2006.
6 Anstead, Nick, and Ben O'Loughlin, "The Emerging Viewertariat and Bbc Question Time: Television Debate and Real-Time Commenting Online," *The International Journal of Press/Politics* 16, no. 4 (2011): 440–62.
7 Kalsnes, Bente, Arne H. Krumsvik, and Tanja Storsul, "Social Media as a Political Backchannel," *Aslib Journal of Information Management* 66, no. 3 (2014): 313–28.
8 Anstead, Nick, and Ben O'Loughlin, "The Emerging Viewertariat and Bbc Question Time: Television Debate and Real-Time Commenting Online,", Pedersen, Sarah, Graeme Baxter, Simon Burnett, Ayse Göker, David Corney, and Carlos Martin, "Backchannel Chat: Peaks and Troughs in a Twitter Response to Three Televized Debates During the 2014 Scottish Independence

Referendum Campaign," Paper presented at the CeDEM15: Conference for E-Democracy and Open Government, 2015.

9 D'Heer, Evelien, and Pieter Verdegem, "What Social Media Data Mean for Audience Studies: A Multidimensional Investigation of Twitter Use During a Current Affairs Tv Programme," *Information, Communication & Society* 18, no. 2 (2015/02/01 2014): 221–34.

10 Buschow, Christopher, Beate Schneider, and Simon Ueberheide, "Tweeting Television: Exploring Communication Activities on Twitter While Watching Tv," *Communications - The European Journal of Communication Research* 39, no. 2 (2014): 129–149.

11 Yardi, Sarita, "The Role of the Backchannel in Collaborative Learning Environments," In *Proceedings of the 7th international conference on Learning sciences*, 852–58. Bloomington, Indiana: International Society of the Learning Sciences, 2006.

12 Ebner, Martin, Conrad Lienhardt, Matthias Rohs, and Iris Meyer, "Microblogs in Higher Education - a Chance to Facilitate Informal and Process-Oriented Learning?," *Computers and Education* 55, no. 1 (2010): 92–100.

13 McCarthy, Joseph F, and dana boyd, "Digital Backchannels in Shared Physical Spaces: Experiences at an Academic Conference," Paper presented at the Conference on Human Factors and Computing Systems (CHI 2005), Portland, Oregon, USA, April 2–7, 2005 2005, Reinhardt, W, M Ebner, G Beham, and C Costa, "How People Are Using Twitter During Conferences," Paper presented at the Creativity and Innovation Competencies on the Web, Proceedings of 5, EduMedia conference, Salzburg, 2009, Grosseck, Gabriela, and Carmen Holotescu, "Microblogging Multimedia-Based Teaching Methods Best Practices with Cirip.Eu.," *Procedia - Social and Behavioral Sciences* 2, no. 2 (2010): 2151–55.

14 Harry, Drew, Joshua Green, and Judith Donath, "Backchan.nl: Integrating Backchannels in Physical Space," In *Proceedings of the 27th international conference on Human factors in computing systems*, 1361–70, Boston, MA, USA: ACM, 2009.

15 Bisker, Solomon, Hector Ouilhet, Steve Pomeroy, Agnes Chang, and Federico Casalegno, "Re-Thinking Fashion Trade Shows: Creating Conversations through Mobile Tagging," In *CHI '08 extended abstracts on Human factors in computing systems* (Florence, Italy: ACM, 2008), 3351–56.

16 Hawthorne, Joshua, J. Brian Houston, and Mitchell S. Mckinney, "Live-Tweeting a Presidential Primary Debate: Exploring New Political Conversations," *Social Science Computer Review*, 31, no. 5 (2013): 552–62.

17 Vieweg, Sarah, Amanda L Hughes, Kate Starbird, and Leysia Palen, "Microblogging During Two Natural Hazards Events: What Twitter May Contribute to Situational Awareness," Paper presented at the Proceedings of the SIGCHI Conference on Human Factors in Computing Systems, 2010.

18 Van Cauwenberge, Anna, Gabi Schaap, and Rob van Roy, ""Tv No Longer Commands Our Full Attention": Effects of Second-Screen Viewing and Task Relevance on Cognitive Load and Learning from News," *Computers in Human Behavior* 38, no. 0 (2014): 100–09.

19 Cameron, Jaclyn, and Nick Geidner, "Something Old, Something New, Something Borrowed from Something Blue: Experiments on Dual Viewing Tv and Twitter," *Journal of Broadcasting & Electronic Media* 58, no. 3 (2014): 400–19.

20 Pynta, Peter, Shaun AS Seixas, Geoffrey F. Nield, James Hier, and Emelia Millward, "The Power of Social Television: Can Social Media Build Viewer Engagement? A New Approach to Brain Imaging of Viewer Immersion," *Journal of Advertising Research* 54, no. 1 (2014): 71–80.

21 Highfield, Tim, Stephen Harrington, and Axel Bruns, "Twitter as a Technology for Audiencing and Fandom: The# Eurovision Phenomenon," *Information, Communication & Society* 16, no. 3 (2013): 315–39.
22 Lochrie, Mark, and Paul Coulton, "Mobile Phones as Second Screen for Tv, Enabling Inter-Audience Interaction," In *Proceedings of the 8th International Conference on Advances in Computer Entertainment Technology*, 1–2. Lisbon, Portugal: ACM, 2011.
23 Magee, Rachel M., Melinda Sebastian, Alison Novak, Christopher M. Mascaro, Alan Black, and Sean P. Goggins, "#Twitterplay: A Case Study of Fan Roleplaying Online," In *Proceedings of the 2013 conference on Computer supported cooperative work companion*, 199–202, San Antonio, Texas, USA: ACM, 2013.
24 Bore, Inger-Lise Kalviknes, and Jonathan Hickman, "Continuing the West Wing in 140 Characters or Less: Improvised Simulation on Twitter," *The Journal of Fandom Studies* 1, no. 2 (2013): 219–38.
25 Yardi, Sarita, "The Role of the Backchannel in Collaborative Learning Environments," In *Proceedings of the 7th international conference on Learning sciences*, 852–58. Bloomington, Indiana: International Society of the Learning Sciences, 2006.
26 Shamma, David A, Lyndon Kennedy, and Elizabeth F Churchill, "Conversational Shadows: Describing Live Media Events Using Short Messages," Paper presented at the Proceedings of the Fourth International AAAI Conference on Weblogs and Social Media, Washington DC, 2010.
27 Honeycutt, Courtney, and Susan Herring, "Beyond Microblogging: Conversation and Collaboration in Twitter," In *Proceedings of the Forty-Second Hawai'i International Conference on System Sciences*, no page numbers available, Los Alamitos, CA: IEEE Press, 2009.
28 Starbird, Kate, Leysia Palen, Amanda L Hughes, and Sarah Vieweg, "Chatter on the Red: What Hazards Threat Reveals About the Social Life of Microblogged Information," Paper presented at the Proceedings of the 2010 ACM conference on Computer supported cooperative work, 2010.
29 Zhao, Dejin, and Mary Beth Rosson. "How and Why People Twitter: The Role That Micro-Blogging Plays in Informal Communication at Work," Paper presented at the Proceedings of the ACM 2009 international conference on Supporting group work, 2009.
30 Grosseck, Gabriela, and Carmen Holotescu, "Microblogging Multimedia-Based Teaching Methods Best Practices with Cirip.Eu.," *Procedia - Social and Behavioral Sciences* 2, no. 2 (2010): 2151–55.
31 Ritter, Alan, Colin Cherry, and Bill Dolan, "Unsupervized Modeling of Twitter Conversations," Paper presented at the Human Language Technologies: The 2010 Annual Conference of the North American Chapter of the Association for Computational Linguistics, 2010.
32 Twitter. "Twitter About Page," https://twitter.com/about.
33 Posts to services such as Twitter, Weibo and Facebook will have timestamp information appended to them indicating when the post was published. While revealing location data is usually optional, this temporal data is usually automatically generated since it is central to delivering chronologically unfolding 'streams' of content to the ambient audience.
34 Hope, Wayne, "Global Capitalism and the Critique of Real Time," *Time & Society* 15, no. 2–3 (2006): 275–302.
35 Couldry, Nick, "Liveness,"Reality," and the Mediated Habitus from Television to the Mobile Phone," *The Communication Review* 7, no. 4 (2004): 353–61.

36 There is debate about the value of citizen journalism which has been criticized for invoking "the drama of instantaneity, which is compelling and engaging for readers, but not necessarily compatible with fact checking processes of western paradigms of journalism" Papacharissi, Zizi and Maria de fatima oliveira, "Affective news and networked publics: The rhythms of news storytelling on# Egypt", *Journal of Communication*, 62 (2012): 266–282, p. 279.

37 Zappavigna, Michele, "Coffeetweets: Bonding around the Bean on Twitter," In *The Language of Social Media: Communication and Community on the Internet*, edited by P Seargeant and C Tagg (London: Palgrave, 2014), 139–60.

38 Couldry, Nick, "Liveness,"Reality," and the Mediated Habitus from Television to the Mobile Phone," *The Communication Review* 7, no. 4 (2004): 353–61.

39 Zappavigna, Michele, "Ambient Affiliation: A Linguistic Perspective on Twitter," *New Media & Society* 13, no. 5 (2011): 788–806.

40 Bruns, Axel, and Jean Burgess, "Researching News Discussion on Twitter: New Methodologies," *Journalism Studies* 13, no. 5–6 (2012): 801–14.

41 Borra, Erik, and Bernhard Rieder, "Programmed Method: Developing a Toolset for Capturing and Analyzing Tweets," *Aslib Journal of Information Management* 66, no. 3 (2014): 262–78.

42 Antconc (Version 3.4.3) [Computer Software]. Waseda University. Available from http://www.laurenceanthony.net/, Tokyo, Japan.

43 Martin, J.R, and P.R.R White, *The Language of Evaluation: Appraisal in English* (New York: Palgrave Macmillan, 2005).

44 System networks are an alternative to modelling language as a catalogue of structures. This kind of systemic orientation to meaning arose out of the Firthian tradition in linguistics which asserted the need for a distinction between structure and system, that is, between syntagmatic and paradigmatic relations in language (Firth, 1957).

45 Halliday, Michael Alexander Kirkwood, and Christian Matthias Ingemar Martin Matthiessen, *An Introduction to Functional Grammar*, 3rd ed (London: Arnold, 2004).

46 Cunha, Evandro, Gabriel Magno, Giovanni Comarela, Virgilio Almeida, Marcos André Gonçalves, and Fabrício Benevenuto, "Analyzing the Dynamic Evolution of Hashtags on Twitter: A Language-Based Approach," Paper presented at the Proceedings of the Workshop on Language in Social Media (LSM 2011), 2011.

47 Houston, Keith, *Shady Characters: The Secret Life of Punctuation, Symbols, and Other Typographical Marks* (New York ; London: WW Norton & Company, 2013).

48 boyd, D, S Golder, and G Lotan, "Tweet, Tweet, Retweet: Conversational Aspects of Retweeting on Twitter," Paper presented at the Proceedings of 43rd Hawaii international conference on system sciences (HICSS), 5–8 January 2010, Honolulu, HI, United States of America, 2010.

49 Zappavigna, Michele, "Searchable Talk: The Linguistic Functions of Hashtags," *Social Semiotics* 25, no. 3: 274–291.

50 Halliday, Michael Alexander Kirkwood, *Language as Social Semiotic: The Social Interpretation of Language and Meaning* (Baltimore: University Park Press, 1978).

51 Halliday, Michael Alexander Kirkwood, and Christian Matthias Ingemar Martin Matthiessen, *An Introduction to Functional Grammar*.

52 Small caps are used here to differentiate the technical use of these terms from their everyday counterparts.

53 Zappavigna, Michele, "Coffeetweets: Bonding around the Bean on Twitter," In *The Language of Social Media: Communication and Community on the Internet*, edited by P Seargeant and C Tagg, 139–60. London: Palgrave, 2014, Zappavigna, Michele, "Ambient Affiliation in Microblogging: Bonding around the Quotidian," Media International Australia no. 151 (2014): 97–103, Zappavigna, Michele, "Ambient Affiliation: A Linguistic Perspective on Twitter," *New Media & Society* 13, no. 5 (2011): 788–806, Zappavigna, Michele, *Discourse of Twitter and Social Media*. Continuum Discourse Series (London: Continuum, 2012), Zappavigna, Michele, "Enacting Identity in Microblogging," *Discourse and Communication* 8, no. 2 (2014): 209–28.

10 Teaching with Twitter

A Case Study in the Practice of Audiencing

Sue Turnbull and Christopher Moore

Introduction

Being a university student, especially one enrolled in a Media and Communications Studies bachelors degree, involves coming to an understanding that while the technological affordances of personal computational and telecommunication devices are a means for negotiating relations with their higher education institution they are also a pathway to achieving critical professionalism for future careers. Through the techniques afforded by their digital devices, students manage their interconnected memberships between multiple and overlapping audiences, shuttling rapidly between casual social interaction, professional self presentation, formal knowledge formation, and informal information gathering processes. The challenge students face when moving through the university environment, and into employment with an ongoing career trajectory, is how to expand their personal and social online media practices to accommodate an online persona that is better suited to their future professional selves. As we will discuss further, a student's persona is more than a website, a CV, or e-portfolio, it is the hybrid collection of digital objects, including self-mediated and remediated content and expressions that circulate as part of the nominated identity interface that stands in for the individual online.

As a media platform, Twitter has done much to support the development of the 24-hour news cycle while remaining largely popular with celebrities, politicians, journalists, subcultures and fandoms.[1] However, the company itself has done little to support the platform's potential for public research and is rarely considered in relation to its pedagogical role in teaching, despite widespread adoption in higher education by students, academics and institutional public relations and marketing teams.[2] This is hardly surprising given that Twitter's trajectory as a private company and as a public platform is currently oriented towards the continuing search for a viable business model. The future of Twitter, however, is increasingly uncertain when compared to that of Facebook or Google. The platform faces the perennial problem of balancing advertisers' interests with those of their intended and established users.

As it is, the current large-scale quantitative analysis of Twitter data and user information allows for the comparative algorithmic assessment of events in order to distinguish key patterns. As Axel Bruns and Stefan Stieglitz suggest, this increases the potential for new forms of analysis of dynamic audience behaviors.[3] Bruns and Jean Burgess's methodology identifies major themes in the tweets involved in the coverage of events, and can trace their spread over time to consider a range of the activities within networked discussions.[4] To the individual attempting to understand their place in these networks, however, other tools and approaches can also be of use. Twitter data is proving to be significant to those attempting to get a sense of their own audience reach and to understand how their online persona functions as part of larger network formations. For example, Danielle Acosta found Twitter appealing as a means for increasing the social capital of higher education students, whose generational familiarity with social media meant a potential reduction in the barriers to learning from geographic location, socioeconomic status and individual isolation.[5] Twitter can also be used to get a sense of how different self-mediated digital objects, such as that of a tweet from a university classroom, or a Facebook status update about a job application, circulate as part of the larger performance of the presentational self online.[6] In this way, Twitter can be an extremely useful platform for drawing student's attention to the metadata of online persona and personal information that is publicly accessible and can be algorithmically sorted to visualize relationships, interactions and other network activities. The resulting sociograms then serve to reveal important dimensions of a student's role as both a producer of, and audience for, the presentation of an online persona.

Bruns and Burgess have demonstrated how standardized metrics for Twitter analysis are useful for expanding on questions of media and communication studies grounded within a humanities and social sciences methodology that address issues of power relations among actors.[7] They consider the elements of non-repeatable and non-verifiable research methodologies of individual scholarship to lag behind the large scale and more rigorous tools available for more reliable and real time Twitter analysis. Standardized Big Data approaches are indeed crucial, and as researchers it is empowering to have an assortment of technologies for scientifically reliable metric analysis. These are, however, are less useful for undergraduate students attempting to develop literacies for the critical analysis and reflection on their own activities, patterns of behavior and relationships to audiences, institutions and the issues of power. In this chapter we advance simple, repeatable, but non-verifiable approaches to limited data sets drawing on simple social network analysis visualization tools and consider the inclusions of such network exploration and analysis techniques within subject content and learning activities. Students are encouraged to acquire critical literacies in making sense of their personal, professional and media specific connections, interfaces and networks in local, national and global terms. Twitter activity and the visualization of the data thus produced is incorporated into lecture content and seminar discussions with students, leading to what is in fact a phenomenology of 'small data' audience research. This enables a reflection on the ways in which the pedagogical relations between students and teachers as digital media consumers and social media users are transforming the temporalities and spatialities of university teaching and learning practices.

In considering students as an audience, we embrace the notion of audiencing as an active participation in the networks of communication that produce meaning. Indeed, the transformation of the noun 'audience' into the present participle of the non-existent verb, 'to audience' is a clear marker of our view. This is mirrored by our commitment to the notion of students as active participants in the process of learning and knowledge formation, a belief that is underpinned by curriculum transformation within our own institution, but also more broadly in the Humanities and the Arts, and selectively across other disciplines and domains. The global move to the flipped classroom, online courses, and MOOC-style hybrid responses to the challenges of massification in the higher education sector have provided a range of flexible and networked approaches to the processes of knowledge formation with varying degrees of success.

Our attention here is on the professional and public networks of learning that emerge between student, lecturer, tutor, and the institution, which also serve as an interface between students and an audience made up of individuals, organizations, and representatives of the broader cultural and creative industries within which graduates will be seeking employment. It is the gradual awareness of the public and professional dimensions of these online networks that is the game-changer for new students, who, from first year onwards in our program, are required to construct a public identity, or what Kim Barbour, David Marshall, and Christopher Moore identify as an online persona.[8] Our students are required to present and perform their online selves as part of the learning assessment for their coursework and at the same time are encouraged to engage in the management of a public and professional identity that is intended to transcend their university experience.[9]

Within our own university, and across the sector more generally, there are multiple 'official' media platforms and communication technologies that are available as public learning spaces and open experimental teaching environments. However, since 2008 onwards, and with varying degrees of success, Twitter has been employed as a channel for conversation and discussion, commentary, and criticism within the Bachelor of Communication and Media Studies program, and is directly integrated into student learning as a means for reporting on their learning and their research as generated through their studies. Requiring students to present a public persona as part of their learning activities does not make sense for all degrees and disciplines, but in the domain of cultural and creative industries, students are encouraged to generate insight through reflection and peer-support in their early experiments with audiencing and professional network curation with the intention of enabling them to gain industry-relevant experience and equip them with the means to develop a critical professionalism.

The use of microblogging and Twitter in higher education has been well documented. Amandeep Dhir, Khalid Buragga, and Abeer Boreqqah provide a comprehensive summary of the different benefits of micro-blogging across multiple roles in higher education.[10] George Veletsianos' review of the scholar's use of Twitter for professional work suggests the platform is effective in encouraging participation and identity formation through practices of networked learning.[11] Learning is changed in the networked environment, argue Matthew Fuller and Andrew Goffrey, because 'work' is inseparable from the processes of education and learning within it.[12] Bazilah Talip's exploration of the use of Twitter for professional networking purposes in the Information Technology (IT) industry found that IT professionals use the 'information flow' pattern of tweets to contribute to a virtual place that provides a sense of belonging and is conducive for professional development.[13] Performing professionalism, or being professional with social media can then be understood as an information practice, which Talip describes as a continuous series of negotiations between heterogeneous (human and non-human) actors in the process of composing a world defined by standards that are constantly redefined in the circulation between individual and collective properties.

Tweeting the First Year Experience

Students in the first year of their study within the media and communications discipline are required to participate in social media use across two subjects. To begin with, students are encouraged to set up and own their domains for their blogs on WordPress and to establish their online presence on Twitter. Requiring new students to start tweeting on 'Day One', is an on-the-job learning experience for many, as students are presented with the challenge of creating a public and professionally oriented profile from which to engage with the subject material, learning assessment practices and to share the products of their research into new media and communication technologies. From the outset, students are expected to research, analyze, and use Twitter to communicate their mediated responses to learning assessment challenges regarding the concepts and topics that they encounter in the course of their studies, and to tweet relevant sources that connect to, or problematize, these issues.

In this way, Twitter is used to curate information, develop knowledge through criticism and review, participate in discussion using hashtags to manage information flow and aggregate these performative practices into a cohesive online persona. This Twitter activity accompanies the students' weekly blogging activity on WordPress, documenting their investigation and response to the subject materials in more detail. The transformation of the student's everyday social media practice into a personally reflective and critical activity, which is informed, competent, creative, ethical, and innovative is a gradual process that continues throughout their enrolment and beyond. The goal is to encourage the student's development of research and analysis skills, digital and media literacies, and the professional requirements of the public presentation of the self.

It should be noted that our early attempts to teach with Twitter were not met with great success. Back in 2008, many students were quite reluctant to consider their social networking activity as scholarly, or as a suitable location to be seen as being a student, or to use their precious bandwidth and data caps for lecture, seminar, and assessment related activities. Facebook and Twitter were particularly resisted, although we had more success with smaller community focused sites, the majority of which had the tendency to fold, commercialize or simply disappear. Many students at that time did not have access to a smartphone or an internet enabled phone, which also limited the experiment. As a result, there was dissatisfaction with the use of Twitter and its role in the learning assessment strategies of the subject, as we required students to make a certain number of tweets per week, and expected commentary and discussion. The regular, not quite daily, assessment related activity and practice was challenging to students, but over time this became normalized as it reflected what has come to be recognized as the professional practice of celebrities, highly regarded experts, political figures, and strategic social media users.

In 2016, however, students are much more ready to engage in the 140-character-style conversations and hashtag use of Twitter conversation. They now have more consistent access to mobile technologies and are more familiar with many of the features and limitations of the devices they use. Students enrolling in the courses we teach demonstrate significantly more familiarity with the structures, limitations, and sophisticated user practices of social networking platforms, if not Twitter use itself. Indeed, in one lecture in 2016, students suggested that they were the 'online generation', born into an online world of connectivity that they both expected and occasionally resented. Students who identify as the 'online generation' are already familiar with the material demands of mobile internet access, from the endless balancing of hardware and connection costs (although at 18 this may not be the reality for some), to the management of battery and memory capacity, and the constraints of an app-based operating system. In many ways, our students are also more familiar with the current trends in social media use than we are, but by concentrating on Twitter and formalizing its role through assessment, we take learning public. The Twittersphere is a simultaneously private and public space, which is constrained by an important set of utilities, affordances, and pedagogically useful limitations, all of which form the basis for the learning assessment strategy in the discipline's digital communication major.

Students often express an initial hesitancy in discussing course related content publicly (a key reason we avoid Facebook); others have expressed difficulties with integrating pedagogical participation into public professional self presentation. Very few have come to their studies acutely aware as to what degree their social media data is quantified, analyzed, and ultimately owned and sold by the platforms and services they rely on for the majority of their daily social interactions, communication activity, and media consumption. Students do not always understand that their public activities online are surveilled and scrutinized, and to what degree control over their self-representative practices are extensions of their personal and political agency. These students do perhaps presume an audience of invisible others, a 'context collapse' between a heterogeneous group of authorities, employees, peers, and rivals considered to be always potentially surveilling their activities as Alice Marwick and danah boyd suggest.[14] In our experience, students are less adroit with the legal and ethical dimensions of the techno-social constructs, otherwise known as 'Big Data', particularly in terms of what it means for individual agency. Exposed to constant and unrelenting public surveillance from all online and institutional services, students are largely unperturbed by the extensive use of industrial data analytics they are exposed to and the more insidious dimensions of government spying and metadata analysis enabled by social media and mobile telephony. However, by integrating an analysis of the student cohort Twitter activity and visualizing the learning network being performed in lectures, seminars and tutorials, students are offered a highly effective demonstration of the status of their online persona and how this might be pursued and tracked over time.

Visualizing, Audiencing, and Performing Persona

Understanding how a student, institutional, or academic persona interacts with others and manages their micro-public of attention is useful for interpreting their 'intercommunicative self'.[15] The management of a persona's audience constitutes a highly intensive investment of energy in presentational media strategies and the tactics of impression management. The intercommunicative self involves an individually directed distribution of presentational media and assembly of images, locations, transactions, and connections to the self, intended for an audience comprised of followers and the followed.[16] The term 'micro-public' refers to the reach of the online persona and its attendant networked audiences, and it is used by Marshall to indicate the audience's ability to participate in the performance of a public self, contributing to the presentation and circulation of the persona across multiple media platforms and communication services that can be described as moving intercommunicatively.[17] Students for example have been known to tweet lecturers about emails sent via another platform regarding issues with blogs. The audience in this model

> ...are the followers and friends that are connected to a range of content via a particular individual that is simultaneously a 'private' network, but regularly and publicly updated and responded to in the tradition of broadcast and print media forms that makes it a quasi-public network.[18]

The concept of the intercommunicative self acknowledges the necessity of linking the offline identity to the online presence. Intercommunication involves, say, the movement of photos from the smartphone device through Instagram or Facebook to Imgur and Reddit; it presumes the comment or post becomes an element of a retweeted meme, or animated gif, and is involved in the circulation and reputational economies of prestige and engagement in the practices of likes, shares, posts, and hits.[19] The concept also signals the persona's fragmented nature and that a student's persona is not limited to any single site, or performed in any one space.

We begin by applying Bruno Latour *et al.'s* 'counterintuitive' research strategy, which inverts the common move from claims about simple structures and interactions to more complex ones.[20] This starts instead with the overlapping complex entities that are comprised of other complex entities, and locates shared attributes. This approach draws on the digital tools and algorithmic analysis of social network analysis (SNA) as a means for visually navigating and steering a course across the complexity of a micro-public in order to make the performativity of the student's persona visible to themselves and to the cohort generally. Twitter activity and the networks of connections this forms, which we can variously term audiences or micro-publics, can be rendered graphically to assist in considering their intersecting features. These socio-graphic representations are, however, heterogeneous and only representative on a provisional basis. Instead of generalizing about insights into global patterns of audience activity, professional network formations and the ethics of online learning, the focus here is on the way we make use of a series of intellectual, algorithmic and technical instruments that assist in producing an understanding with students about the overlapping positions of their audiences, without attempting to unify or collapse these audiences into a single notion.

The 'small' data sets we can idiosyncratically capture therefore reveal intersecting features without being generalizable. We can, however, cluster the Twitter data and draw frames around intensities of connections in the student-generated micro-publics to help recognize the role these play in the overall communicative landscape.[21] The amount of Twitter data freely available to the public researcher is limited and highly costly to access at a large scale. However, the value for the researcher, for the student, for the actor in the professional network, or the university, is the potential for visual analysis of this network activity as a means for rendering one perspective or dimension more visible than others. This involves the application of algorithmic processes to distill complex representational frameworks of networks into simple two-dimensional planes, from which it is then possible to offer interpretations and explanations of recurring patterns and attributes.[22] This visualization process can assist in critical qualitative analysis and network exploration in order to complement anthropological, ethnographic, phenomenological and other quantitative methodologies. The graphs thereby produced are by no means definitive datasets: they are simply snapshots capturing a moment of network operation and subject to the same selection processes that are part of any act of interpretation.[23]

Network visualization techniques are only as revealing as the research question that prompted them and the design of the software that enables them will permit. As it is, we have applied a necessarily limited selection of social network analysis techniques to inscribe and to annotate the roles of those students in key positions in the micro-publics their activities form, and to consider the centrality of information hubs and other key performers in the network. As we attend to the visualization of the structures of knowledge, using the tools to turn the gaze on our own activities as teachers and students, and as producers and audiences, we understand the ways that the software (both the communication platform and the visual analysis tools) directs, limits and controls what can be discovered. The tools for the analysis of network activities thus structure the production of the knowledge that can be produced, as do the platforms and services from which the data is collected. It is, therefore, the phenomenological dimension of the visual analysis of small data, and the snapshots they provide of the larger flow of mediated communication, that makes Twitter an intriguing platform with which to explore the micro-publics and forms of intercommunication that occur between individuals, small groups and networking clusters.[24]

Small data is not representative, indeed it can be entirely misconstrued, and yet we see it masquerading as Big Data across the socially distributed newsfeeds of Facebook, the trending patterns of Twitter's media flow, and in the mainstream coverage of broadcast news. Meanwhile, the growth in infographic content has increased the demand for visually literate audiences, critical of the normalized circulation of misinformation and socially agreed on interpretations, which magnifying the equally misrepresentative metrics of common ranking systems such as likes, favorites, stars and other rating systems. As Ned Rossiter suggests:

> ...when data is understood to operate within, and indeed, constitute, regimes of truth, a secondary empirical quality emerges in the shaping of social practices and material conditions in ways not so dissimilar from how policies of various kinds result in forms of action.[25]

In order to have any hope of encouraging resistance to the command and control influence of network architectures, it is first a requirement that we become familiar with the dynamics of the environment we are attempting to understand. In our example this takes the form of independent student-led research, investigating a media technology or platform as part of their learning assessment activity.

Hashtags: Markers of Audiences

In the following section we present the analysis of a number of sociograms and other infographics generated during the course of the teaching session, in this case focusing on the subject-related hashtag #BCM112. The aim of this case study analysis is to illustrate how the students in the weekly seminars are encouraged to engage with these visualizations and to consider and explore their role in the network. This weekly exercise suggests that even brief exposure to social media analysis and visualization tools serves to increase the network literacies of these students, but more importantly to support the development of their own career strategies to target specific audiences. Each week the students are asked to Tweet about their own inquiries into the relevant issues or concepts from the subject materials.

Bruns and Stieglitz consider hashtags to be an important mechanism for coordinating conversations around identified themes and events.[26] Bernhard Reider and Theo Röhle suggest that visualizing the users' networks of hashtags can render certain perspectives more visible and more accessible than others.[27] This helps to render the complex framework of interaction into more accessible and workable representational forms through processes of selective reduction and also assists in making interpretation and explanation feasible. The hashtag is thus our primary method of understanding the shape of the student cohort and its weekly activity. The hashtag also facilitates communication with the subject coordinators, lecturers and guest lectures, tutors and alumni, acting as a broader knowledge community with clear public interface points. The use of the subject hashtag therefore indicates students' public availability, with their Twitter activity revealing glimpses into the types of learning that are usually hidden by carefully constrained learning management systems. The use of sponsored university hashtags, carefully curating the social media profile of the institution, represents one degree of the students' role as audience, while the subject-identifier hashtags signal an entirely different order of relationship. The hashtag translates the requirements of individual participation into a public space, and serves as an interface to a series of entities, including the university, the course content and curriculum, and brings together the student's learning experience and public presentation of self as a micro-public[28].

The hashtag is therefore an important socio-cultural assemblage that is performed by the university and is contested and confirmed by students, whose previous modes of interaction with the institution have largely been dominated by internal procedures, closed communication loops, and bureaucracies. Students are thus able to make themselves heard in public in ways that were unavailable to previous generations. Hashtags, retweets (RTs), and @replies, argues Jose Van Dijck, are woven into the social fabric of 'idiosyncratic microsyntax'.[29] In this way, students enact multiple roles on Twitter as participants, producers, and as an audience, both translating and modifying behaviors that complicate the usual student, teacher, institution triad. This enables the Twitter platform to function as a *mediator*, in terms of actor-network theory (ANT), rather than as an *intermediary*, as it contributes directly to shaping the performance of social acts. Social network analysis and visualization tools represent predetermined sensibilities and modalities, and therefore already undermine the aim of ANT to avoid making *a priori* distinctions based on assumptions about the understanding of the foundations of knowledge and how these must be formed. The social, we are reminded, is not a pre-existing object of enquiry, but rather network effects of the assembly of a separate domain. There is a contagious diaspora to the tools of ANT, argues John Law in the analysis of the social as a continuously generated phenomena, an arrangement that is entirely dependent on its continued enactment.[30] This quickly becomes obvious by turning our attention to the punctuated temporal existence of the university schedule as the punctilious notion of the semester continues to be the defining element of learning and continues to artificially structure the student's progress.[31]

Social network analysis tools can trace and point to phenomena across the network, such as the connections to international celebrities, national news networks, local businesses, and personal relationships and the interactions between them. Coupled with visualization applications, they also suggest gaps and draw attention to associations, from the social to the material, that would be otherwise overlooked. The assemblages revealed by the graphs provide a means for students to investigate their own performance, to reflect on priorities, practices, objects, flows, and other connections, from the personal to the professional.[32] The network exploration and overview software NodeXL is a 'plug-in' for MS Exce that collects small data samples of Twitter data and is able to analyze and algorith-mically represent the connections in the network of learning activity and provide simple but effective measurements of group density and diversity. For example, the graphs assist in revealing the individuals who function as highly connected 'hubs', while 'bridges' are those individuals with fewer but more strategic connections.[33] The attraction of tools like NodeXL is the automatic features for gathering and visualizing of data that assist in the rapid assembly of simple but meaningful graphs, which can be explored to gain insight into the organization and activity of the network. As plat-forms like Twitter continue to monetize and make unpredictable changes to their application programming interface (API), the tools and the means and perhaps the relevancy for such analysis will also change. In the disci-pline of Media and Communication Studies, the process is perhaps more acutely attuned to the obsolescence of communication and media techno-logies and platforms, and the migratory practices of audiences.[34]

Visualizing Audiences in Networks of Learning

Marc Smith *et al.* describe the method for network visualization using NodeXL as being similar to aerial photography, or the drone footage of crowded public spaces and political events, which enables a social as well as spatial domain to be pictured and examined in order to reveal infor-mation.[35] Such information would include the size, structure, and flow of interactions in the networks, including whether a network is composed of large groups or many sub-groups, and just how connected those groups are. The general techniques that can then be used to identify information hubs and bridges, to chart degrees of centrality, and locate key agents in the field of connections are immensely useful to consider in a pedagogical context.

Take for example, the first graph (Figure 10.1), which visualizes the captured Twitter activity of @messages, favorites, follows, and retweets featuring the hashtag #BCM112 in the third week of the 2014 session. Each of the 'vertices' or nodes, represented by the Twitter 'avatar' or profile image are individual actors connected by the thin lines or 'edges', which indicates a social relationship. During tutorials, students are in-vited to examine and discuss the graphs, following a brief introduction to social networking analysis and asked to convey their own interpretation. Visual analysis of small data sets makes this process fast and effective, as the students are able to quickly distinguish differences between the algo-rithmically sorted clusters. The first cluster from the right in Figure 10.1 is dominated by subject tutors and lecturers, as well as the media platforms, new media technologies, and online news and information sources, that students inevitability turn to when first establishing their Twitter ac-counts and are seeking to emulate professional practice. The center cluster represents a group of students who connected early on in the session or prior to the subject and the third group on the far right is a collective of individuals using both the #BCM110 and #BCM112 hashtags, the two first-year subjects which include Twitter in their learning assessment.

A couple of basic social network analysis concepts are very useful for guiding informal but critical investigation of the graphs in consultation with students and other audiences. The actors in the network, who act as central information brokers or hubs, are connecting to a significantly large number of individuals in the network and are thus revealed. Bridging roles can also be considered in terms of locating individual nodes with a high frequency of non-redundant information passing through them; individuals with high 'betweenness centrality' (BC) function as a bridge between different parts of the network. These individuals possess key network positions in the forwarding of information, and the types of roles they play in the network are of significance to the network overall. Those with a higher 'eigenvector centrality' (EC) measure tend to attract greater attention from others in the network; the more followers an actor has typically indicates that they are attracting more attention, and reflects, to some degree, a measure of esteem in the network. Those with a higher EC are most often individuals who have attention paid to them by other individuals who have a similar high degree of attention paid to them, in the same way the Google PageRank algorithm works.[36] Not all individuals in a network attract a huge following, and yet their position in the network can greatly influence the flow and movement of information through that network. Those on the network with a high attention but low centrality may be simply passing on redundant information. Conversely, those with both high attention and a high betweenness centrality may turn out, with further investigation, to be notable figures within that network. As has been noted, asymmetric attention is key to Twitter celebrity, given that those with a higher degree of EC may have more people's attention, but those who are asymmetric, represent those for whom attention only flows one way, towards them.[37]

Figure 10.1 Network visualisation of the Twitter hashtag search results for #BCM112 following week three of the thirteen week session, March 14, 2014.

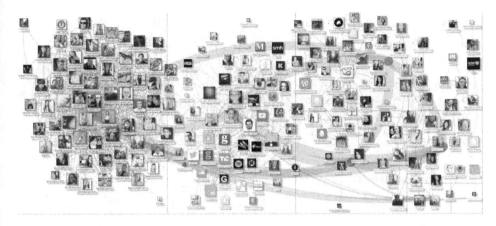

Figure 10.2 Network visualisation for the Twitter hashtag search results for #BCM112 following week four, March 23, 2014.

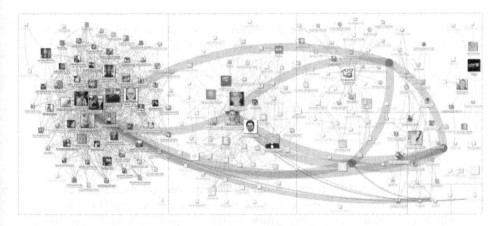

Figure 10.3 Network overview for the Twitter hashtag search results for #BCM112 March 23, 2014. The vertex sizes are scaled according to betweenness centrality values and vertex opacities are based on eigenvector centrality values.

The comparison between Figures 10.2 and 10.3 reveals the early emergence of students and tutors as significant figures in the network, an effect produced by students audiencing themselves and their peers as followers, intensifying their positions in the learning network and occupying locations in the networks as both hubs and bridges. This includes their contribution to the production of knowledge through conversation as well as relaying practical information about session dates, links to materials and retweeting non-redundant information from the lecturers and institutional actors. The official university Twitter account retains high EC and BC values as indicated by its opacity and size occupies a peripheral location in the hashtags network in Figure 10.3.

Figure 10.4 Network visualisation for the Twitter hashtag search results for #BCM112, in week six April 5, 2014.

Figure 10.4 shows a peak period of activity at the mid-point of the university semester, and features a higher number of more densely interconnected relationships still connected in three general clusters. This graph reveals a healthy expansion of the learning network to include a number of media platforms, technologies, and organizations relevant to the learning assessment task and the broader interests of students looking to develop careers in media and the creative industries. A greater number of news organizations and social media platforms and apps have appeared, indicating that students are expanding their own networks by becoming audiences for other significant actors.

The visualization software provides simple frequency analysis of the word pairs associated in the text of the tweets containing the hashtag #BCM112, which reveals that student Twitter conversations at this mid-point in the semester are still navigating the fundamentally structural experience of university learning. The content of the clusters' tweets (Table 10.1) are largely concerned with the public discussion of blogging assessment for both subjects that were due at this time (the third most tweeted word pair indicates this), suggesting a highly information-driven learning network concerned with the parameters of the task and not its depth.

This analysis is further supported by the data recorded by Tweet Archivist, a paid service that records all tweets labeled with a specific hashtag, shown in Figure 10.5, indicating the density of tweets over time occurred in the 'catch-up' period leading to the first learning assessment. Being able to share this information with students assists in revealing the artificiality of the temporal compression of the learning network in the university semester, because ideally an engaged network shape would be less bunched with wild peaks and troughs of activity around assessment due dates.

Table 10.1 Top word pairs in tweet in entire graph

bcm110,bcm112	jessbinx_,uni
bcm112,bcm110	uni,life
blog,post	life,nutshell
bcm112,lecture	nutshell,bcm110
check,out	bcm112,blog

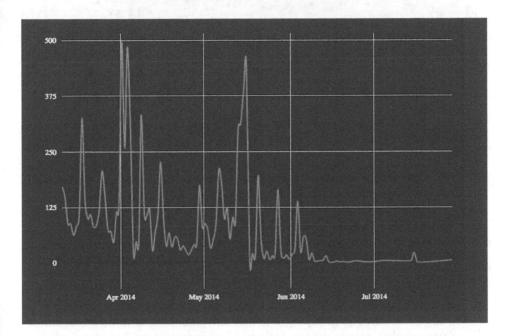

Figure 10.5 This plots the Tweet volume of the hashtag #BCM112 mentionedoverthecourseoftheuniversitysemesterin2014.Generatedwith TwitterArchivist.

In terms of thinking of the student as simultaneously a participant and producer in the experience of a learning network, the student is both connected as an audience to other learners, professionals, organizations and industry agents, with audiences of their own, as expressed in their micro-publics of followers and connections. It's not until later in the session, following the cycles of assessment submission and feedback, that students begin to demonstrate an internalization and normalization of their understanding of how these dimensions of audience activity serve to demonstrate more considered strategies of participation. The graphs begin to fill with connections featuring tweets sharing news and information communicating the cohort's research related to the technologies and media platforms under investigation outside of the more perfunctory and expositional tests that students engage in simply to pass the requirements of the exercise.

Figure 10.6 Network visualisation for the Twitter hashtag search results for #BCM112 in week ten, May 20, 2014.

The graph in Figure 10.6 provides an overview of the transformation and increasing density of the learning network over time and it reveals that the students are now the audience for a much wider range of news and media organizations, apps, technologies, and industry actors, including public intellectuals and celebrities. In exploring and discussing the graph, students were quick to recognize the formation of a cluster in the lower middle, grouping together the technologies and the media platforms they were sourcing for news and information and the media platforms and technologies examined in their shared research. Technologies and new media platforms like Twitch.tv, Spotify, Steam, Pinterest, and Amazon have now become part of the conversation, with some individual students continuing to function as high centrality figures, and by this later stage in the semester these roles are starting to be spread more equally across the graph.

To date, the majority of the learning network graphs produced in this way reveal what Smith *et al.* describe as a 'tight crowd' formation, a network that features discussions characterized by highly interconnected audience members, with few 'isolated' participants.[38] According to Smith *et al.*, these 'tight crowd' formations are seen to occur when networks lead to the formation of communities of interest that attract focused debate and discussion. Such tight crowd formations might include conference attendees and professional networks around specific topics, as well as hobby and fan groups. From these results, distinct and overlapping audience formations are observed to occur in the tight crowd cohort each year. Students form into large, interconnected audience communities and networks; they also develop an audience of followers including those brands, labels, social media managers, and other Twitter operatives attracted by the content of the student's tweeted research who are in turn met with the student's evolving public presentation of the self. Finally, there is a smaller audience of lecturers, tutors, and guests that form a micro-public of pedagogically oriented actors and agents. Over the course of the session, general patterns of behavior emerge, and have been observed in each of the three years that data has been collected. One of the most common is the evolution of a more professional online identity. Those Twitter profile names that initially border on the offensive and profile images (often called avatars or avis) and that feature potentially inappropriate content are very soon revised, without request, as the students enter into a professional sphere of interest and discussion.

Conclusion

In this chapter we have considered a small data approach to understanding the transformation of audience using techniques appropriated from social network analysis in order to engage undergraduate students in reflexive patterns of self-surveillance. We have argued that to be part of an audience now means to present a public persona as an interface to a network of connections. Students need multiple techniques for effectively mapping their own audiences, determining who follows them and what the patterns involved in those relationships might reveal when visualized from the network perspective. Our approach is a useful means for individuals seeking to investigate and better understand their own relationships to micro-public formations that we find ourselves part of, through online learning networks, social media groups, niche fandoms or internet games. As Nick Couldry has observed, the practice of 'audiencing' is best understood as part of a practice that is not itself 'about' media.[39] It is, therefore, particularly of use to students attempting to produce themselves professionally for the first time and unlike other information collected about them during the cumbersome, perfunctory, and often restricted university feedback mechanisms, it provides real time overview of their location in the institution's own micro-public of attention. Similarly, this approach offers the lecturer and the classroom teacher working with social media and microblogging platforms a means for generating an overview to explore and expand reflection on their own roles and positions in the learning network. By inviting students to scrutinize and learn how to interpret their own online activities and audience behaviors, it engages the learner as a producer of knowledge about their own learning. In other words, it does two things at once, as it teaches them about the ways in which online media function and can be analyzed, it also invites them to share in the production of that very knowledge.

Notes

1 Axel Bruns and Jean Burgess, "New Methodologies for Researching News Discussion on Twitter," *The Future of Journalism*, 8–9 September (Unpublished, Cardiff: Cardiff University, 2011) http://eprints.qut.edu.au/46330/; Axel Bruns and Jean Burgess, "Notes Towards the Scientific Study of Public Communication on Twitter," in *Science and the Internet*, eds. Alexander Tokar, Michael Beurskens, Susanne Keuneke, Merja Mahrt, Isabella Peters, Cornelius Puschmann (Düsseldorf: Düsseldorf University Press, 2012): 59–169; Page, Ruth, "The linguistics of self-branding and micro-celebrity in Twitter: The role of hastags," *Discourse and Communication* 6, no 2. (2012): 181–202; Axel Bruns and Stefan Stieglitz, "Quantitative Approaches to Comparing Communication Patterns on Twitter," *Journal of Technology in Human Services* 30 (2012): 160–185.
2 Lupton, Deborah, *Feeling Better Connected: Academics' Use of Social Media* (Canberra: News and Media Research Centre, University of Canberra, 2014).
3 Bruns and Steiglitz, "Quantitative Approachs," 162.
4 Bruns and Burgess, "New Methodologies,"; "Notes towards the scientific," np.
5 Danielle Morgan Acosta, "Tweet Up? Examining Twitter's Impact on Social Capital and Digital Citizenship in Higher Education," *About Campus* 18, no. 6 (2014): 10–17.
6 P. David Marshall, "Persona Studies: Mapping the Proliferation of the Public Self," *Journalism*, 15, no. 2 (2013) 153–170.
7 Bruns and Burgess, "New Methodologies,"; "Notes towards the scientific," np.
8 Kim Barbour, P. David Marshall and Christopher Moore, "Persona to Persona Studies," *M/C Journal: A Journal of Media and Culture* 17, no. 3, (2014): 1–6.
9 See P. David Marshall and Kim Barbour, "The Academic Online: Constructing Persona Through the World Wide Web," *First Monday* 17 no. 9 (2012), np. http://firstmonday.org/ojs/index.php/fm/article/view/3969/3292.
10 These include enhancing social interactions, facilitating educational activities, continuous and transparent communication, immediate feedback, adding transparency to the learning process, informal learning via informal communication, easy and free from many restrictions, informal support for collaboration, and meaningful interaction beyond classrooms. See, Amandeep Dhir, Khalid Buragga and Abeer Boreqqah, "Tweeters on Campus: Twitter a Learning Tool in Classroom?" *Journal of Universal Computer Science*, 19, no. 5 (2014): 672–691.
11 George Veletsianos, "Higher Education Scholars' Participation and Practices on Twitter,". *Journal of Computer Assisted Learning* 28 (2012): 336–349.
12 Learning, Fuller and Goffey argue, is inherently performative and mediated, it is a "...theatre where the self encounters its own becoming, and engages in relays of value with the materials, media organizations, and networks by which it is engaged and evaluated...Thus lifelong learning operates via a double movement: first the interiorization, the claiming of the self, of what was previously the work of the state, church and family; and second an opening up of possibilities to other kinds of actors and nonstandard learning events." Matthew Fuller and Andrew Goffey, *Evil Media* (Cambridge, Massachusetts: The MIT Press 2012): Loc 3408–09.
13 Bazilah A. Talip, "Twitter as a Medium for Professional Networking," *MARA Innovation Journal*, 4, no 2. (2015): 1–19.

14 danah boyd, "Social Network Sites as Networked Publics: Affordances, Dynamics and Implications", in *Networked Self: Identity, Community, and Culture on Social Network Sites*: Zizi Papacharissi, ed., (New York: Routledge, 2011): 39–58; Alice Marwick and danah boyd, "I Tweet Honestly, I Tweet Passionately: Twitter Users, Context Collapse, and the Imagined Audience, *New Media & Society* 13, (2011): 114–133.

15 See P. David Marshall "Personifying Agency: the Public/Persona/Place/Issue Continuum," *Celebrity Studies*, 4, no. 3 (2013): 369–71. Also, the concept is similar to what Zizi Papacharissi (2015) calls the 'networked self', expressed in the practice of the everyday forms of connectivity and conversation, which is both privately imagined and collectively aspired to. The network self recognizes the implicit understanding of audience connected to the presentation of personally defined and politically directed performance, which is phatically presented, individually motivated and civically responsive as a public facing identity. Zizi Papacharissi, *Affective Publics: Sentiment, Technology and Politics*. Oxford Studies in Digital Politics. (New York: Oxford University Press, 2015): 101.

16 P. David Marshall, "Monitoring Persona: Mediatized Identity and the Edited Public Self," *Frame: Journal of Literary Studies* 28, no. 1 (2015): 115–133.

17 P. David Marshall, "Persona Studies: Mapping the Proliferation of the Public Self," *Journalism* 15, no. 2 (2014): 153–170.

18 P. David Marshall "Personifying Agency," np.

19 P. David Marshall, "Persona Studies," 42.

20 Bruno Latour, Pablo Jensen, Tommaso Venturini, Sébastian Grauwin and Dominique Boullier, "The Whole is Always Smaller than its Parts' – a Digital Test of Gabriel Tardes' Monads" *The British Journal of Sociology* 63, no. 4 (2012): 590–615.

21 Latour et al. "The Whole," 13.

22 Bernhard Rieder and Theo Röhle, "Digital Methods: Five Challenges', In *Understanding Digital Humanities*, ed. David M. Berry (New York: Palgrave Macmillan, 2012): 67–84.

23 For further discussion see Christopher Moore, "Invigorating Play: The Role of Affect in Online Multiplayer FPS Game", in *Guns, Grenades, and Grunts: First-Person Shooter Games*. Gerald A. Voorhees, Josh Call, and Katie Whitlock eds. book (New York: Continuum 2012): 341–363; Christopher Moore, "Screenshots as Virtual Photography: Cybernetics, Remediation and Affect," in *Advancing Digital Humanities*. Paul Longley Arthur and Katherine Bode eds. (UK Palgrave Macmillan 2014).

24 P. David Marshall, "Persona Studies", np.

25 Ned Rossiter, *Materialities of Software: Logistics, Labour, Infrastructure*, in *Advancing Digital Humanities*, Paul Longley Arthur and Katherine Bode eds. (UK: Palgrave Macmillan 2014) 221–240.

26 Bruns and Steiglitz, "Quantitative Approaches," 162.

27 Rieder and Röhle, "Digital Methods" 72–74.

28 Kim Barbour, P. David Marshall, and Christopher Moore, "'Persona as method: exploring celebrity and the public self through persona studies," *Celebrity Studies* 6, no. 3 (2015): 288–305.

29 Jose Van Dijck, *The Cultures of Connectivity: A Critical History of Social Media*, Oxford University Press, New York. 2013.

30 John Law, "Actor Network Theory and Material Semiotics," (Lancaster: Lancaster University, 2007) (2007:595), 1–21. http://www.heterogeneities.net/publications/Law2007ANTandMaterialSemiotics.pdf.

31 Rowan Wilken and Christian McCrea, "University Life, Zombies States and Reanimation," in *Zombies in the Academy, Living Death in Higher Education*, Andrew Whelan, Ruth Walker, and Christopher Moore (Chicago: Intellect, The University of Chicago Press, 2013): 39–52.
32 Many of our students are already engaged in their own micropublics that are monetized as YouTube channels, DeviantArt profiles, Twitch streams, or My Little Pony podcasts, and bring with them a massive range of media and digital literacies, skills and experiences about how such associations are made and unmade very quickly in the highly saturated media communication industries and the increasingly unpoliced divide between amateur and professional creative practitioners and media producers.
33 See Lee Rainie and Barry Wellman, *Networked The New Social Operating System* (Cambridge Massachusetts: The MIT Press 2012).
34 Henry Jenkins, *Convergence Culture*, (New York: New York University Press, 2006) 7.
35 Marc Smith, Lee Rainie, Ben Shneiderman, and Itai Himelboim, *Mapping Twitter Topic Networks: from Polarized Crowds to Community Clusters* (Pew Internet Research Centre, 2014): http://www.pewinternet. org/2014/02/20/mapping-twitter-topic-networks-from-polarizedcrowds-to-community-clusters/.
36 Barash, V. and Golder, S. "Twitter: Conversation, Entertainment, and Information, All in One Network!", in *Analyzing Social Media Networks with NodeXL: Insights from a Connected World*. Derek Hansen, Ben Shneiderman, Marc Smith, eds. (Morgan Kaufmann Publishers. 2010): 143–164.
37 Barash and Golder "Twitter: Conversation", 151.
38 Smith et al. "Mapping Twitter" np.
39 Nick Couldry "Theorising Media as Practice," *Social semiotics 14*, no. 2 (2004), 125.

11 Migration and Mediatization

Three Cohorts of Dutch Migrants to Aotearoa / New Zealand

Joost de Bruin

Introduction

The contemporary media landscape provides audiences with a raft of opportunities to consume media content from all over the world and connect with people in different places. Scholarship on the notion of 'mediatization' has argued that in the last couple of decades societies have become permeated with digital media and that media more than ever before exert an influence over how people conduct their social lives.[1] The pervasiveness of digital media results in a plethora of reference points that audiences can draw on to construct a sense of belonging. For international migrants who have physically moved their lives from one country to another but want to retain connections, developments of mediatization have had a profound impact. Migrants can now exploit satellite, internet, and mobile phone-based platforms to stay in touch with the people and places that they have left behind, while at the same time using these platforms to make connections with the country that they have moved to, as well as other locations.[2] 'Mediatized migrants'[3] are in a unique position to take advantage of the widespread availability of digital media to position themselves in relation to a variety of cultural fields.

This chapter discusses the results of a small-scale qualitative interview study with migrants who have moved from the Western European country of the Netherlands to Aotearoa / New Zealand. The aim of the chapter is to take a historical approach to mediatization and use an audience research project to illustrate how developments in the digital media landscape affect particular cohorts of migrant audiences. The analysis distinguishes between three cohorts of Dutch migrants: 'post-war immigrants' who arrived in the 1950s and 1960s, 'skilled immigrants' who arrived in the 1970s and 1980s, and 'transnational professionals' who arrived from the 1990s onwards.[4] The findings of the study show that the three cohorts relate and respond to developments of mediatization in different ways. Post-war immigrants use some digital media to connect with the Netherlands, but they do this in specific ways and for specific reasons. Skilled immigrants have taken up new opportunities that have arisen with the arrival of digital media to reconnect with Dutch media.

The consequences of mediatization are most strongly felt, however, by the transnational professionals cohort. Their experience of migration is, to use Andreas Hepp's expression, 'molded by media'[5]: from consulting media pre-migration and carrying media with them while travelling to their new home country to consuming Dutch media via the Internet and staying in contact with people left behind through social media, email, phone, Skype, and other digital technologies, this cohort of migrants exemplifies how mediatization has changed the nature and experience of migration. Using the interview study with Dutch migrants, this chapter illustrates that different cohorts of audiences can respond to developments of mediatization in dissimilar ways and it will argue that qualitative audience research is instrumental in making these kinds of differences visible.

Mediatized Migrants

In recent discussions about the current field of media and cultural studies, 'mediatization' has gained traction as a useful concept to analyze the consequences of the enormous changes that have occurred in the media landscape with the introduction of digital media technologies.[6] Mediatization can be defined as a meta-process of cultural change on the same level as individualization, commercialization or globalization.[7] A state of mediatization has been realized in (large parts of) Western societies in the late 2000s with the increased availability of smartphones, wireless internet, online search capacity, blogs and social media.[8] For many people, digital media have become the main reference point for obtaining information, relating to other people and constructing identities.[9] Stig Hjarvard outlines the focus of mediatization in four key ideas: contemporary media extend people's abilities to communicate in time and space; they substitute activities that used to take place face to face; they infiltrate everyday life with a raft of opportunities; and people adapt their behavior to structures of the media.[10] The media's role in the audiences' lives has thus shifted direction; as Nick Couldry states, mediatization 'points to the *changed dimensionality of the social world in a media age*'.[11]

Migrants' media cultures, more specifically, have changed dramatically over the last couple of decades. While until the 1980s the main channels to stay in touch with friends and family in former home countries were letters and audio cassettes, which had to be sent by postal mail, contemporary migrants can, if they have the means to do so, access a range of media technologies that connect them with places all over the world.[12] As a consequence, migrant cultures are increasingly influenced and defined by their media consumption. According to Hepp, migrant cultures are 'cultures of mediatization: that is, cultures that are molded by the media'.[13] These developments can have life-changing consequences for migrants who are invested in maintaining connections with different places:

> migrants can participate simultaneously in different communication spaces: watching satellite and Internet TV, downloading films, listening to internet radio or reading online newspapers – all of these open up the possibility of participating, in parallel, in political and popular cultural discussions taking place in the country of origin, [the country of residence] and elsewhere in the world.[14]

'Mediatized migrants' use the affordances of contemporary mediascapes to their full potential. Media hence become constitutive of the social reality of migrants: making sense of migrant cultures is impossible without thinking about media.

This does not mean, however, that all migrants use media in the same way. It is important to consider the multidimensionality of migrant cultures while at the same time acknowledging patterns of media use within migrant groups.[15] Based on their own research with different migrant communities in Germany, Hepp and his colleagues Cigdem Bozdag and Laura Suna distinguish between three types of migrants: origin-oriented, ethno-oriented, and world-oriented migrants.[16] Origin-oriented migrants use media to stay connected with the culture of their former home country. They use media as a bridge to the 'homeland'. Ethno-oriented migrants see themselves as part of two cultures. They use media for bicultural networking, both with their culture of origin and with German culture. World-oriented migrants identify as 'citizens of the world' and their media use traverses across a range of cultures. Origin-oriented migrants tend to be older than ethno-oriented migrants, whereas world-oriented migrants are relatively young.[17]

While this typology is useful in demonstrating that not all migrants navigate the digital media environment in the same way, it does not provide an explanation for *why* different migrants have particular priorities. Other authors have pointed out that mediatized identities depend on migrants' specific sociocultural resources and life histories and that migrants' media practices are intertwined with other social practices, activities and interactions.[18] Sudesh Mishra advocates for a perspective of 'archival specificity' when analyzing migrant experiences, which distinguishes between experiences of distinct cohorts of migrants and thus shows awareness that migrant cultures are characterized by 'historically-motivated differences and discontinuities'.[19] Adrian Athique proposes a framework for analyzing media consumption that sees audiences as interacting with 'cultural fields'.[20] A cultural field is 'defined by the imaginative work of its participants'[21]: people form imagined communities through the consumption of media products. A shared interest in a media product can enact diverse cultural dialogues. For migrants, positions in relation to the cultural field are informed by specific migration histories and cultural affiliations, familiarity with media technologies and personal or communal interests that people want to satisfy.

Locating Dutch Migrants

Following previous work by Suzan van der Pas and Jacques Poot, people who have migrated from the Netherlands to Aotearoa / New Zealand can be grouped in three cohorts, depending on when they moved: postwar immigrants (1950s and 1960s), skilled immigrants (1970s and 1980s), and transnational professionals (1990s to the present).[22] The first cohort of migrants moved shortly after the Second World War at a time of economic hardship in in the Netherlands. This cohort quickly assimilated into dominant New Zealand culture. While first cohort migrants were mostly from working class backgrounds, second cohort migrants were generally middle class and highly educated. This cohort moved for environmental and lifestyle rather than economic reasons. Third cohort migrants are also professionals in search of a different lifestyle, but they maintain closer links with the Netherlands than the previous two cohorts. This cohort is more transient than the previous two. In general, for Dutch migrants to Aotearoa / New Zealand, there has been a shift from permanent migration to migration for temporary work and study.

The estimated size of the Dutch community in Aotearoa / New Zealand is 116,700 people, which makes the Dutch the second-largest European migrant group after people from the UK.[23] Due to differences between cohorts of Dutch migrants and constant new arrivals, the Dutch community in New Zealand is in transformation and there is great variety in how people relate to their Dutch background.[24] Dutch migrants are seen as 'invisible migrants'[25]: unlike other migrant groups they are not part of the national imaginary. Dutch people in Aotearoa / New Zealand are not clustered in ethnic communities but live all over the country.[26] One of the few visible signs of a Dutch presence are the Dutch food stores. Participants for the interview study were contacted trough the Dutch Shop in Petone, Lower Hutt. This store sells food products which have been imported from the Netherlands, such as cheese, liquorice, sweets, bread toppings, and spices. Through its slogan, featured on its website[27], 'For all your Dutch delicacies', the Dutch Shop invites customers to connect with Dutch food culture and find enjoyment in this experience, in a way similar to other food stores established by migrants. Purnima Mankekar writes about Indian grocery stores in the San Francisco region: 'Indian grocery stores form a crucial node in the transnational circulation and consumption of commodities and discourses about India. (...) Indian grocery stores invoke and produce powerful discourses of home, family and community'.[28] The same notion applies to the Dutch Shop. It is a place where people can consume not just food products from the Netherlands, but also discourses about what 'Dutch culture' consists of. By engaging with these, they position themselves in relation to ideas about 'home', the Netherlands, and other Dutch people in Aotearoa / New Zealand.

The notion of 'cultural field' can be used to interpret how audiences consume media products, but also to make sense of what happens when people visit a food store and interact with the products there. My aim in contacting people through a Dutch food store was to find migrants who have an interest in interacting with Dutch cultural fields, to analyze the implications of developments of mediatization, and to uncover continuities and discontinuities between different cohorts of migrants. On three consecutive Saturdays, I stood outside the Dutch Shop and talked with people leaving the store. My first question to them was: 'Are you originally from the Netherlands?' and if the answer was affirmative, I asked: 'Do you use media to stay in touch with the Netherlands?'. If the answer was 'Yes' I asked them if they wanted to participate in an interview. As a result, I conducted sixteen interviews in which twenty people participated. Twelve interviews were with individuals, four with couples. Seven interviews took place at people's homes, seven at people's workplaces and two in cafés. Eleven participants were men and nine were women, seventeen were white Dutch and three were Indonesian Dutch. Participants represented a range of ages: some were in their 20s, others in their 30s, 40s, or 50s and 60s. In terms of the aforementioned cohorts of Dutch migrants to Aotearoa / New Zealand, three individuals and one couple arrived in the 1950s-1960s, four individuals in the 1970s–1980s and five individuals and three couples in the 1990s or later. Interviews lasted for 45 minutes to 1.5 hours. The conversations were characterized by what Mieke Bal has termed 'migratory culture'[29]: a context in which being a migrant is not just accepted, but is the norm. I had moved from the Netherlands to Aotearoa / New Zealand several years earlier, so I could personally relate to many experiences that the participants were talking about.

The objective of qualitative interviewing as a research method is to encourage people to talk at length in order to gain insight into how they make sense of the world around them. For Media Studies scholars, specifically, the qualitative interview is 'a vehicle for bringing forward the media-induced meanings of the informants' lifeworld'.[30] The goal of the interview study was to invite Dutch migrants to talk about how they use different media to connect with the Netherlands in a context where the media landscape is rapidly changing. There was no expectation that all participants would navigate the media landscape in similar fashion; on the contrary: the aim was to hear different migrant's unique stories about media consumption, paying particular attention to how they respond to recent developments of mediatization.

Dutch Migrants' Use of Digital Media

A cultural field is a dynamic site and not all participants relate to the object of interest in the same way: 'agents engage in *particular* and *relative* forms of social imagination'.[31] Audiences determine their positions in relation to cultural fields through practices of imagination. In the case of the Dutch migrants interviewed for this study, their media consumption is informed by migration histories, media literacies, and specific interests that people aim to satisfy, such as being curious about the news or being a fan of sports or popular music. Despite a variety in affiliations, the study found similarities in digital media use between people who belong to the same cohort of Dutch migrants to Aotearoa / New Zealand. It is evident that developments of mediatization have had a dissimilar impact on the post-war immigrants, skilled immigrants, and transnational professionals in terms of how migrants use media to connect with the country that they have physically left behind.

Post-war Immigrants

Participants belonging to the post-war immigrants cohort, who arrived in the 1950s and 1960s, were forced to assimilate into dominant New Zealand culture. Many stopped speaking Dutch and, due to the limited means of communication at the time, were unable to retain a connection with the Netherlands. Having lived in Aotearoa / New Zealand for the majority of their lifetime, they have a limited interest in connecting with the Netherlands. At the start of every interview, I asked participants if they wanted to talk in Dutch, English, or both. Out of the four interviews with migrants who arrived in the 1950s and the 1960s, three were conducted in English and one in Dutch. Trudy and Piet made the decision to stop speaking Dutch to each other as soon as they left the ship they had arrived on:

JOOST: So the two of you speak English together?
TRUDY: Yes.
JOOST: Not Dutch anymore. So when did you stop doing that?
PIET: When we arrived here.
TRUDY: Yeah.
JOOST: Straight away?
TRUDY: Straight away (...)
PIET: It's always been easier to speak English. And we were rather proud of the fact I think that people said 'oh you're not Dutch, you don't speak like a Dutchman'. (...). What did they say when we first got here? We were Canadian. Because we have a, sort of a North American twang...

This cohort of migrants has been living in Aotearoa / New Zealand for 45 years or more and arrived at a time when migrants were expected to assimilate into society and leave their original languages and cultures behind.[32] For Willem, who arrived as a ten-year-old child, this means that he experiences very few connections with the Netherlands at all:

WILLEM: My attitude has always been one of basically just acceptance of here I am in New Zealand. I speak English, that's the language of the country. I like this place. Holland is where my life started, I have some basic memories of it but not too many. And I never had a strong enough motivation to try to get back there (...) I think I have just been accepting of the way things are.

Willem does not use any digital Dutch media. He talked about reading Dutch books and occasionally listening to Dutch access radio in the past, but he has never watched Dutch television programs and does not use the internet. He is aware that the media landscape has changed enormously in the past decade, but feels that it is too late for him to start using digital media. The other participants who belong to the post-war immigrant cohort use some digital media to connect with the Netherlands, but they do so selectively. Aad, who like Willem migrated when he was a child, talks about his general attitude of selectivity when using media:

AAD: My relationship with the media is a little bit utilitarian. When I need it, I know where it is (...) My relationship with the media is more what do I need rather than do I want everything that's available.
JOOST: So along similar lines, the media are probably not that important for you in terms of maintaining a relationship with the Netherlands or Dutch culture?
AAD: Ehm, no. I think my connection... there is a strong emotional connection, it's a connection with people, people that I know, people whose faces I can see in my mind. It's nice to see them on Skype but I don't think my relationships are really depending on having all the media there all the time.

Aad sometimes uses media to engage with Dutch media. He has a strong interest in particular types of musical instruments from the south of the Netherlands and he uses the internet to research them by browsing websites and watching YouTube clips. He talks about the enjoyment of finding a Dutch language book about these instruments online:

AAD: We had a lot of fun finding a book that was published in Holland I think, about musical instruments. So there was a crazy thing, again from the south called a (...) rommelpot. With a pig's bladder and a stick. Used in a parade. Terrible noise but it was good fun. (...) So we had some fun in recent years making these things. And (...) my job was to translate the book while we worked on it.

Annie uses more Dutch media than Aad but for quite a different reason. She watches the Dutch and the Belgian news (which is also in the
Dutch language) on a daily basis through the satellite television channel
Stratos.[33] Despite this daily habit, watching the news serves to maintain
her distance from the Netherlands and find reassurance that migrating
to Aotearoa / New Zealand was the right choice:

ANNIE: We watch the news from Holland and from Belgium. That's at
    12:30 and at 1:00. And then you see what's happening there. And
    the troubles that they're having.
JOOST: What kind of troubles?
ANNIE: Immigrants over there. (...)
JOOST: Do you find it important to watch the news?
ANNIE: Well, it's enjoyable to watch. Not that I would ever want to live
    there. But it's fun to see what's going on over there. And what they're
    doing, what's bothering them and that they can't get a government
    and those kinds of things. (...) It's kind of interesting. Because other-
    wise you wouldn't hear anything, because on TV here you hardly
    hear anything about Holland. (...). Unless something really bad hap-
    pens, but otherwise you won't hear anything. And it's the Euro of
    course, my God how expensive everything has become there since.

Participants from the post-war immigrants cohort find themselves at quite
a distance from Dutch media and their engagement with digital media in
general is limited. In all interviews, participants talked about media that
they had used in the past to stay connected with the Netherlands. These
were mainly paper media such as books, newspapers, magazines and letters, and audio-based media such as radio and cassettes. Developments
of mediatization have not had much impact on this cohort of migrants.
They are aware that the media landscape has changed and that there is
now a range of digital media available, but they use these media in selective ways and for particular purposes.

Skilled Immigrants

The skilled immigrant cohort arrived in Aotearoa / New Zealand in the
1970s and the 1980s. This cohort is positioned in between the other two
cohorts, the post-war immigrants and the transnational professionals.
Out of the four interviews with participants from this cohort, three were
carried out in Dutch and one in English. Possibly because of the nature
of being an in-between cohort, several participants talked about how the
media landscape has changed over time:

GERARD: I think the most relevant thing about it is, if you think about
    migration, that for people that were to immigrate or emigrate now,

staying in contact is so much easier, you know. And I think that was probably quite a difficult thing when we went in 1982. There wasn't really the ability to stay in touch so therefore you just simply didn't, other than a few letters in the first few years. But that soon wears off and then that's like *that's it*, then it's forgotten. I think it'd be a hell of a lot easier if people move now because the channels are there.

Participants who belong to this cohort talked about taking up new opportunities that have arisen with the arrival of digital media. During his interview, Thijs, like Gerard, compared the media available when he arrived with the media he uses now. He talked about how he and his siblings used to send each other audio cassettes and letters via the mail and how they can now video chat with each other on Skype.[34] He also explained how difficult it used to be to find a Dutch newspaper, while these days he receives news notifications through his iPhone every couple of minutes. Thijs follows the Dutch football avidly and reflects on how digital media have allowed him to reconnect with his passion for football:

JOOST: At the shop you said you still follow the football.
THIJS: Yeah, yeah.
JOOST: How does that go?
THIJS: Well good, when we're talking about nowadays, I forgot about it for a long time. But now... [Thijs shows me his iPhone] (...) What I've got on here, it's got *Voetbal International*. I used to buy that magazine every week [in the Netherlands]. (...) Now I have an app, it's on here and you can select your favorite club. (...) So Ado is my favorite club and all the news just appears here. (...) About the matches, who has scored and who is being transferred. So you just get the news.

Participants from this cohort seem the most confident in liaising with both New Zealand and Dutch media. They can be compared similar to the ethno-oriented migrants from Hepp, Bozdag, and Suna's study, who use media to engage in bicultural networking. Several participants from the skilled immigrants cohort spoke about consuming news from both countries.[35] One reason for their focus on Dutch news is their dissatisfaction with New Zealand news sources:

MISHA: The news in New Zealand is too much like, almost like Privé [a Dutch gossip magazine], that type, Women's Weekly...
JOOST: Gossip magazines.
MISHA: Yeah, sensationalizing what has happened. Whether it's murders, whether it's accidents or that fire in the mine, that was important of course but if I want to know about things like Greenpeace or important things, for example about the Obama administration,

I just find that that I get provided with more detail and more factual knowledge [in Dutch media]. (...) I don't know what kind of world I live in sometimes, because New Zealand is so isolated and I want to know what's happening.

Compared to the post-war immigrants, the skilled immigrants seem more confident in thinking across cultures and coordinating their media use accordingly. Their middle class background and higher level of education may have an influence here. Another example of thinking across cultures was provided by Gerard, who has recently discovered gay fiction in the Dutch language through the internet:

GERARD: It is nice to read Dutch stories. (...) There is lots of gay fiction and stuff out, but it's always in English and it's always like [the same], you know. And you sort of go: 'Oh I wonder what it'd be like to read something in Dutch'. So you start looking for that. And it's actually quite good for your Dutch because I think the more you read and the more you write the better it is.

In a different part of his interview, Gerard makes a broader point about his media use, which sums up the general attitude of this cohort of migrants. The skilled immigrants arrived in Aotearoa / New Zealand at a time when there were limited options to connect with Dutch cultural fields. With the arrival of a raft of digital media technologies, they seek to benefit from the newly arisen opportunities:

GERARD: I think that's the best thing about media and actually the result of that being that I'm accessing a lot more Dutch things than I ever would have. You know, I'm much more actively looking at Dutch things and talking Dutch and emailing Dutch (...).
JOOST: More than ten years ago you would say?
GERARD: Yeah, absolutely because media wasn't there, the technology wasn't there to easily do it. (...) And the easier it becomes, I think the more you start using it.
JOOST: So are media important in staying in touch with the Netherlands?
GERARD: Absolutely, essential. Yeah, I don't think you would have that opportunity without the media being around.

The skilled immigrant cohort, who have been in Aotearoa / New Zealand for 25 years or more, were relatively well-positioned to start using digital media when these became more easily available. Developments of mediatization have facilitated a change in how they relate to their own experience of migration. Whereas opportunities for connection used to be limited, they can now engage with Dutch cultural fields to broaden their horizons and pursue particular interests. Because they are more fluent in Dutch than the post-war immigrants, this is something they can do without much effort.

Transnational Professionals

For the cohort of transnational professionals, who arrived in the 1990s or later, the consequences of mediatization are more strongly felt than for the post-war immigrants and the skilled immigrants. Their experience of migration is shaped by media consumption in several ways: from consulting media before they left the Netherlands and taking media with them while migrating, to using digital media on a daily basis and staying in contact with people in the Netherlands through social media, email, phone, and Skype. This cohort is in the best position to benefit from the 'amalgamation of opportunities'[36] that contemporary mediascapes offer and transitional professionals also seem to relate the closest to their Dutch background. All of the eight interviews in this category were conducted in the Dutch language and all participants regularly use media to stay in touch with the Netherlands. While the post-war and skilled immigrants made a conscious choice to permanently move to a country on the other side of the world, the transnational professionals are relatively transient and comfortable with living their lives affiliating with two, if not more, countries.

Esther and Paul are a couple with children who are planning to stay in Aotearoa / New Zealand for only one year. They talked about their hard drive, on which they saved books and other documents before they left the Netherlands. After they arrived in Aotearoa / New Zealand, they subsequently printed everything off again:

ESTHER: For the kids, before we left Paul downloaded about 1500 books from a colleague onto the hard disc.
JOOST: 1500?
ESTHER: Yeah something like that.
PAUL: That kept me busy for a while.
ESTHER: But part of those are children's books, because the kids they... well of course they will need to keep up their Dutch. And especially Stijn, because he's going to school in New Zealand for a year (...) and next year he would like to return to his old class.
JOOST: So he needs to keep up.
ESTHER: He needs to keep up. And I copied the school books and everything, we have those digitally as well because we scanned them. We took them on the hard disc and I printed them off here and then, then I do them together with him.
PAUL: Sheet music too. All of the sheet music I scanned at the same time. In PDF format and ...
ESTHER: And we printed those here too.

The practice of scanning and saving essential documents at one location and printing them off at the next location is an intriguing example of the mediatization of migration. Esther and Paul told me that they travelled to Aotearoa / New Zealand with only a couple of suitcases and that their hard drive was the most important item they took with them. Paul also reflected on the difference that broadband internet has made in being away from the Netherlands for an extended amount of time, claiming that in the current media landscape he can carry out his job from almost anywhere:

PAUL: I think because there is broadband internet now, that it has become so much easier to maintain contact with people and continue to do a lot of things. Let me put it this way, I think that if we wouldn't have had broadband internet that my boss wouldn't have liked me going away for a year.

JOOST: Right, so that really makes a difference.

PAUL: Yes. (...) Because I can continue doing my job. Because now, when it's necessary... I even logged on to clients' computers a couple of times to solve a problem.

Several participants talked about the role that media played at the time they made their decision to move to Aotearoa / New Zealand. Wouter's decision to migrate was spurred by watching a television program in the Netherlands about a couple that had migrated to Aotearoa / New Zealand. He also talked about the use of immigration websites in preparing for the move:

WOUTER: There were those two big ones, *Immigrate.org* and *Move to NZ*. (...) *Move to NZ* had about 20,000 members.

JOOST: Oh right, what do people talk about?

WOUTER: Like 'I live in England, who can give me a tip for the best mover'? 'What's the best place to live if I'm looking for good schools, or sunny weather?', really quite basic [questions].

This cohort of migrants is very media literate. They are fully aware that there is a range of digital media at their disposal which they can use to connect with Aotearoa / New Zealand, the Netherlands as well as other countries. Jean and Albertje have bought a satellite dish to watch BVN, a worldwide service with Dutch television programs, but they also get access to services from other nations:

JEAN: Press TV from Iran. And Russian television.

JOOST: Is that also on the satellite?

JEAN: Yeah, and one from Japan has just been added. (...). It's all in English. (...) It's sixty channels and out of those about thirty are from Asia so also non-English language ones. And also, as I was saying before, just the well-known New Zealand channels (...) and BVN.

Jean and Albertje use the same satellite to listen to Radio Netherlands Worldwide, an international radio station for Dutch expats. They have installed speakers in different areas of their home so they can listen to Dutch radio wherever they happen to be. Their home is truly mediatized; it has been set up to allow easy access to Dutch media through digital technologies. Several other participants talked about similar arrangements:

JOOST: Do you listen to Dutch radio programmes?
FEMKE: Yeah, that's often, I listen regularly. Also over the internet. You live stream over the internet and most of all Radio 3. It's just there. And then you have the night programming when you listen during the day, the Dutch night programming. (...) So that's kind of funny. (...)
JOOST: And how do you do that, with a PC or a laptop?
FEMKE: Laptop. (...) We have two laptops, one for each of us. And they're just there, wherever we're working or doing stuff. (...) We have loudspeakers in one room, so we can connect to those.

This cohort of Dutch migrants has the media literacies to arrange for their homes in Aotearoa / New Zealand to be filled with sounds and images from the Netherlands. Continuous access to digital media is taken for granted, as Femke comments: 'It's just there'. Participants express a great sense of control over the media that they select from the broad variety of media that are available. Jeroen talks about subscribing to RSS feeds to ensure that he receives news stories that he is interested in:

JEROEN: That's RSS. And, well there [shows his phone] it shows you all the headlines. (...)
JOOST: And those news stories (...), where do they come from?
JEROEN: From all different sites. If you have a website you can offer all news items on your site as an RSS feed. Other people can then follow that RSS feed. So when you publish something they get it instantly. It's like you have a newspaper and you determine what information appears in your newspaper. (...)
JOOST: And how many different sites do you link to, through your RSS feed?
JEROEN: I think somewhere between 60 and 100.
JOOST: Are they Dutch, or European, or from here?
JEROEN: I have no idea, it's from everywhere.

Jeroen positions himself as a 'world-oriented migrant'[37]: to him, it does not matter where news stories come from. More generally, it is striking how comfortable these migrants are with living in a global world and having affiliations with a range of places. The widespread availability of digital media allows them to position themselves in relation to a variety of cultural fields.

Conclusion

Through adopting a perspective of 'archival specificity'[38], this chapter has argued that three cohorts of Dutch migrants to Aotearoa / New Zealand have been influenced by developments of mediatization in dissimilar ways. The post-war immigrants, who moved in the 1950s and 1960s, were forced to assimilate into dominant New Zealand culture and for the majority of their lifetime they had limited media at their disposal to retain a connection with the Netherlands. Some of the participants belonging to this cohort use digital media now, but they do this for specific purposes. The skilled immigrants, who arrived in the 1970s and 1980s, are an in-between cohort. Several participants belonging to this cohort talked about benefitting from new opportunities that have arisen with the advent of digital media. The transnational professionals, who arrived from the 1990s onwards, can be most confidently labeled as 'mediatized migrants'. Participants belonging to this cohort talked about how their lives, and consequently their experiences of migration, are saturated by digital media.

Mediatization scholars contend that with the introduction of digital media and the increased availability of satellite, internet, and mobile phone-based platforms the shape and conduct of social life has irrevocably changed.[39] However, this claim is not generally backed up by audience research; most scholars arrive at conclusions based on an analysis of the digital media landscape rather than audiences' interactions with it. After reviewing the available research on mediatization, David Deacon and James Stanyer conclude that besides a lack of specificity about what the term encompasses, mediatization research is rather weak on analyzing historical processes and questions of media influence.[40] It is particularly with regards to the latter issue that audience research can make a contribution; the goal of audience research has always been to interrogate the notion of media effects by illustrating that audiences actively negotiate what the media offer to them.[41]

The interview study with Dutch migrants illustrates that audience members navigate digital media by drawing on their personal histories, specific cultural affiliations, familiarity with media technologies, and personal or communal interests. As previous research has indicated, there is great variety in how Dutch migrants to Aotearoa / New Zealand relate to their Dutch background[42] and this is articulated in patterns of media consumption. The notion of 'cultural field' is helpful in analyzing how different audience members relate to the same object. Audiences determine their positions in relation to cultural fields through practices of imagination and these practices are particular, relative and context-specific.[43] Qualitative research methods are best suited to analyze these kind of practices because they facilitate a detailed look into how people experience the world around them.[44]

The notion of mediatization allows us to see digital media consumption as informed by a meta-process of cultural change which has only just started. The introduction of digital media has resulted in profound changes in the media landscape. Within a mediatized environment, audiences engage in cultural consumption across a range of spaces. For audiences who have a certain level of media access and media literacy, digital media reshape everyday social practices and notions of belonging. At the same time, media practices are intertwined with other social practices, activities and interactions.[45] Qualitative audience research has a role to play in showing that the implications of mediatization are not uniform.

Notes

1 Paula Cordeiro, Manuel Damásio, Guy Starkey, Inês Botelho, Patrícia Dias, Carla Ganito, Catia Ferreira and Sara Henriques, "Networks of Belonging: Interaction, Participation and Consumption of Mediatised Content," in *Audience Transformations: Shifting Audience Positions in Late Modernity*, eds. Nico Carpentier, Kim Schrøder, and Lawrie Hallett (New York: Routledge, 2014), 101–119; Nick Couldry, *Media, Society, World: Social Theory and Digital Media Practice* (Cambridge: Polity, 2012).
2 Mirca Madianou and Daniel Miller, *Migration and New Media: Transnational Families and Polymedia* (London: Routledge, 2012).
3 Andreas Hepp, Cigdem Bozdag and Laura Suna, "Mediatized Migrants: Media Cultures and Communicative Networking in the Diaspora," in *Migration, Diaspora, and Information Technology in Global Societies*, eds. Leopoldina Fortunati, Raul Pertierra and Jane Vincent (New York: Routledge, 2012), 172–188.
4 This distinction is derived from Suzan van der Pas and Jacques Poot, *The Transformation of Immigrant Communities: The Case of the Dutch Kiwis* (Auckland: Integration of Immigrants Programme, Massey University, 2011).
5 Andreas Hepp, *Cultures of Mediatization* (Cambridge: Polity, 2013).
6 Nick Couldry and Andreas Hepp, "Conceptualizing Mediatization: Contexts, Traditions, Arguments," *Communication Theory* 23: 191 202.
7 Hepp, *Cultures of Mediatization*, 69.
8 Couldry and Hepp, "Conceptualizing Mediatization," 192.
9 Cordeiro et al., "Networks of Belonging," 112.
10 Stig Hjarvard, *The Mediatization of Culture and Society* (London: Routledge, 2013).
11 Couldry, *Media, Society, World*, 137.
12 Madianou and Miller, *Migration and New Media*, 57.
13 Hepp, *Cultures of Mediatization*, 2.
14 Hepp, *Cultures of Mediatization*, 97.
15 Hepp, Bozdag and Suna, "Mediatized Migrants," 172.
16 Hepp, Bozdag and Suna, "Mediatized Migrants," 177.
17 Hepp, Bozdag and Suna, "Mediatized Migrants," 182.
18 Magnus Andersson, "Multi-Contextual Lives: Transnational Identifications under Mediatised Conditions," *European Journal of Cultural Studies* 16, no. 4 (2013): 387–404.
19 Sudesh Mishra, *Diaspora Criticism* (Edinburgh: Edinburgh University Press, 2006).

20 Adrian Athique, "Media Audiences, Ethnographic Practice and the Notion of a Cultural Field," *European Journal of Cultural Studies* 11, no. 1 (2008): 25–41.
21 Athique, "Media Audiences," 38.
22 van der Pas and Poot, "Immigrant Communities".
23 van der Pas and Poot, "Immigrant Communities," 9.
24 Tanja Schubert-McArthur, "Second and Third Generation Dutch in New Zealand," paper presented at the Melbourne Migration Conference, Melbourne, Australia, 15 November 2013.
25 Hank Schouten. *Tasman's Legacy: The New Zealand – Dutch Connection* (Wellington: New Zealand-Netherlands Foundation).
26 van der Pas and Poot, "Immigrant Communities," 7.
27 See http://dutchshop.net.nz/.
28 Purnima Mankekar,"India Shopping: Indian Grocery Stores and Transnational Configurations of Belonging," *Ethnos: Journal of Anthropology* 67, no. 1 (2009): 75–98.
29 Mieke Bal, "In Your Face: Facing Mothers of Migrants Through Migratory Aesthetics," keynote at the Crossroads: Europe, Migration and Culture Conference, Network for Migration and Culture, University of Copenhagen, Denmark, 24–25 October 2013.
30 Kim Schrøder, Kirsten Drotner, Stephen Kline and Catherine Murray, Researching Audiences (London: Arnold, 2003).
31 Athique, "Media Audiences," 38.
32 Ineke Crezee, "Language Shift and Host Society Attitudes: Dutch Migrants Who Arrived in New Zealand Between 1950 and 1965," *International Journal of Bilingualism* 16, no. 4 (2012): 528–540; van der Pas and Poot, "Immigrant Communities," 13.
33 The STRATOS channel broadcasts news programmes from different countries all over the world. At the time of the interview, the Dutch news was aired at 12.30 p.m. every day and the Belgian news at 1:00 p.m.
34 See Madianou and Miller, *Migration and New Media*, 57.
35 Hepp, Bozdag and Suna, "Mediatized Migrants," 182.
36 Couldry and Hepp, "Conceptualizing Mediatization," 192.
37 Hepp, Bozdag and Suna, "Mediatized Migrants," 177.
38 Mishra, *Diaspora Criticism*, 18.
39 Couldry, *Media, Society, World*, 137; Cordeiro et al., "Networks of Belonging," 112; Hjarvard, *Mediatization*, 11.
40 David Deacon and James Stanyer, "Mediatization: Key Concept or Conceptual Bandwagon?" *Media, Culture and Society* 36, no. 7 (2014): 1032–1044.
41 Sonia Livingstone, "Media Audiences, Interpreters and Users," in *Media Audiences*, ed. Marie Gillespie (Maidenhead: Open University Press, 2005), 9–50.
42 Schubert-McArthur, "Dutch in New Zealand," 3.
43 Athique, "Media Audiences," 38.
44 Schrøder, Drotner, Kline and Murray, *Researching Audiences*, 143.
45 Andersson, "Multi-Contextual Lives," 387.

List of Contributors

Adrian Athique is Associate Professor in Cultural Studies and Deputy Director of the Institute for Advanced Studies in Humanities (IASH) at the University of Queensland. Adrian has written extensively on media audiences in a range of locations, addressing the empirical, methodological and theoretical dimensions of audience research. He is author of *The Multiplex in India: A Cultural Economy of Urban Leisure* (Routledge 2010, with Douglas Hill), *Indian Media: Global Approaches* (2012, Polity), *Digital Media and Society* (2013, Polity) and *Transnational Audiences: Media Reception on a Global Scale* (2016, Polity).

Axel Bruns is an Australian Research Council Future Fellow and Professor in the Digital Media Research Centre at Queensland University of Technology in Brisbane, Australia. He is the author of *Blogs, Wikipedia, Second Life and Beyond: From Production to Produsage* (2008) and *Gatewatching: Collaborative Online News Production* (2005), and a co-editor of the *Routledge Companion to Social Media and Politics* (2016), *Twitter and Society* (2014), *A Companion to New Media Dynamics* (2012) and *Uses of Blogs* (2006). His current work focuses on the study of user participation in social media spaces such as Twitter. His research blog is at http://snurb.info/, and he tweets at @snurb_dot_info. See http://mappingonlinepublics.net/ for more details on his research into social media.

Joost de Bruin is Senior Lecturer in Media Studies at Victoria University of Wellington in Aotearoa / New Zealand. He teaches in the areas of audience studies, television studies, and media and cultural identity. He has published articles in media and cultural studies journals such as *Television and New Media, Continuum, Media International Australia* and *Participations*. With Koos Zwaan, he co-edited a volume on the *Idols* format: *Adapting Idols: Authenticity, Identity and Performance in a Global Television Format* (2012, Ashgate). He has published chapters in anthologies on global television formats and indigenous media. His current research interests include migrant cultures, indigenous media and language learning, and the cross-cultural consumption of television, film, and news.

Gerard Goggin is ARC Future Fellow and Professor of Media and Communications at the University of Sydney. His research interests lie in new media uses, cultures, and audiences (especially concerning mobile media and Internet); media policy and regulation; and disability and digital technology. Gerard's books include *Disability and the Media* (2015; with Katie Ellis); *Global Mobile Media* (2011), *Cell Phone Culture* (2006), and, with Christopher Newell, *Disability in Australia* (2005) and *Digital Disability* (2003). Among his edited collections on mobile media are *Locative Media* (2015; with Rowan Wilken), *Routledge Companion to Mobile Media* (2014; with Larissa Hjorth), and *Mobile Phone Cultures* (2008). Gerard has also published three edited volumes on the Internet with Mark McLelland, *Routledge Companion to Global Internet Histories* (2017), and *Internationalizing Internet: Beyond Anglophone Paradigms* (2009), and *Virtual Nation: The Internet in Australia* (2004).

Ian Goodwin is a Senior Lecturer in the School of English and Media Studies, Massey University. With a background in cultural studies his research is wide ranging and often inter-disciplinary, yet centers on understanding the societal changes associated with the rise of 'new' media technologies. He is interested in exploring intersections between contemporary media forms, identity politics, popular culture, activism, citizenship, media policy, consumption, health and well-being, and space/place.

Christine Griffin is Professor of Social Psychology at the University of Bath in the UK and a member of the UK Centre for Tobacco and Alcohol Studies funded by the UK Clinical Research Collaboration. Chris has a long-standing interest in young people's experiences, as shaped by gender, class, race, and sexuality, and the relationship between identity and consumer culture. She is currently investigating alcohol marketing to young people via social media in a project funded by Alcohol Research UK.

Ramaswami Harindranath is Professor of Media at the University of New South Wales, Sydney, Australia. He has published widely on various topics, including audience research; global media, economy and culture; diasporic media and cultural politics; multicultural arts and cultural citizenship; South Asian politics and culture; and post-coloniality. His major publications include *Approaches to Audiences* (co-edited with Roger Dickinson and Olga Linne) (Arnold, 1998), *The 'Crash' Controversy* (with Jane Arthurs and Martin Barker) (Wallflower Press, 2001), *Perspectives on Global Cultures* (Open University Press, 2006), *Re-imagining Diaspora* (co-edited with Olga Guedes Bailey and Myria Georgiou) (Palgrave Macmillan, 2007), and *Audience-Citizens* (Sage, 2009). He is currently completing a manuscript entitled *Southern Discomfort*, which re-assesses the concept and politics of cultural imperialism.

Craig Hight is an Associate Professor in Communication at the University of Newcastle, NSW. His research interests have focused on audience research, digital media and documentary theory. His most recent books are *Television Mockumentary: Reflexivity, satire and a call for play* (Manchester University Press, 2010) and *New Documentary Ecologies: Emerging Platforms, Practices and Discourses* (co-edited with Kate Nash and Catherine Summerhayes) (Palgrave Macmillan, 2014). His current research focuses on the relationships between digital media technologies and documentary practice, especially the variety of factors shaping online documentary cultures.

Antonia Lyons is a Professor at Massey University, Wellington, New Zealand where she teaches health and social psychology. Her research has explored issues around health, gender, embodiment, and identity, and she is particularly interested in the social and cultural contexts of health behaviors such as alcohol consumption.

Tim McCreanor is a Senior Researcher at SHORE & Whariki Research Centre, Massey University, Aotearoa New Zealand. He has a track record of qualitative research around young people and alcohol within a critical public health paradigm.

Christopher Moore is a Lecturer in Digital Communication and Media Studies at the University of Wollongong, Australia. His published work in Game Studies examines the affective dimensions of multiplayer and first person experiences. He is currently researching the potential for game engines and Virtual Reality interfaces to support archival curation and knowledge production in open and collaboratively-assembled spaces. Most recently co-editing the journal of Persona Studies, his research in the Digital Humanities explores the role of digital objects in the presentation and personal surveillance of the public self online.

Adon C. M. Moskal is a Professional Practice Fellow in the Higher Education Development Centre at the University of Otago in New Zealand. He researches broadly in the fields of Higher Education and Educational Technology, with specific research interests in social media/network analysis; staff and institutional technology adoption and integration; and academic practice and culture.

Erika Pearson is a Senior Lecturer in the School of Communication, Journalism and Marketing at Massey University Wellington, New Zealand. She researches in areas of social capital, online networks and trust, as well as online image cultures, surveillance, and privacy. She is also a regular commentator for the media in the areas of technology in society.

Katie Prowd is cofounder of Hypometer Technologies and a visiting researcher at Queensland University of Technology (QUT). Katie's research within the Social Media Research Group at QUT has focused on the application of 'Big Data' and social media trends in commercial decision making and public interest, namely the predictive capabilities such data has for large-scale and televised events in Australia and internationally.

Andy Ruddock is Senior Lecturer in Media and Communications at Monash University. He is author of *Understanding Audiences, Investigating Audiences* and *Youth and Media*. He has published numerous journal articles and book chapters applying cultivation analysis to topics such as politics, sport, alcohol advertising, media violence, pornography, cultural industries, and rampage murders.

Sue Turnbull is Professor of Communication and Media Studies at the University of Wollongong where she is Discipline Leader for the Creative Industries and Director of the Research Centre for Texts, Culture and Creative Industries. Her current research projects include a study of media use amongst migrants, and the transnational career of the TV crime drama. Her recent publications include *The Media and Communications in Australia* (2014) with Distinguished Professor Stuart Cunningham and *The Television Crime Drama* published by Edinburgh University Press (2014). Sue is joint editor of the online journal *Participations: Journal of Audience and Reception Studies* and a frequent media commentator who also writes on crime fiction for *The Sydney Morning Herald* and *The Age*.

Darryl Woodford is co-founder of Hypometer Technologies and Visiting Fellow at Queensland University of Technology. With a background in Engineering and Data Science, he has published extensively on both the methodologies of 'Big Data' social media research and the analysis of its results through his work as a research fellow in QUT's Social Media Research Group, while also developing social media measurement tools featured in Channel 7's G20 coverage and ABC News 24's coverage of the Queensland Election.

Michele Zappavigna is a Lecturer in the School of Arts and Media at the University of New South Wales. Her major research interest is the discourse of social media and she has published two books in this area: *Discourse of Twitter and Social Media* (Continuum, 2012) and, with Ruth Page, Johann Unger and David Barton, *Researching the Language of Social Media* (Routledge, 2014). Her work also engages with the practical concerns of applied linguistics. Key publications with this focus include, *Tacit Knowledge and Spoken Discourse* (Bloomsbury, 2013), and *Discourse and Diversionary Justice: An Analysis of Ceremonial Redress in Youth Justice Conferencing* (Palgrave, forthcoming) with JR Martin and Paul Dwyer.

Index

9 780367 878191